I0800181

IMAGES
of America

ISLE OF HOPE

WORMSLOE AND BETHESDA

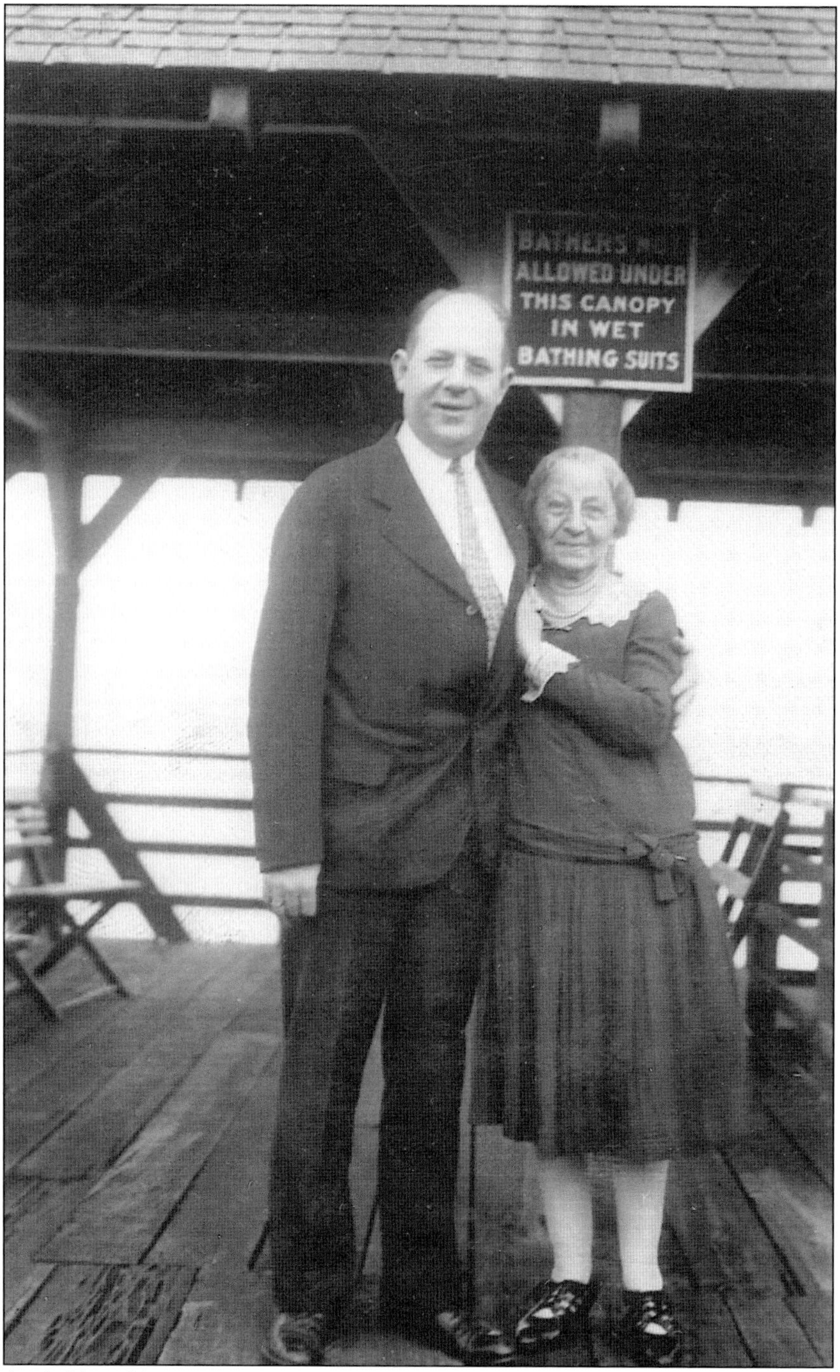

Irwin Rothschild and his wife, Aleen, of Columbus, Georgia, often visited their relatives, the Solomons, on Bluff Drive. Mr. Rothschild was in the textile business. Here, Mrs. Solomon, known as "Carrie B.," poses with Mr. Rothschild on the Solomon dock at Liberty Hall under a "No Wet Bathing Suit" sign. Bathing suits of the 1920s were often made of knitted wool and had so much material that swimmers would get the shivers while waiting in the shade for them to dry.

IMAGES
of America

ISLE OF HOPE
WORMSLOE AND BETHESDA

Polly Wylly Cooper

ARCADIA
PUBLISHING

ISBN 978-0-7385-1414-7

Published by Arcadia Publishing
Charleston, South Carolina

Printed in the United States of America

Library of Congress Catalog Card Number: 2001097591

For all general information contact Arcadia Publishing at:
Telephone 843-853-2070
Fax 843-853-0044
E-mail sales@arcadiapublishing.com
For customer service and orders:
Toll-Free 1-888-313-2665

Visit us on the Internet at www.arcadiapublishing.com

This book is dedicated to the children of Isle of Hope, in hopes that they will grow to appreciate how special this island is, that they will stand firm against the destruction of historic houses for parking lots, and that they will protect our treasured trees, the health of our river, and the fragile ecosystem.

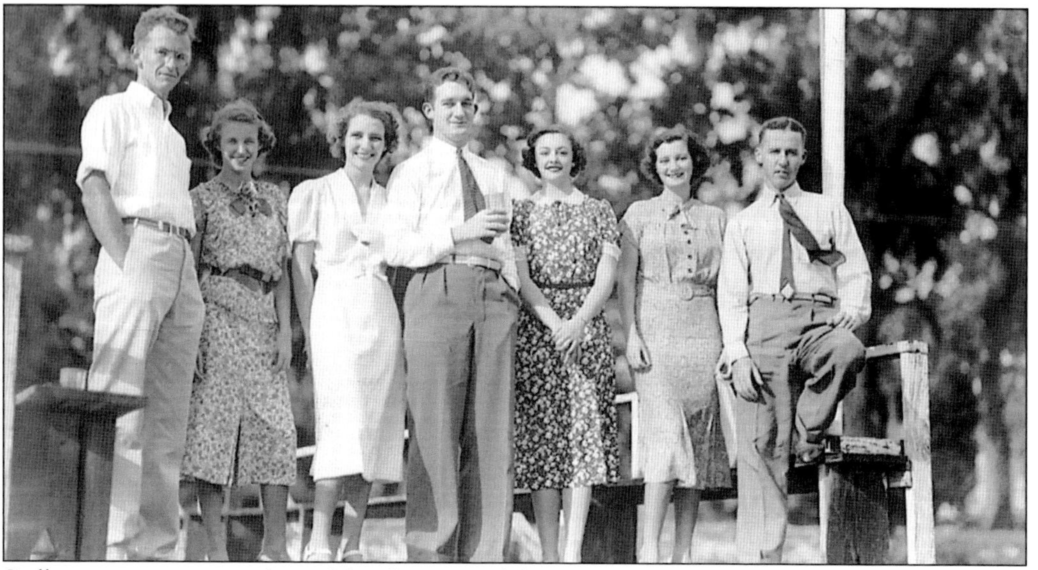

Sailboat races were popular at Isle of Hope and drew crowds out from the city on the streetcars. For this celebration, Corinne Stevens gave a dock party in 1937 for Josephine Pennimen of Washington, D.C. From left to right are Walter "Mutt" Carson, Ethel Davidson (Carson), Josephine Pennimen (Strang), Hugh Nash, Corinne Stevens (Johnson), Ann London (Nash), and James Cope. The group had a super peachy-keen time.

Contents

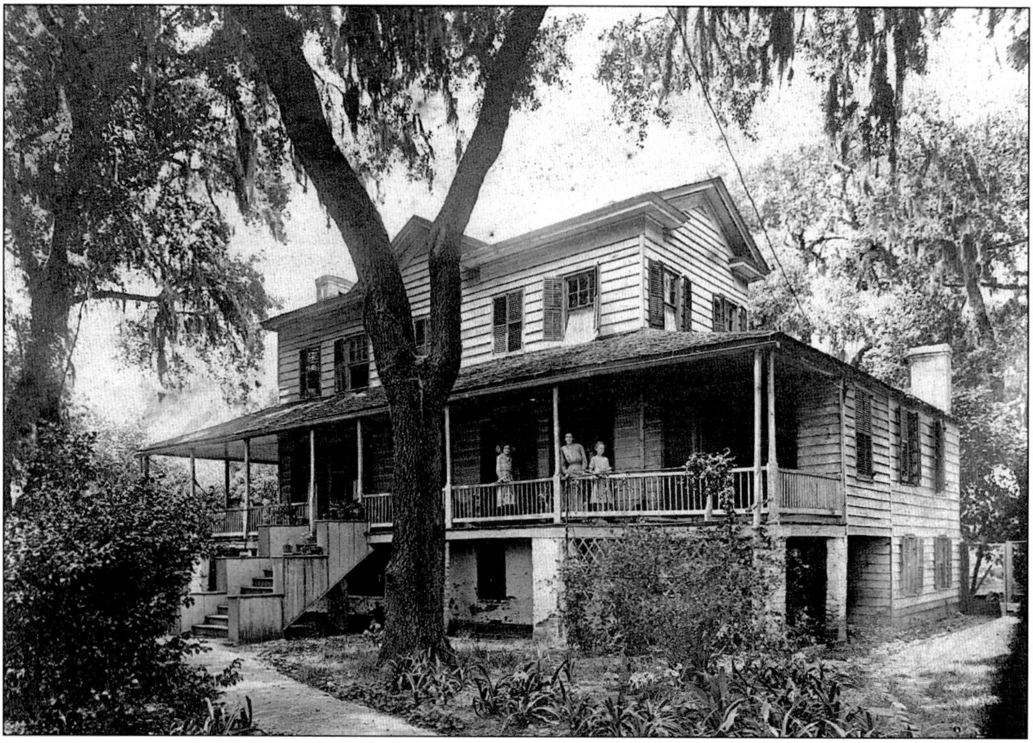

The Lebey house was built in 1854. While slaves were building the foundation, they discovered an iron chest amidst human bones. Terrified, they hastily covered it over, not wanting to disturb the spirits of the departed. Some believe that the chest may contain the treasure of the pirate, Destrade. Clementine Lebey and her daughters, Mary and Ella, are buried in the Isle of Hope Methodist Church graveyard.

ACKNOWLEDGMENTS

Many people rolled up their sleeves and helped edit the raw material for this book. It has been a community effort to stop Isle of Hope history from washing away with the ebb tide.

Thanks go the following individuals for their contributions to this book: Lagare Hucks, Carson Hucks, Harriet Barras, Dr. Julian Kelly, Dr. William Harris Bragg, Sue Wylly, John McIntosh, Nash McIntosh, Pam McCaslin, Al and Anita Quante, Honey Ryan, Alex and Beanie Barbee, Gertrude Barbee, Joe Thompson, Terry Shaw, Craig Barrow, Laura Lawton, Noel and Ruthie Wright, Carolyn Solana, Charlotte Glendye, Thad Dixon, Frank "Sonny" Seiler, Brother Herbert Kemp, Robert and Emmeline Cooper, Randy Brooks Jr., Carl Weeks, Jewell Dalrymple, Mandi Johnson, Tim Cooper, Julian and Hali Cooper, Polly Brooks, Betty Collins, and Gillian Brown.

Others, too numerous to list, have generously contributed their photos and precious memories to this project. I sincerely express my gratitude.

INTRODUCTION

The Isle of Hope, fifteen minutes southeast of Savannah, is a special place. Here, the wonders of nature are combined with serenity. Century-old oaks shade formal and natural gardens. Palms rustle in the breezes while pines grow ramrod tall next to magnolias with blossoms of ethereal sweetness. A natural habitat for woodpeckers, hummingbirds, owls, and seabirds, the island is an oasis away from crowded streets, honking cars, and city crime.

In 1986, part of the older settlement, which dates back to 1736, was declared a National Historic District. Locals are fiercely protective of the character of the island and have waged—and won—intense battles to deter condominium construction. Everywhere, joggers wave to friends rocking on screened porches. Now and then, a tour bus silently creeps along the bluff with cameras flashing through darkened windows.

The architecture is a mixture of Greek Revival, Victorian, and Neoclassical, and tidy white fishermen's cottages neatly lining the bluff. Islanders grow camellias of infinite varieties. Blazing azaleas color the roadsides in springtime, while gladiolas, gardenias, jonquils, and jasmine take turns in the spotlight throughout the year. Fragrant tea olive and wisteria scent the night air, but loveliest of all is a full moon rising over the marshes at sunset.

In 1990, there was a request for the city to erect modern streetlights on the island. In response, Gordon Cross, a builder, wrote, "The Isle of Hope Historical Association believes this would be alien to the lifestyle evolving here since the original land grants of 250 years ago. Evening walks along the river are a favorite pastime. A full moon never goes unappreciated. People walk alone at night to gaze at the stars and listen to the river. These are not commonplace happenings anywhere else in Chatham County."

Isle of Hope—such an intriguing name! The name expressed the colonists' hopes of prosperity. Some moved to the island to escape the deadly malaria and dysentery taking lives in Savannah. Inhaling salty breezes, known as "taking the salts," was believed to be healing for body and soul. It is possible that Noble Jones, an early settler, originally named the island. Jones came from Surrey, England near the River Thames. A community nearby, Stanford le Hope, had the same river configuration as Jones's new home in Georgia.

In London in 1732, James Oglethorpe, a prison reformer and military man, urged King George II to sign a charter for the new colony where people "of decayed circumstances" could begin a fresh life. The name, of course, would be Georgia to honor His Highness. Oglethorpe had compelling reasons. One was the prospect of business opportunities transpiring from a new source of silk and wine. Another was to provide protection for South Carolina from the Spaniards in Florida. Convinced, ink flowed from the royal quill on April 21, 1732, as King George signed the charter for the 13th, and last, British colony in America. On November 16, 1732, the *Anne* sailed down the Thames with London at her stern and new beginnings off her prow. Noble Jones and his family were among the 114 passengers. At once, the colonists set about building houses, roads, and churches. They were befriended by the Native Americans living there, but battled suffocating heat, malaria, and stinging insects. They called their new town "Savannah."

From the onset, Oglethorpe feared an attack from the Spaniards in Florida. The colony of Georgia was geographically in the path of an attack on South Carolina. Oglethorpe's spies reported that the Spaniards resented the colonists in Georgia for settling on land they claimed as theirs. If an attack came, it would have to be by water because there was no road.

Col. William Stephens, a member of Parliament, was sent from England to study the complaints of the colonists. In 1741, he was appointed president of the colony by the Trustees. To build fortifications, 1,500 acres were deeded equally to three worthy men on the Isle of

Hope. Noble Jones called his share "Wormsloe." On Oglethorpe's orders, Jones built a small fort to guard the Skidaway Narrows and 18 men were stationed there. After Stephen's death in 1751, Henry Parker, the assistant bailiff, was appointed as the new president of the colony to await the arrival of the new governor. He died within a year and Ann, his widow, was granted ownership of his land by King George II. John Fallowfield, a naval officer, received an adjoining share. Hard luck befell when his house burned to the ground. After nine years, weary of unsettled affairs in the colony, he and his family moved to Charleston and Noble Jones acquired his land.

The plan was to create a staging area for the communication route to the south because Isle of Hope was the last stop before 100 miles of uncivilized waterway patrolled by the Spaniards. The invasion did take place in 1742. However, Oglethorpe thwarted it before Savannah was affected in a battle on St. Simons Island. The salt water ran red with Spanish blood. This victory ended the threat to Georgia and King George awarded Oglethorpe the rank of brigadier general. There was no military action on Isle of Hope during the Revolution when the colony was trying to shrug off the yoke of British control. In 1808, French refugees from Santa Domingo arrived, including the Dupons, who became large landholders. Dr. Stephen Dupon donated land to build the Union Church (now the Methodist church) and the Catholic church. He then moved to Harrock Hall, the mainland across the marsh. If someone on Isle of Hope needed a doctor, the man of the family would ride his horse to the edge of the island and "Hallooooooo" across the marsh. Dr. Dupon would throw his medical bag into his buggy and trot off at a fast clip to the patient. People further away fired their guns three times to summon the good doctor.

Later, the Civil War (1861–1865) brought unrest. Citizens were constantly on the alert for threatened attacks during those unsettled days. The Chatham Artillery, stationed at Fort Pulaski, rode the steamer *Ida* to Camp Claghorn at Isle of Hope on September 28, 1861. There, horses and men drilled intensely. Gen. Robert E. Lee pronounced them "inferior to none in the Confederate Service." Brig. Gen. Alexander Lawton was so impressed that he gave the 121 men a steel rifle Blakely gun brought in by a blockade-running ship. With deadly accuracy, the men practiced shelling Burntpot Island across the Skidaway River. Anxious as they were for combat, they were reserved for coastal defense. Many Confederate soldiers are buried next to the Methodist church, which functioned as a hospital. The Union troops of General Sherman's army, who were stationed there later, melted the bell to use for ammunition. It was later reinstalled by George Washington Wylly.

More residents and farms appeared during the 1800s. By 1870, daily trains brought visitors to this resort area. Barbee's Pavilion at the terminus became highly popular and many large homes were built. Today, Isle of Hope is a year-round community with churches, a school, a marina, swimming pools, and longtime residents who wouldn't live anywhere else.

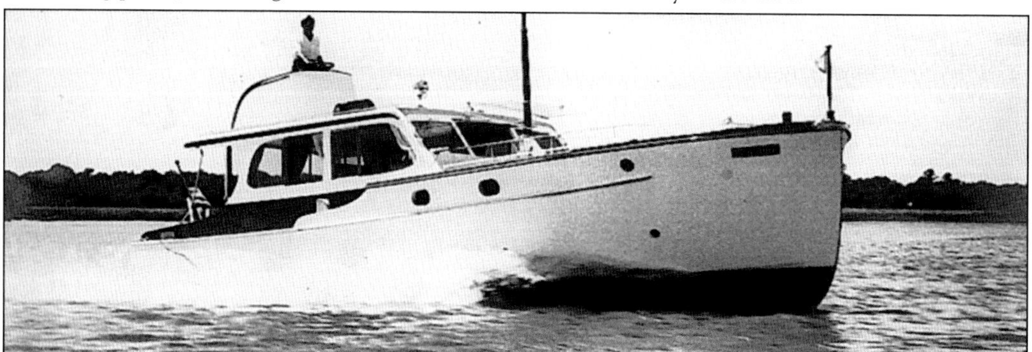

Mike Wright, an employee at Brady's Boat Works in the 1950s, pilots the *Georgia May*, a Matthews cruiser owned by Dale Critz Sr. Critz and Homer Peeples Sr. had gone out fishing on the *Peter Pan*, which broke down in Wassaw Sound. Wright and Lukie Stein came to the rescue and got the *Peter Pan* sputtering again.

One

Days Gone By and the Glorious Present

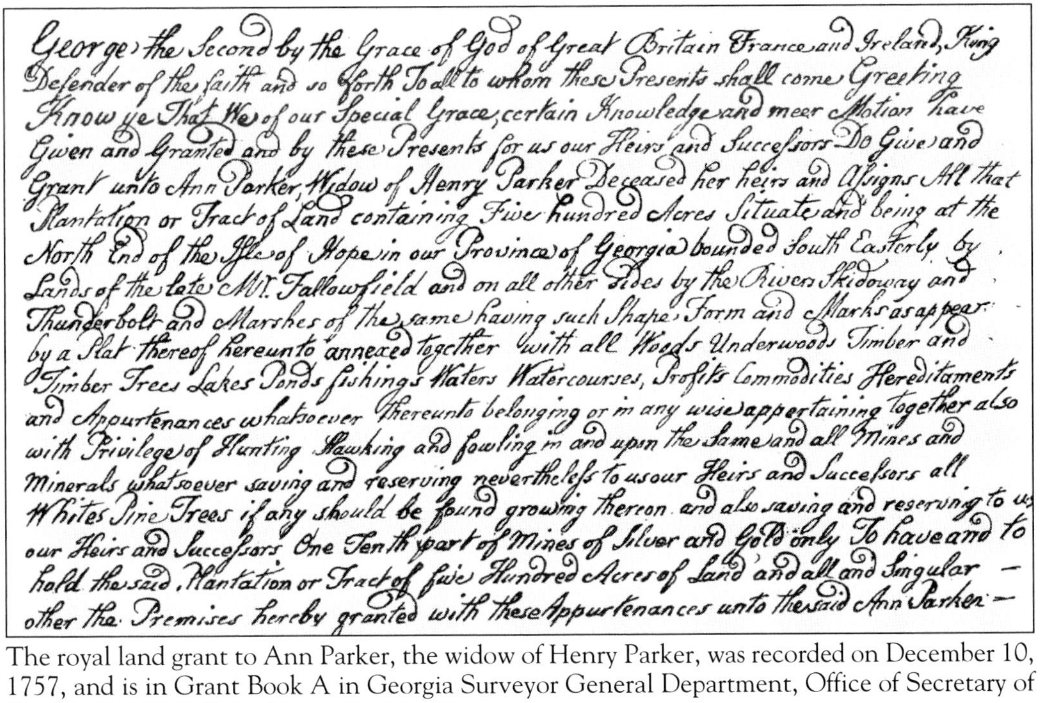

George the Second by the Grace of God of Great Britain France and Ireland, King
Defender of the faith and so forth To all to whom these Presents shall come Greeting
Know ye That We of our Special Grace, certain Knowledge and meer Motion have
Given and Granted and by these Presents for us our Heirs and Successors Do Give and
Grant unto Ann Parker, Widow of Henry Parker Deceased her heirs and Assigns All that
Plantation or Tract of Land containing Five hundred Acres Situate and being at the
North End of the Isle of Hope in our Province of Georgia bounded South Easterly by
Lands of the late Mr. Fallowfield and on all other sides by the Rivers Skidoway and
Thunderbolt and Marshes of the same having such Shape Form and Marks as appear
by a Plat thereof hereunto annexed together with all Woods Underwoods Timber and
Timber Trees Lakes Ponds fishings Waters Watercourses, Profits Commodities Hereditaments
and Appurtenances whatsoever thereunto belonging or in any wise appertaining together also
with Privilege of Hunting Hawking and fowling in and upon the same and all Mines and
Minerals whatsoever saving and reserving nevertheless to us our Heirs and Successors all
White Pine Trees if any should be found growing thereon and also saving and reserving to us
our Heirs and Successors One Tenth part of Mines of Silver and Gold only To have and to
hold the said Plantation or Tract of five Hundred Acres of Land and all and Singular —
other the Premises hereby granted with these Appurtenances unto the said Ann Parker —

The royal land grant to Ann Parker, the widow of Henry Parker, was recorded on December 10, 1757, and is in Grant Book A in Georgia Surveyor General Department, Office of Secretary of State in Atlanta, Georgia.

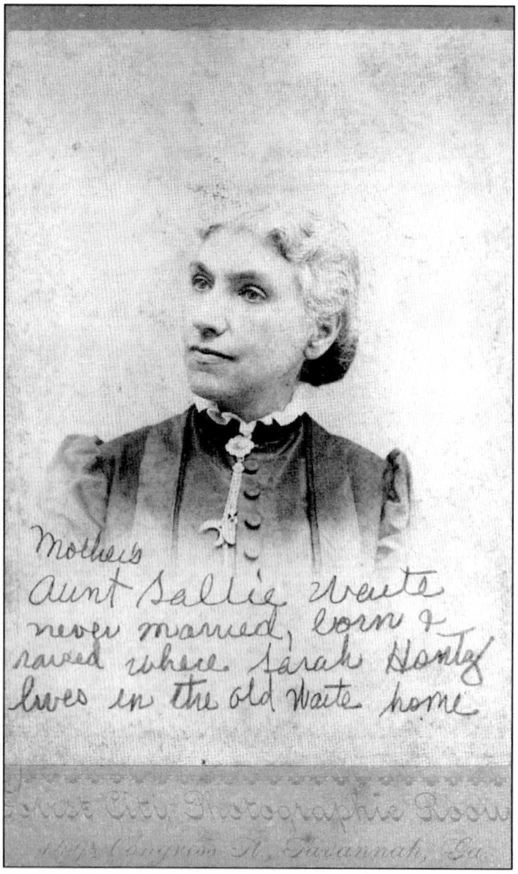

Sally Waite and her siblings grew up in the old Waite home on Grimball Point in the late 1800s. Her niece Lula started the first Sunday School at the Methodist church. The Waite home was later owned by T.J. Rourke, proprietor of Rourke Iron Works in the city. Sarah and Lord Hontz were caretakers. Allen Paulson, Chairman of Gulf Stream Aerospace, built his home in that location.

As Maj. John Gallie and his invalid wife were building their home on the bluff in 1852, a similar house was being built in Biloxi, Mississippi. Called *Beauvoir*, it was to be the home of Jefferson Davis. Scottish-born Gallie was a partner in the Gallie & Wilden Steamship Line. He was in the navy in the 1830s and was later in the Chatham Artillery and Georgia Hussars militia units. During the War Between the States, Gallie commanded Fort McAllister on Genesis Point. He was killed during a Union bombardment. George Wylly bought the house when Mrs. Gallie died in 1854. In 1942, Olin McIntosh Sr. bought the house, and the Noel Wright family purchased it in 1945.

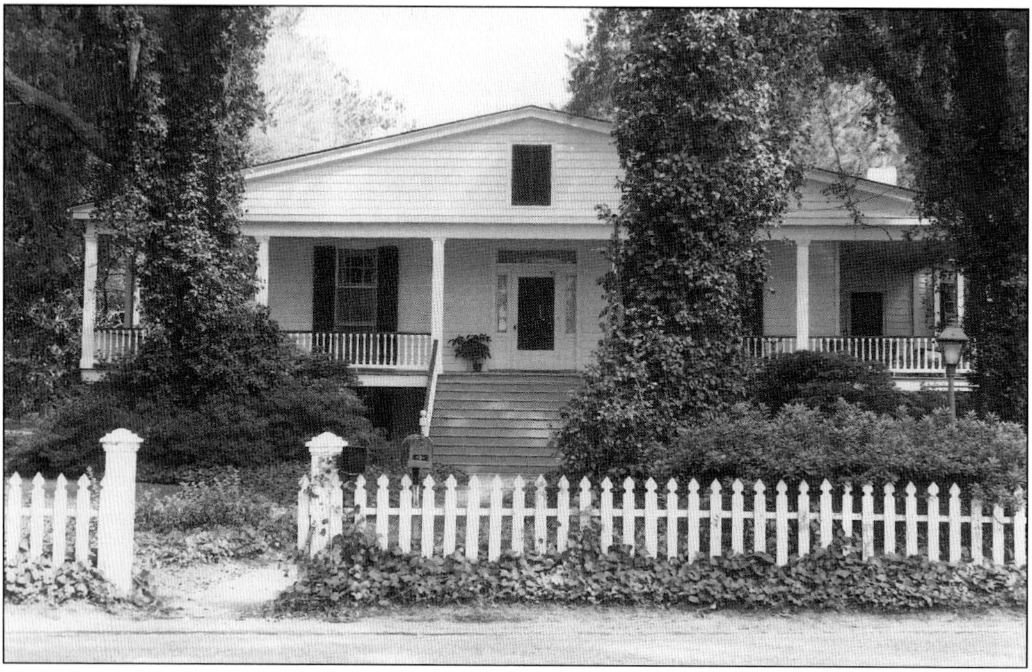

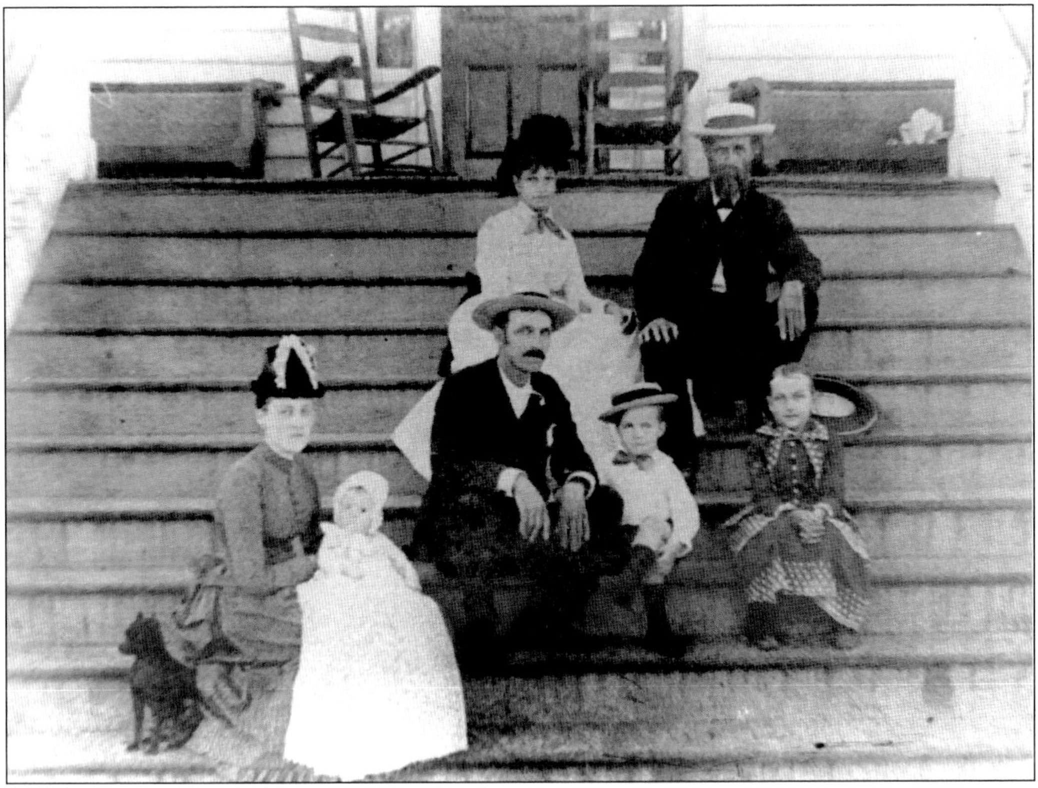

George Washington Wylly Sr. and his family were some of the earliest Isle of Hope residents. Mr. Wylly was the first clerk of the city market, the sheriff of Chatham County, and a member of the Pulaski Guards, the Savannah Volunteer Guards, the Sons of the Revolution, and the Society of the Cincinnati. As a council member during the Civil War, he was appointed to surrender the city to General Sherman. Pictured from left to right are (top) Alzina Johnson (Wylly's second wife) and George Wylly Sr.; (middle) Fred Wylly, Lucian Dawson Wylly, and Naomi Alzina Wylly; (bottom) Emma Lucian Dawson Wylly and baby Georgia.

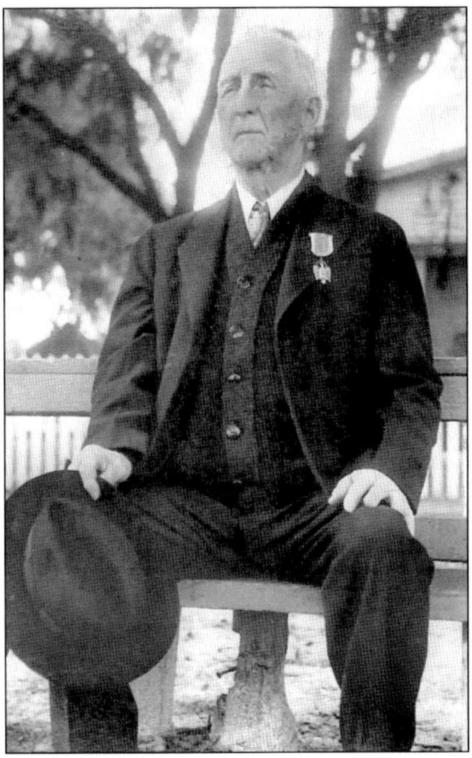

George Washington Wylly Jr. ponders life in front of his home at 3 Bluff Drive. He was a descendent of Capt. Thomas Wylly, who was deputy quartermaster general of the Georgia troops in the Revolutionary Army under George Washington—for whom he and his father were named. "Mr. Wash" joined the Society of the Cincinnati in 1906 and the medal is visible on his coat.

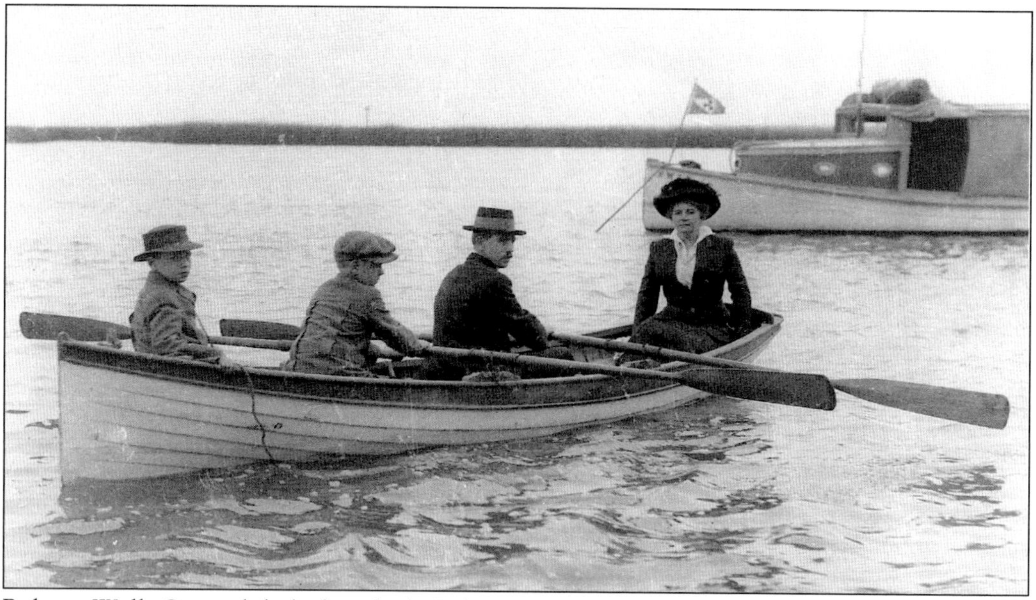

Ralston Wylly Sr., with help from little Ralston, rows his wife, Birdie, ashore after shelling and picnicking on Wassaw Island. His younger son, Albert, nicknamed "Skeet," rides in the prow. Their naptha-fueled pleasure launch, the *Nola W.*, is anchored in the Skidaway River.

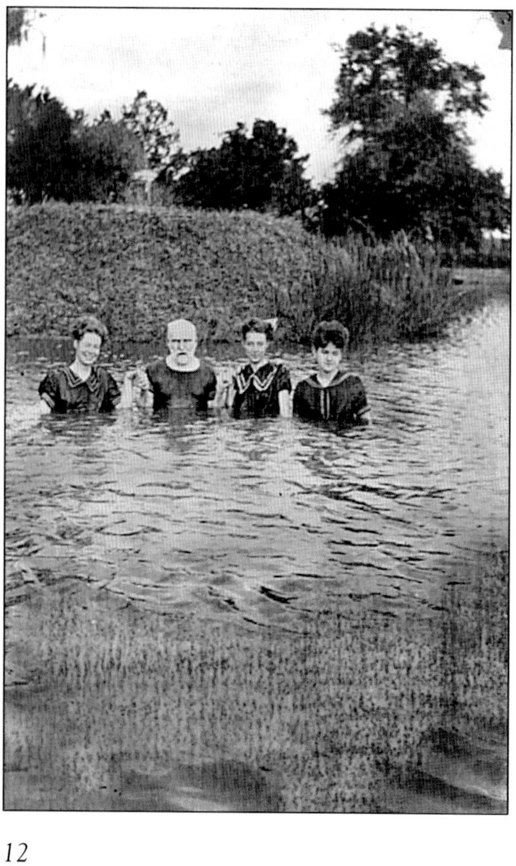

Notations on this early photo identify the swimmers as (left to right) Katie B. Moore, Judge Norwood, Mary Moore, and Hop-See.

Dick and John Rosenbrook arrived from Germany in the late 1800s and sailed the inland waterway pedaling clothes, oars, shoes, blankets, smelling salts, pickles, jerky, fishing tackle, and pocketknives. The floating store was such a success that they opened a general store on the corner of Bluff Drive and Rosenbrook Avenue. Hermann Diedrich Mueller, grandfather of George and Hermann Coolidge, married a Rosenbrook sister and worked in the store for many years.

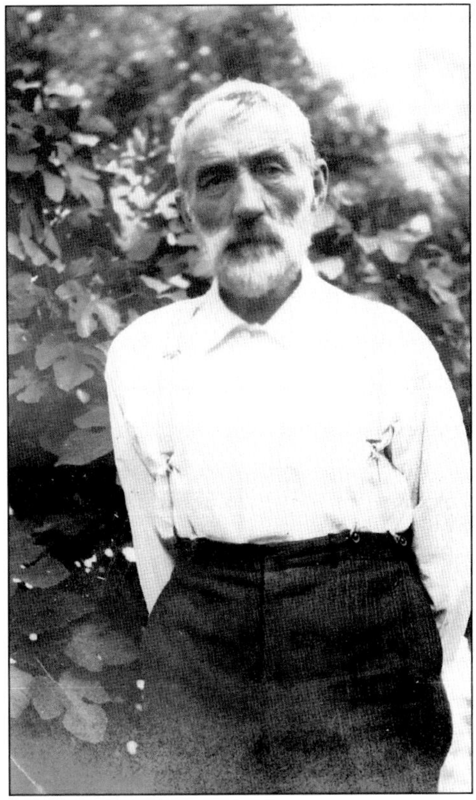

This fascinating photo shows Mr. Mueller leaning on the counter in Mueller's Store. Watermelons and Uneeda biscuits were big business. Notice the scrubbing board hanging on the back wall. The legs of the scrubbing board were placed in a washtub full of soapy water. The dirty clothes were rubbed up and down over the corrugated ridges to get the stains out.

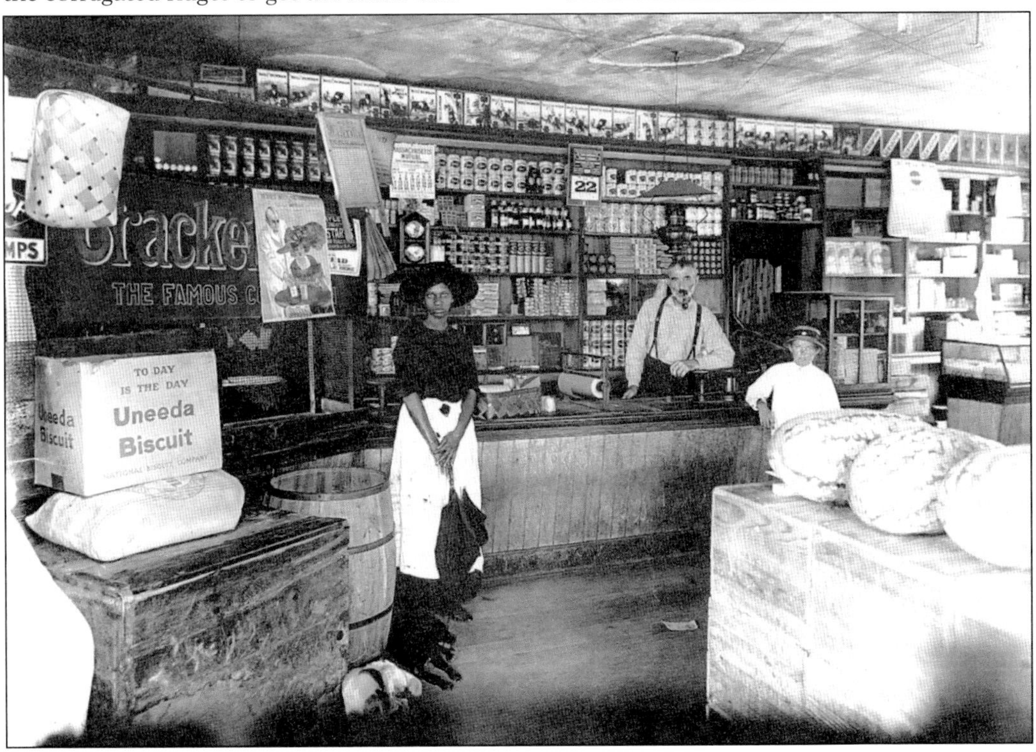

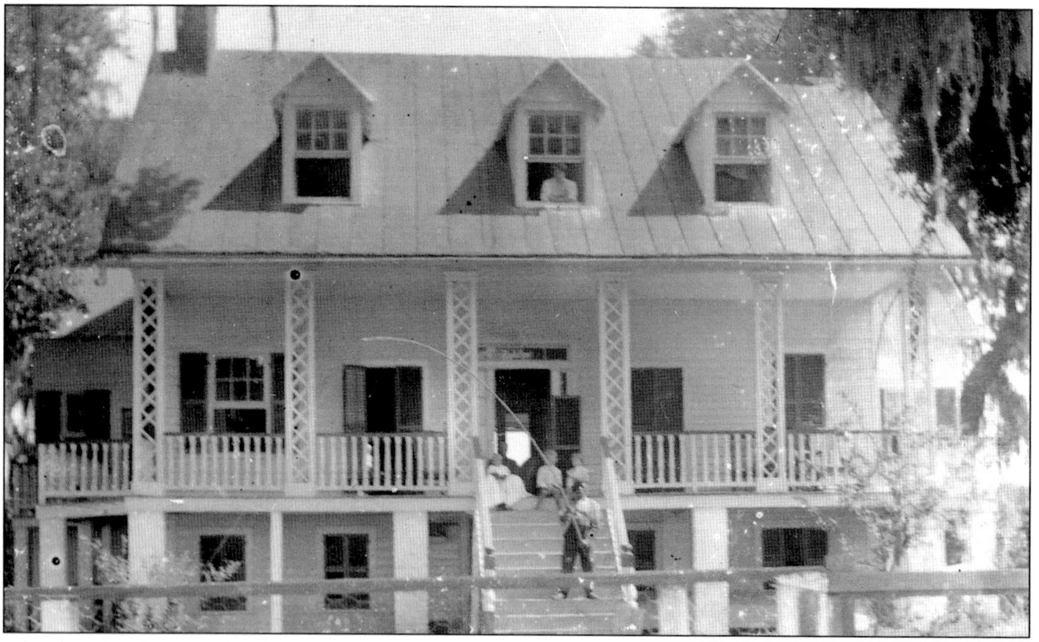

Charles Hardee and his family moved to Isle of Hope in 1873. After renting from Annie Stubbs, he purchased this home at a sheriff's sale and remodeled it. Fleeing yellow fever in the city, relatives Henry and Alice Backus—and their children—moved in. More relatives, the Robert Erwins and their children, came to live there as well, bringing the household occupancy to a total of 18 people. The Hardees happily welcomed all into their home. Mr. Hardee lived well into his 90s. In 1920, ex-mayor Wallace Pierpont became the owner of the house. Subsequent owners were Jim and Margaret Barnett, David and Peggy Johnson, Julian and Linda Kelly, and Roy and Linda Baker.

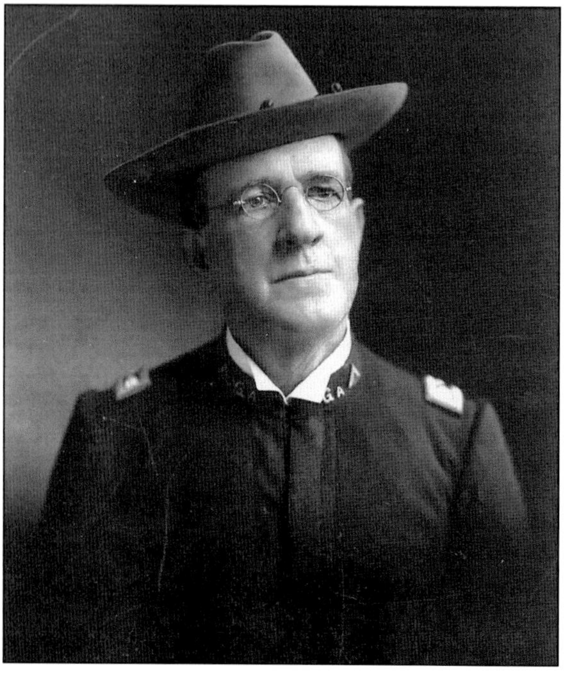

Young John Holbrook Estill was a "printer's devil" setting type at the *Savannah Morning News* and later became the owner and publisher. He owned the mansion called Wymberley (seen on the following page)and folks addressed him as "Squire." Judge George Tiedeman bought the mansion in 1909 and renamed it Carsten Hall. The mansion burned in 1933. In 1940, William Flynn purchased the land as docking for his timber operation on Skidaway Island. In 1946, Jim Richmond, with financial backing from J.D. McLamb, bought the property. He and Maxwell B. Hostetter created the Wymberley subdivision.

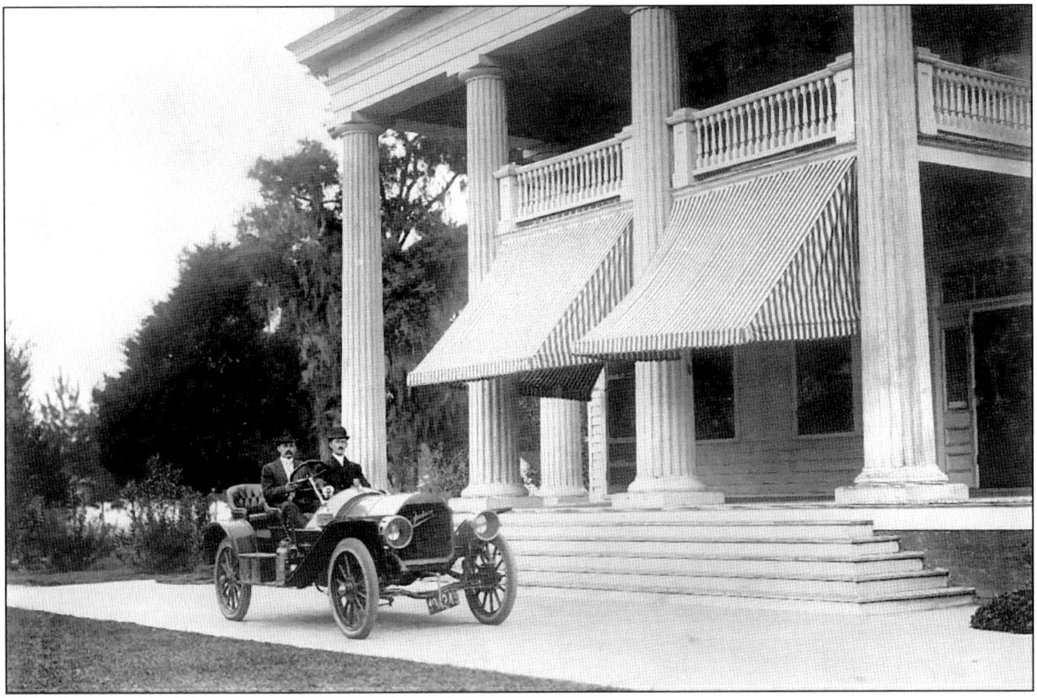

This mansion has had many owners including the Bullochs, the Claghorns, the Joneses, the Hunters, the Bacons, and the Glens. It was a gardener's haven with pecan orchards, pear trees, cedar trees, and palm trees, plus riding stables, tennis courts, a bowling alley, and a boathouse. Sir Thomas Lipton was a great friend of Squire and visited often. This photo shows one of the first cars on the island and the glory of the old mansion.

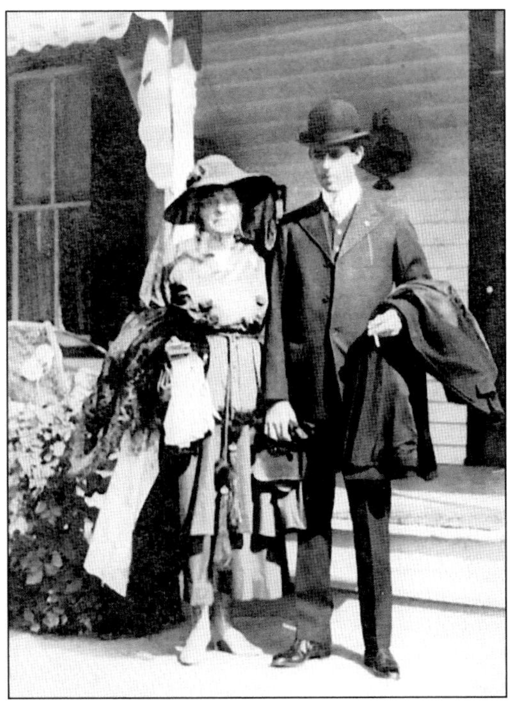

Maude Hill (Estill), Colonel Estill's widow, stands beside her second husband, Douglas Scarborough from Virginia. They lived on Whitaker Street.

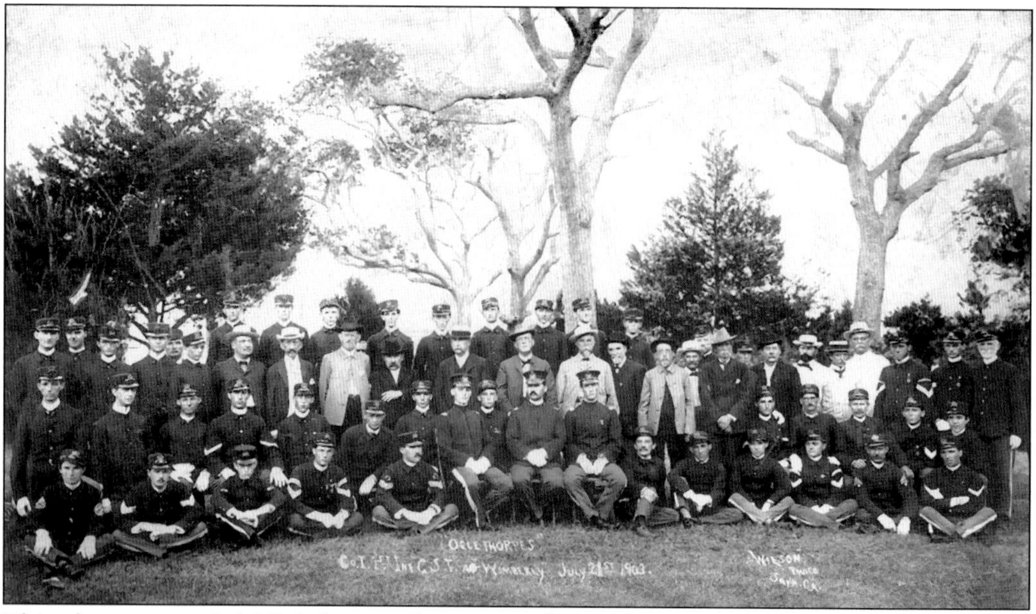

This photo is entitled "Oglethorpes Company I, lst Inf. C.S.T. @ Wimberly, July 21, 1903." Notice that Wimberly had several spellings over the years. Colonel Estill is pictured near the center, standing. During the War Between the States, the area around Wimberly was a Confederate encampment called Camp Claghorn. Soldiers practiced shelling Burntpot Island across the river.

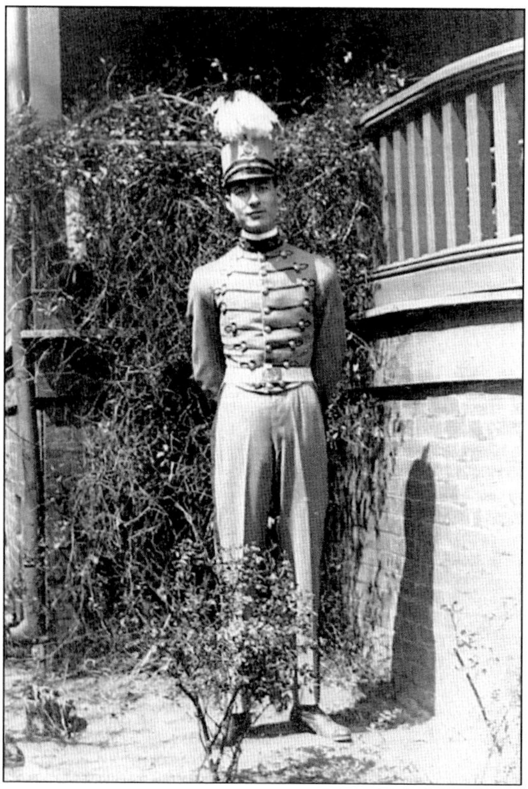

A member of the Chatham Artillery, Pearson Hill Sloan poses at the mansion in 1914. With three degrees in engineering from Georgia Tech, he later became an Episcopal priest and was a driving force in starting St. Thomas Church. His daughter, Jane Lyon, is a prominent Savannah artist today.

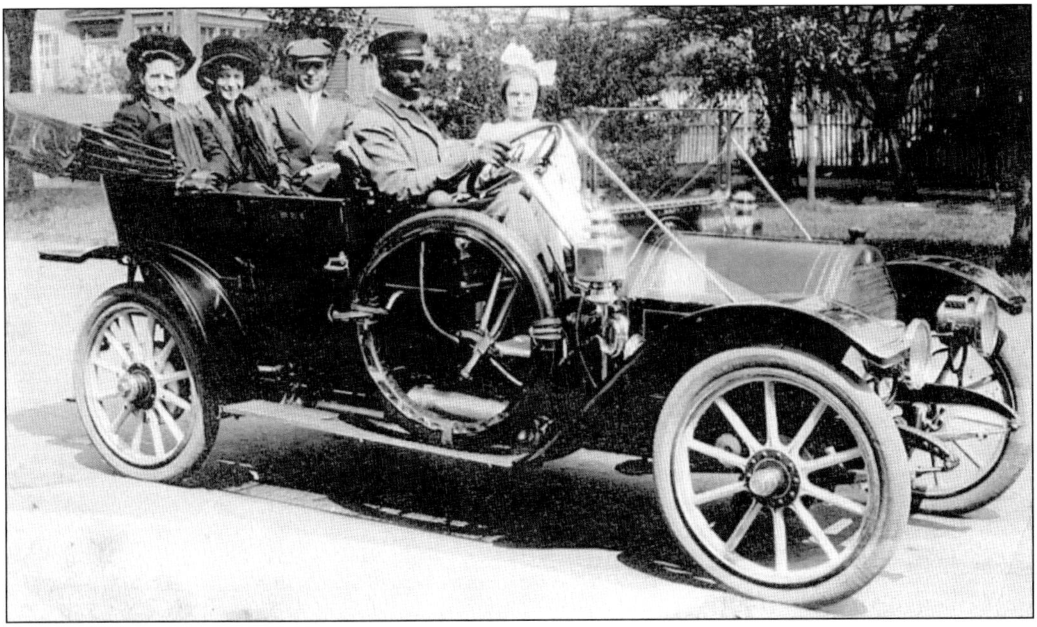

A chauffeur drives the Sloan family (relatives of Colonel Estill) in a 1909 Star. Pearson Hill Sloan (in cap) sits next to Nina Sloan (Lucas) (Yankee) and Jane Hill (Sloan). Jane Maud Sloan (Harty), in her crisply starched hair bow, rides next to the chauffer. The chauffer's house, built in 1820, is thought to be one of the oldest homes on the island. Colonel Estill caved in to pressures from the family to buy a car. Because he did not trust motorcars, he followed it in his trusty horse carriage. Sure enough, the car broke down at the entrance to the estate!

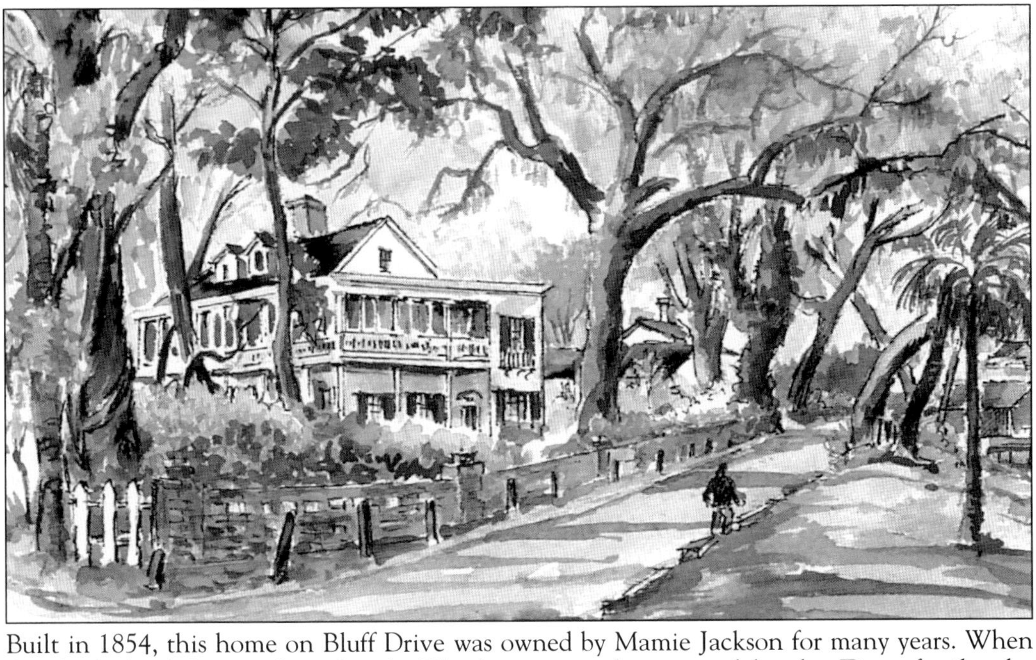

Built in 1854, this home on Bluff Drive was owned by Mamie Jackson for many years. When she died, she left it to her church. The house was then owned by the Tison family, the Watkins, and the Joseph Solanas. Carolyn Solana, grandmother of nine, lives in it today. The grandchildren fish and swim off the dock in fine weather.

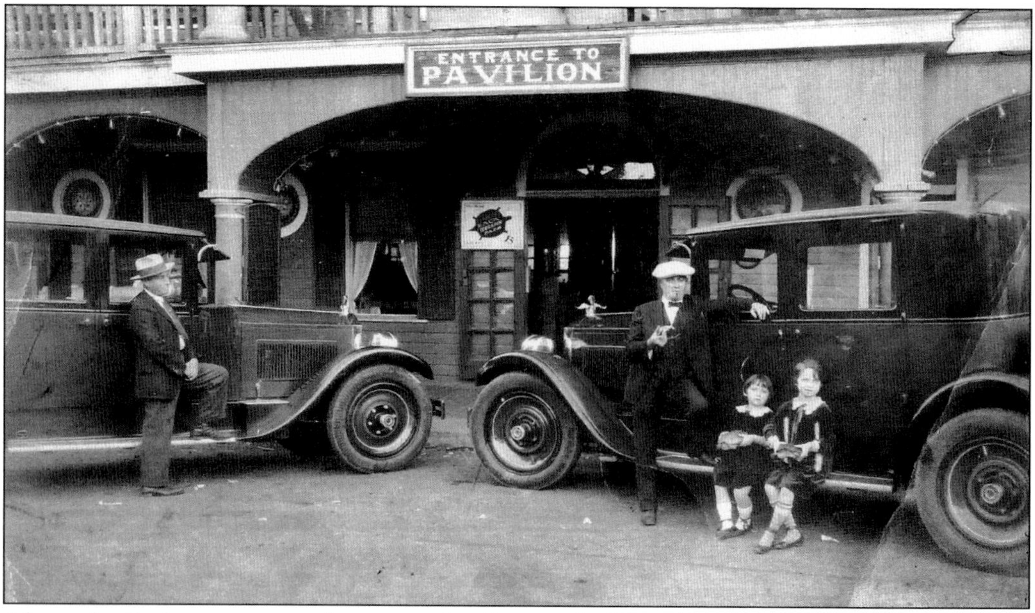

Alexander Barbee was a conductor on the Savannah, Thunderbolt, and Isle of Hope Steam Railroads. He loved terrapin stew, which was made with eggs, butter, cream, nutmeg, and amontillado. In 1898, he decided to raise terrapins, a land reptile. To learn their habits and needs, he bogged at night in the muddy marshes, their natural habitat. His "bulls" and "cows" began to multiply and were soon on the menus of the finest restaurants. Pictured here, from left to right, are William Barbee, Alexander Barbee, and their granddaughters, Ann and Gertrude, on the running board of a classic Packard.

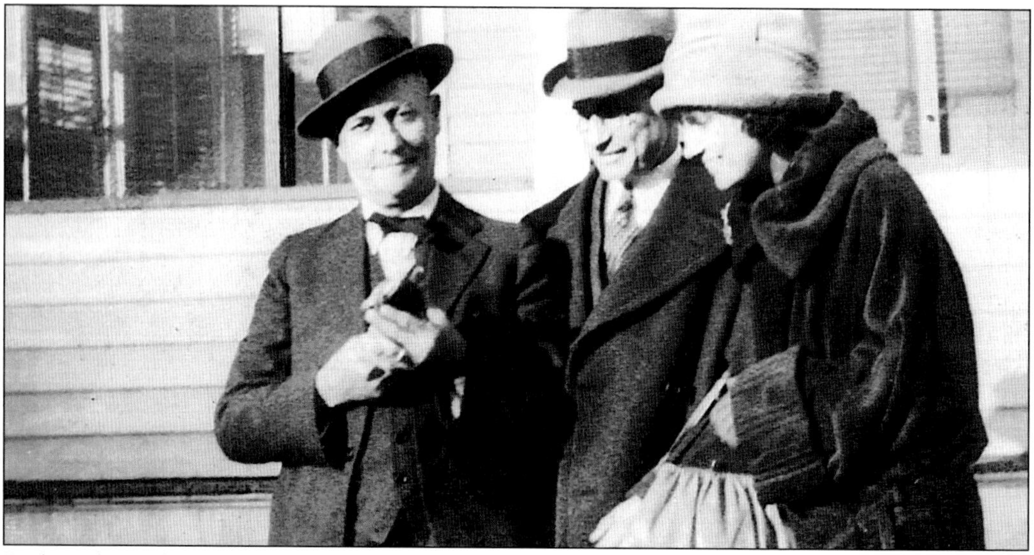

Barbee shows his pet terrapin, Toby, to a pair of curious tourists. The story goes that Toby was hatched in the warm hand of the well-known attorney, William Jennings Bryan. Barbee is quoted as saying, "The most important thing about terrapin meat is its tonic quality. It fills you with fuss, fight, and gumption. It'll make an old rooster out of you!" Savannah temperatures occasionally dip into the 20s, so her warm raccoon coat, very trendy at that time, kept her comfortable.

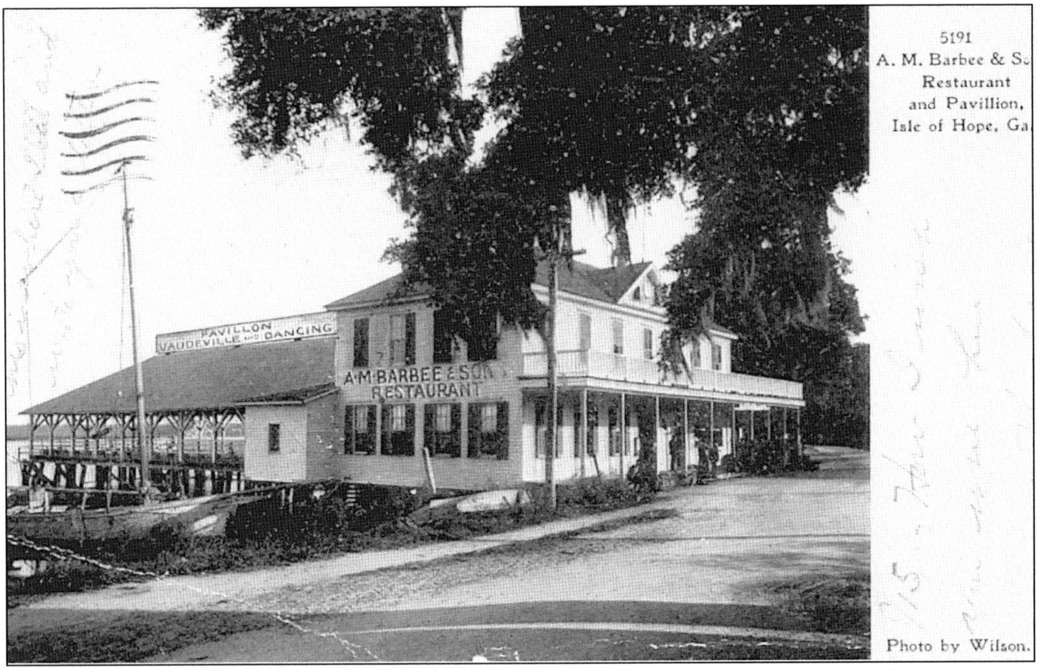

Crowds took the streetcars from the city to Barbee's Pavilion. Bathing costumes and towels could be rented and a seafood factory prepared crabs, oysters, and fish. Fresh shrimp were brought in on two large shrimp boats, the *Gertrude* and the *Ann*. By 9 p.m., couples were doing the box step and waltzing to "Tea for Two," "Deep in My Heart, Dear," and "Does the Spearmint Lose Its Flavor on the Bedpost Overnight?" A sign announced that Barbee's Pavilion was "Where the Pretty Girls Go." Another pavilion was constructed to replace the original one after it burned.

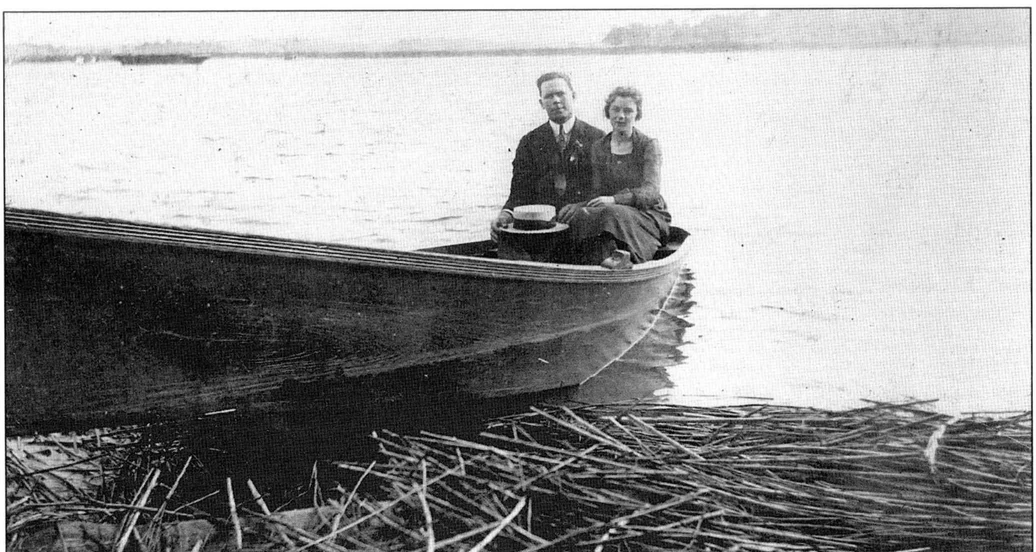

Isle of Hope under a full moon, dancing cheek to cheek on the pavilion, and paddling in the river under the stars drew lots of young romantics. Here, an unidentified couple cozy up to each other in the stern of a long bateau in the Skidaway River.

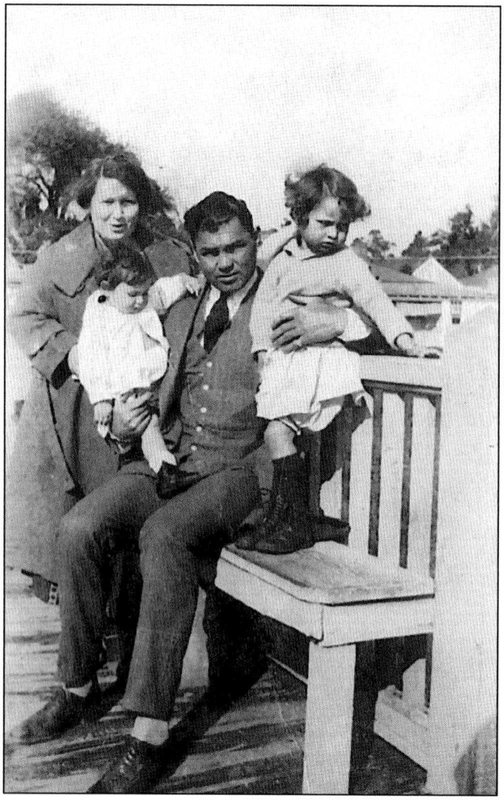

In 1924, Mr. Barbee's son, William, captured more business by bringing in Jack Dempsey, the famous boxer. It was a thrill to the customers but rough on family finances. Pictured from left to right are Mrs. William "Rose" Barbee, Ann Barbee (McIntyre), Jack Dempsey, and Gertrude Barbee (Magee).

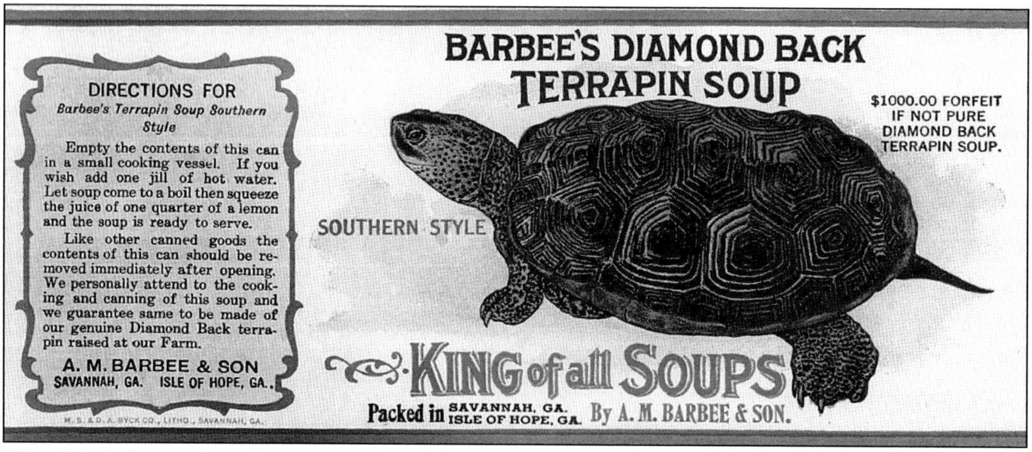

This label shows the characteristics of the terrapin. Multi-colored lines and splotches cover its snake-like head and its shell looks like worn leather. On the carapace are 13 diamond shapes. The underside, or plastron, is smooth like ivory. The magical ingredients in Rose Barbee's famous stew are the following: the meat, heart, and liver of two terrapin, the powdered and sieved yolks of eight hard-boiled eggs, a half pound of butter, two pints of heavy cream, a sprinkle of flour, salt, nutmeg, and a glass of amontillado. This makes about three unforgettable servings.

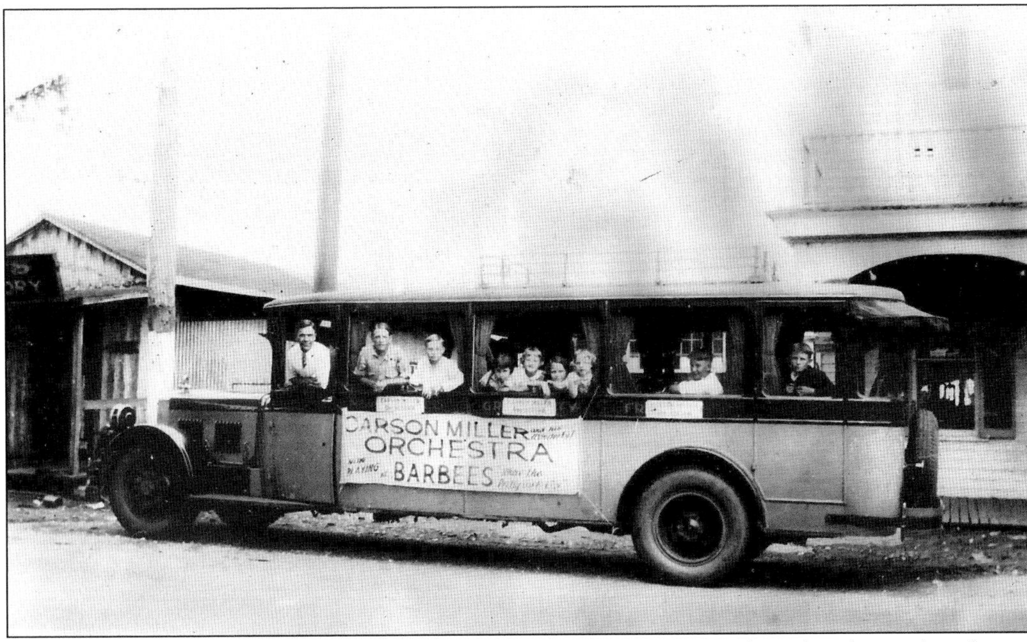

Carson Miller's orchestra pulls up for a gig on the pavilion. Jan Garber's band was also playing there. There was a nickelodeon to provide music when live groups were not available. The pavilion was definitely the "in" place to go.

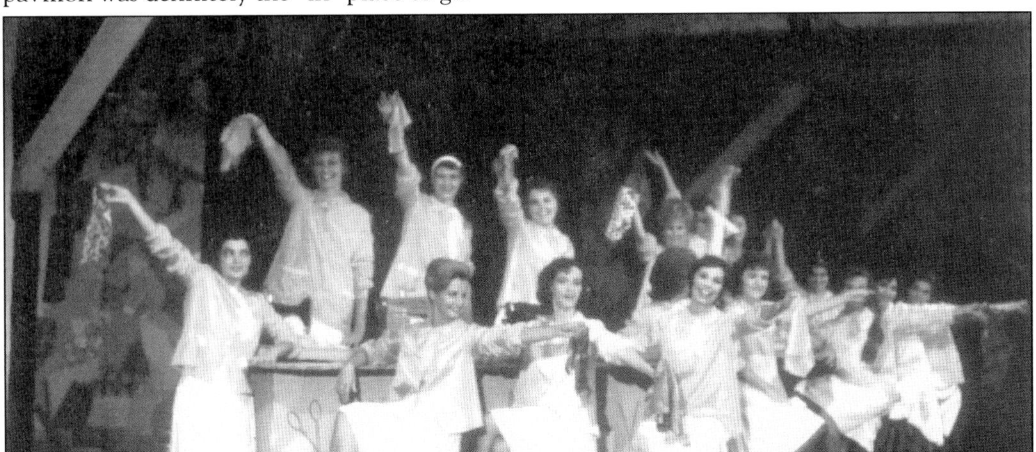

In the 1960s, The Little Theater performed *Pajama Game* on the pavilion. Nancy Keith (Gerard), niece of Savannah's famous songwriter and lyricist Johnny Mercer, is easily recognizable sitting third from the left. Other productions included *My Fair Lady*, *Oklahoma*, *Mr. Roberts*, and *Bye Bye Birdie*. Nearby, Mr. Barbee had a room in his house in which every object played a tune—bed, hat rack, hairbrush, lamps, clocks, and many more. With a touch of the finger, 150 objects came to life and played a tune. Visitors were mesmerized. Today, old-timers recall the days of Barbee's Pavilion with fond nostalgia.

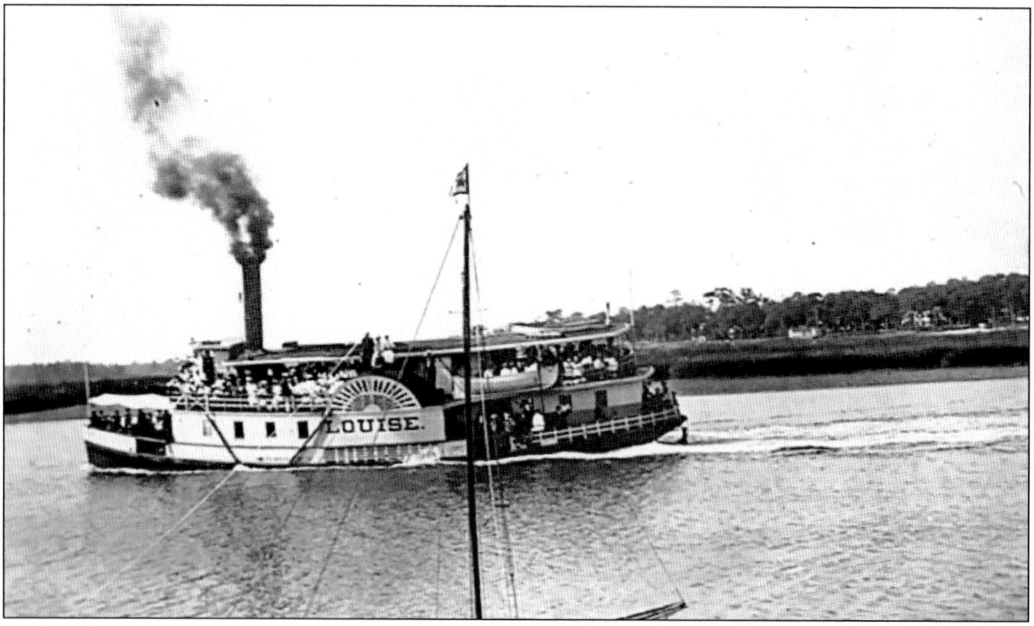

In this photo, a merry crowd from the Methodist Church Sunday school class is aboard the *Louise* motoring to Wassaw for a picnic in June of 1907. The faded notations on this old snapshot read, "Grand surf. Stayed in the water one hour, then took a stroll on the beach. Glorious day and jolly trip. Didn't stick in the mud!"

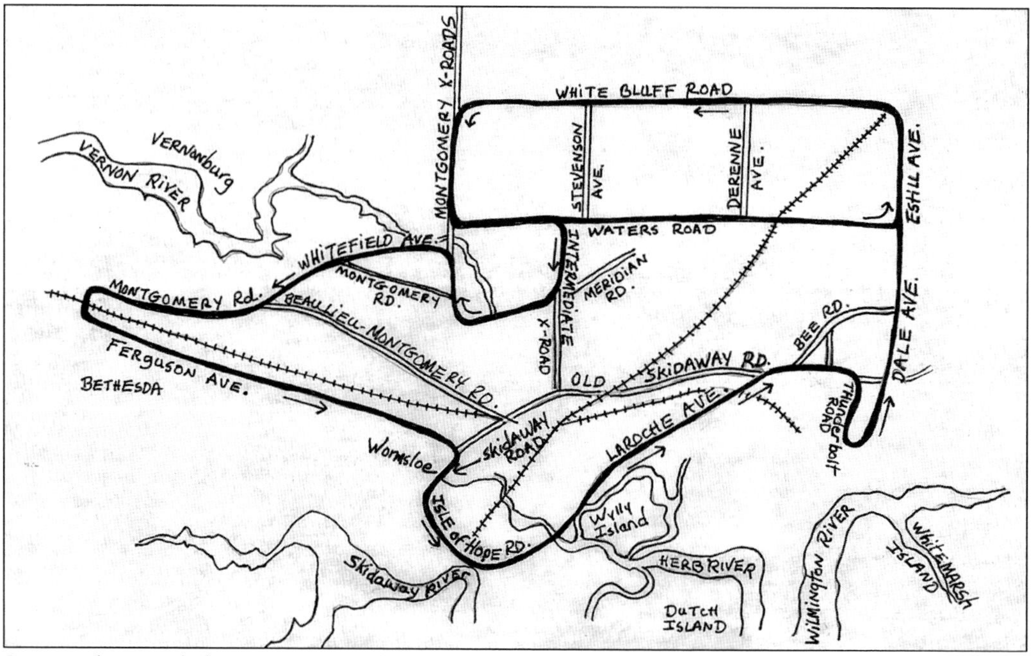

Savannah staged the International Road Race, later called the American Grand Prize Race, with a gold cup prize valued at a whopping $5,000. The 1908 course included Montgomery, Isle of Hope, and Wassaw (Thunderbolt). Ferguson Avenue plunged straight through pine forests for a thrilling four-mile stretch. Goggled drivers hurled their roaring iron monsters at hair-straightening speeds along this straightaway.

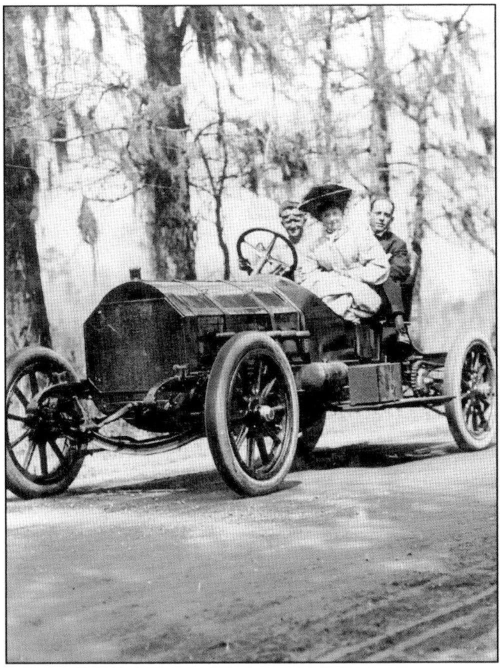

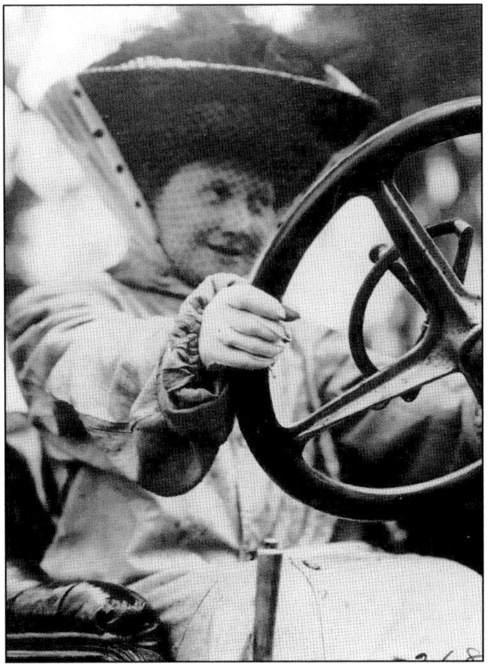

The races were tough on the men who drove in them. The cars had few safety features and crashes were often fatal. Drivers contended with engines roaring and pounding at high speeds, shards being flung up from the dirt roads, and unexpected tire explosions. By contrast, in these two images, the people seem happy as they putt across the causeway from Sandfly to Isle of Hope. The enormous steering wheel overpowers this thrilled young lady on the right.

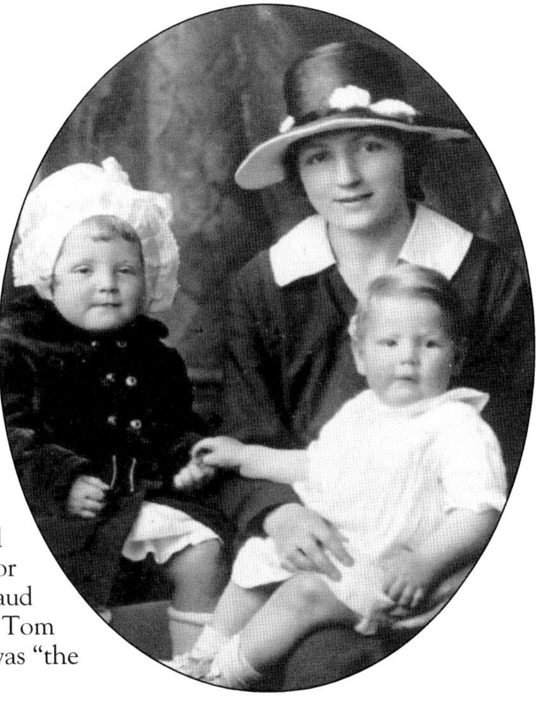

Lillian Chaplin Bragg, born in 1895, is shown here with "Chappie" and Sonny. Lillian Bragg was the catalyst for the political reform movement when her letter to the editor of the *Morning News* blew the whistle on fraud at the voting polls in 1947. According to Tom Coffey, a popular local journalist, her letter was "the shot heard across Savannah."

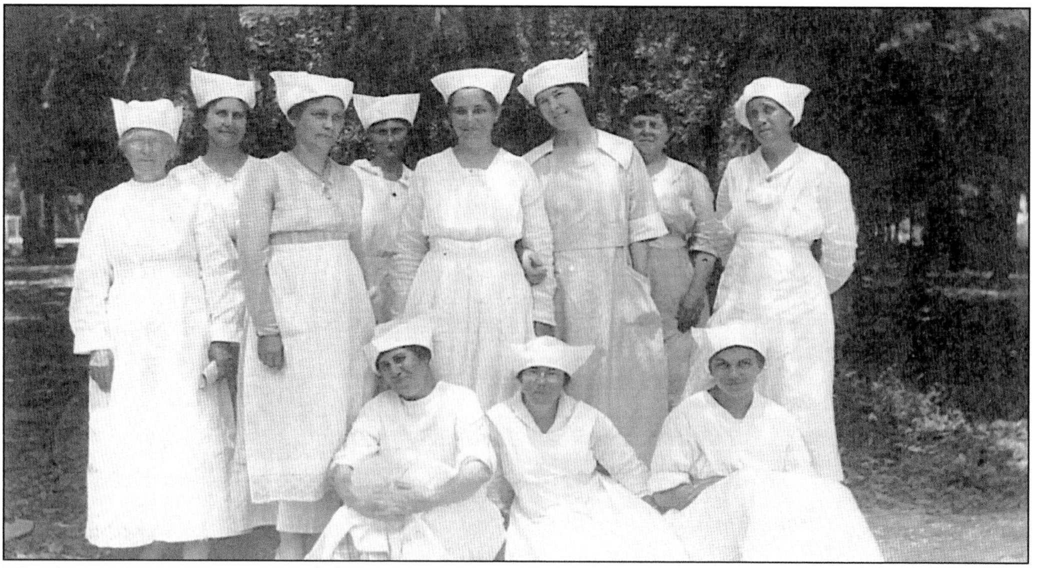

The Home Demonstration Club was an active organization. They often entered their crafts and baked goods in state fairs. They learned to sew, cook, embroider, darn socks, starch shirts, make lye soap, and make cane chairs along with many other useful skills. Club members, from left to right, are (sitting) Josephine Wells, Bess Kinsey, and Martha Boxton McCreery; (standing) Jesie Moore, Mrs. Grice, Mrs. Frank Waite, Alberta Wylly Ellis, Essie Waite, Mary Mittells, unidentified, and Bessie Roberts.

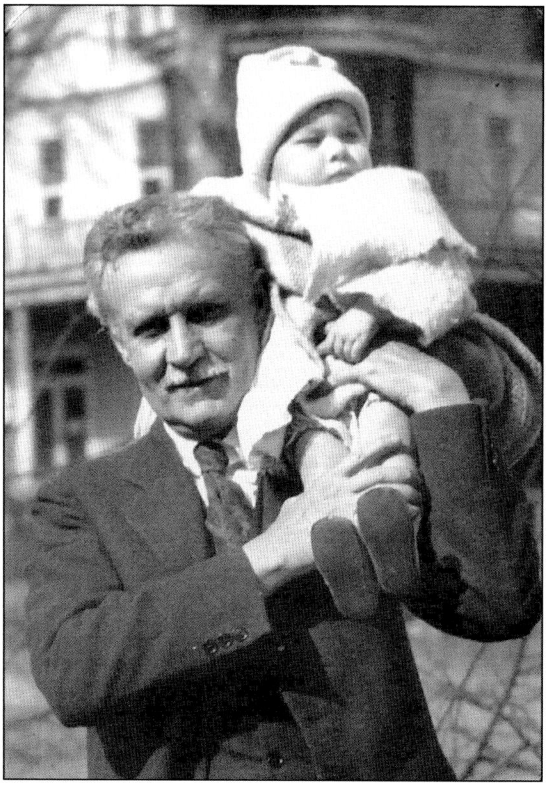

John Arthur Varnedoe hoists his grandbaby, Jane Sloan (Lyon), onto his shoulder. He was proprietor of the Globe Shoe Company on Broughton Street in the 1920s. His wife was Jane Tilton from Charleston. The Varnedoes' house on the bluff burned and the Ben Portmans later built their home on that land. "Baby Jane" grew up to be one of Savannah's most well-known painters.

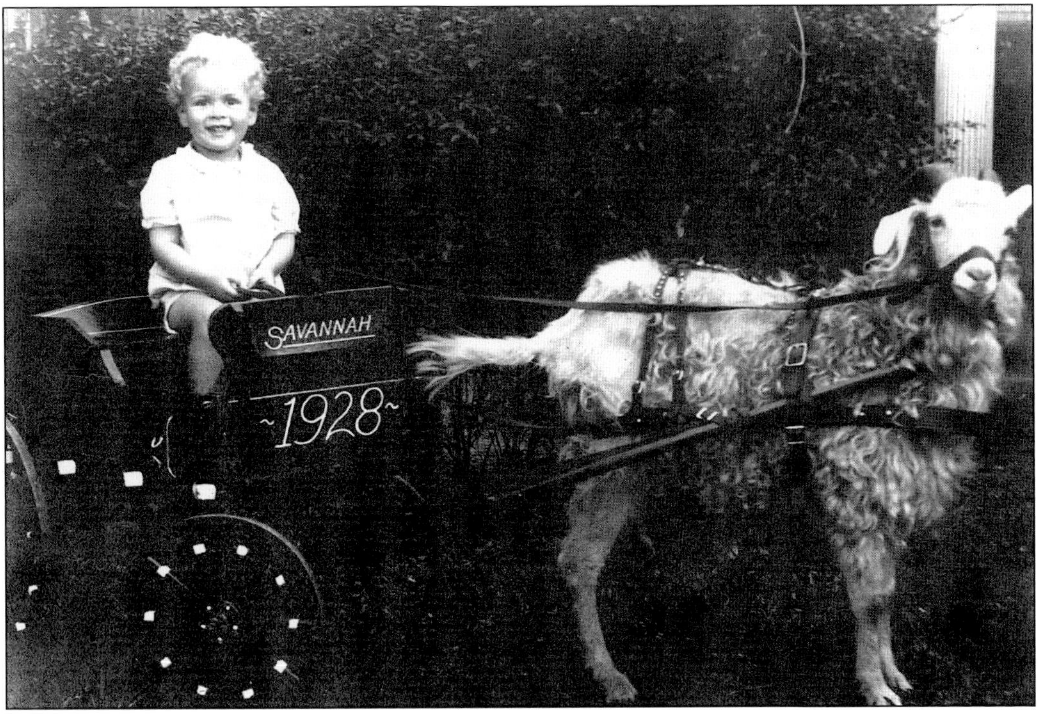

Two-year-old Tommy Johnson beams with delight as he reigns in a billy goat to pose for this "mother's pride" photograph. The Johnson house is at the north end of the bluff. Isle of Hope children learned to swim around the same time they learned to toddle—sometimes even before. Mothers often had to drag their water-logged children out for supper.

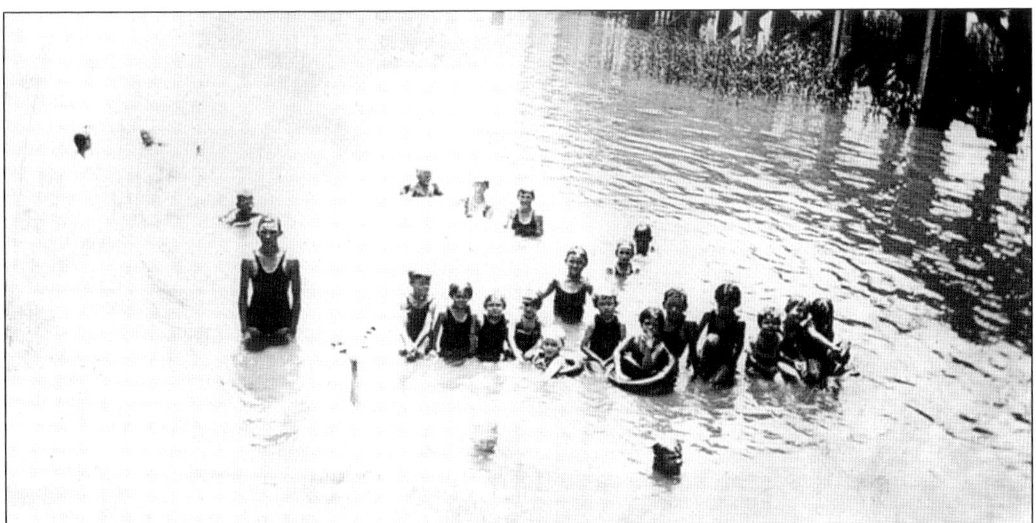

Crowds of bobbing heads, laughter, shrieks, splashes, "cannon balls," and "belly-busters" describe the scene at the "bulkhead" next to a dock on the bluff, owned by Maj. Fred Schwalb. Swimming times depended upon the rise and ebb of the tide.

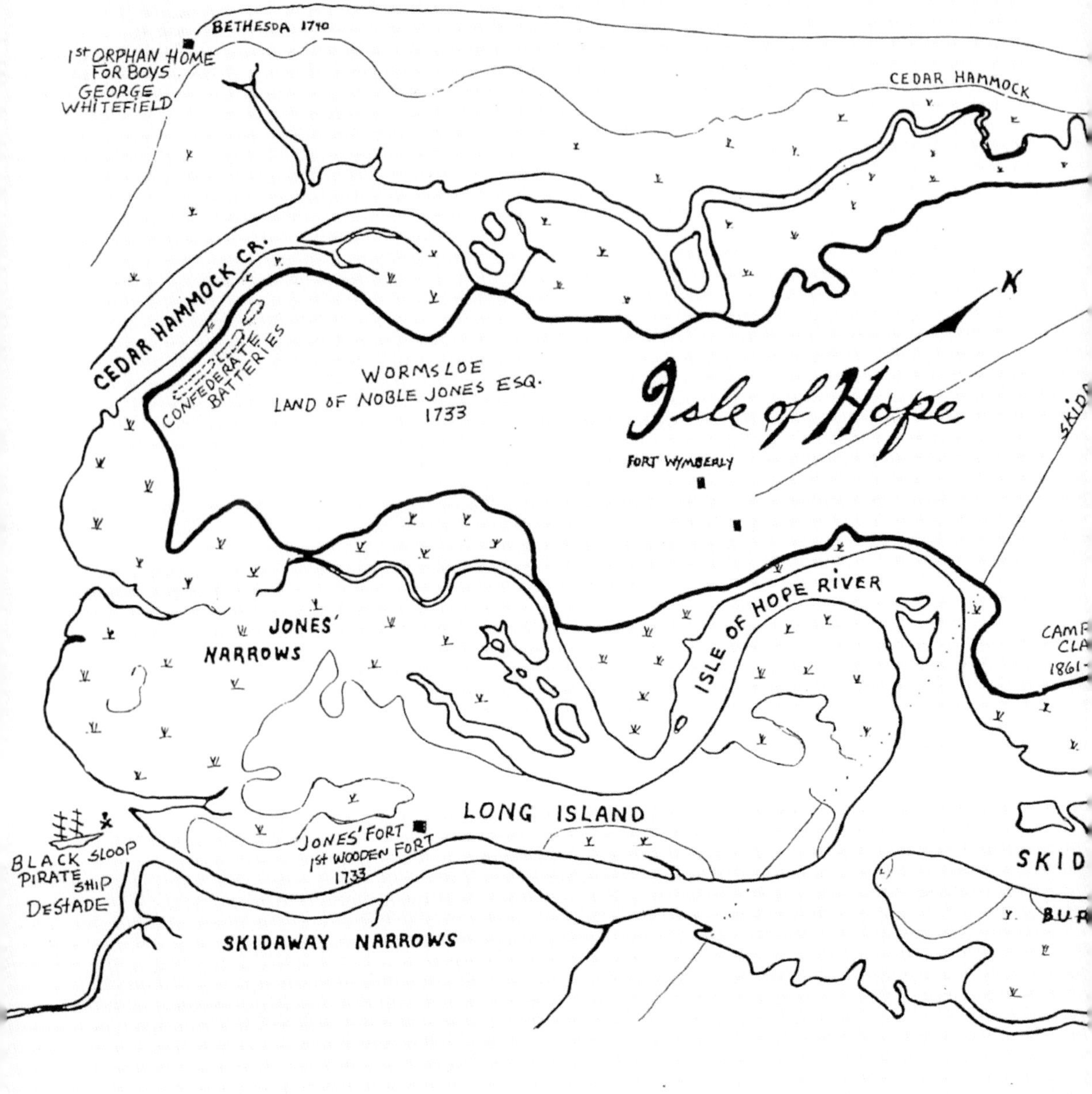

B.T. "Cookie" Byrd was a local historian and drew this map of the area in his own unique style.

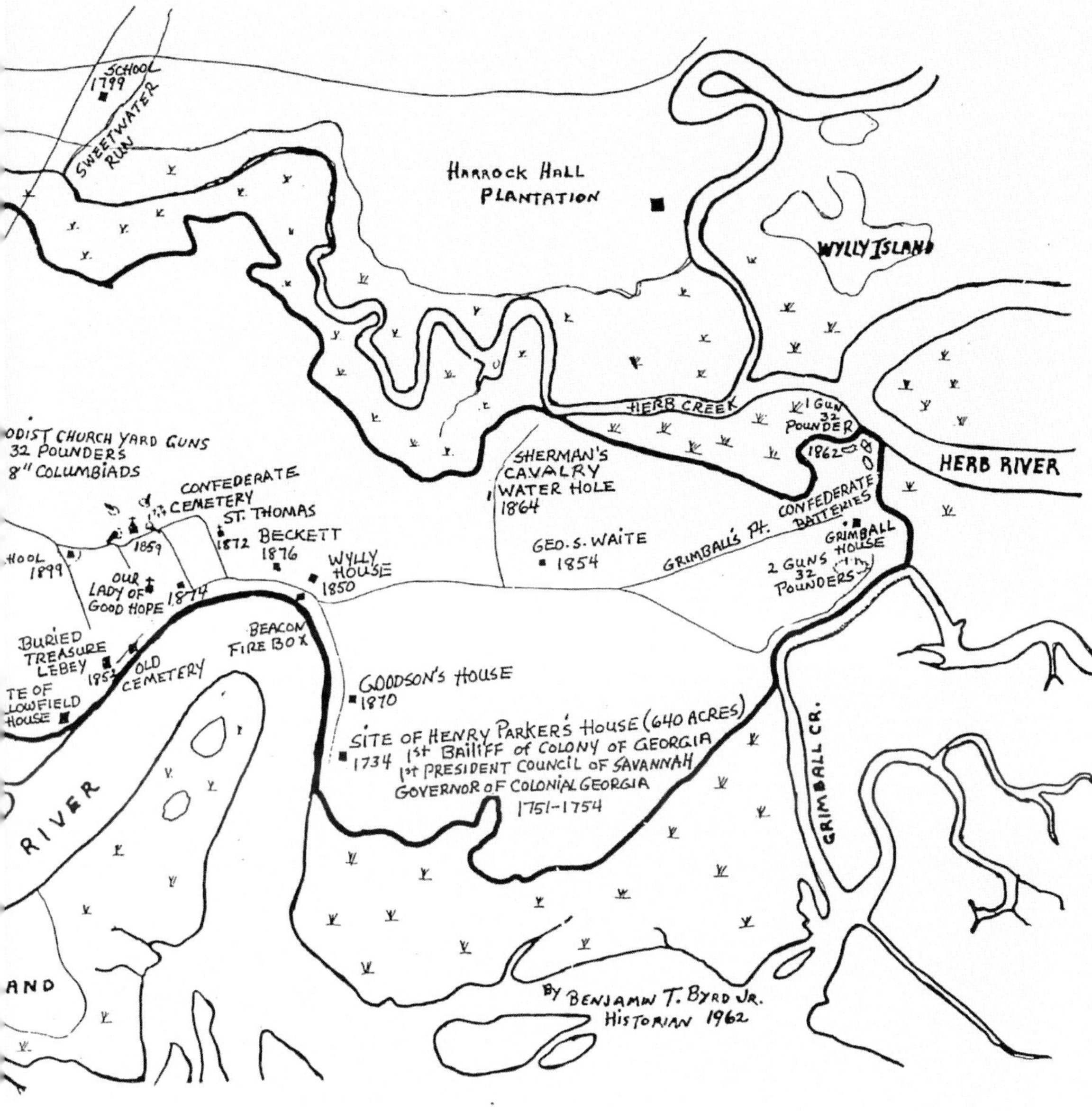
SCHOOL 1799
SWEETWATER RUN
HARROCK HALL PLANTATION
WYLLY ISLAND
HERB CREEK
1 GUN 32 POUNDER
1862
HERB RIVER
ODIST CHURCH YARD GUNS
32 POUNDERS
8" COLUMBIADS
CONFEDERATE CEMETERY
1859
ST. THOMAS
1872
BECKETT 1876
WYLLY HOUSE 1850
SHERMAN'S CAVALRY WATER HOLE 1864
GEO. S. WAITE 1854
GRIMBALL'S Pt.
CONFEDERATE BATTERIES
GRIMBALL HOUSE
2 GUNS 32 POUNDERS
HOOL 1899
OUR LADY OF GOOD HOPE 1874
BURIED TREASURE LEBEY
1852
OLD CEMETERY
TE OF LOWFIELD HOUSE
BEACON FIRE BOX
GOODSON'S HOUSE 1870
SITE OF HENRY PARKER'S HOUSE (640 ACRES)
1734 1st BAILIFF of COLONY OF GEORGIA
1st PRESIDENT COUNCIL OF SAVANNAH
GOVERNOR OF COLONIAL GEORGIA
1751-1754
RIVER
GRIMBALL CR.
AND
By BENJAMIN T. BYRD JR.
HISTORIAN 1962

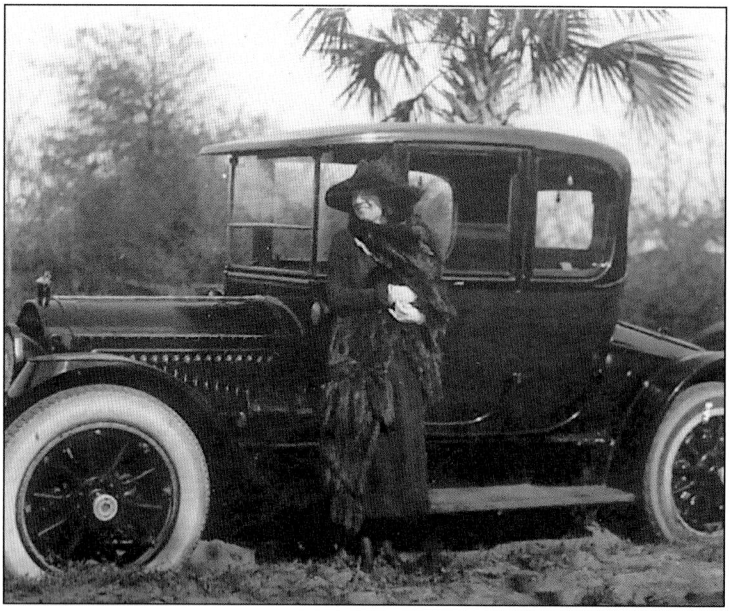

The rutted dirt roads often made driving a nightmare. All dressed up in her hat, minks, and gloves, this lady was on her way to play Parcheesi, a popular board game, when her 1923 Packard became bogged in the mud. This photo was taken on Laroche Avenue before it was paved.

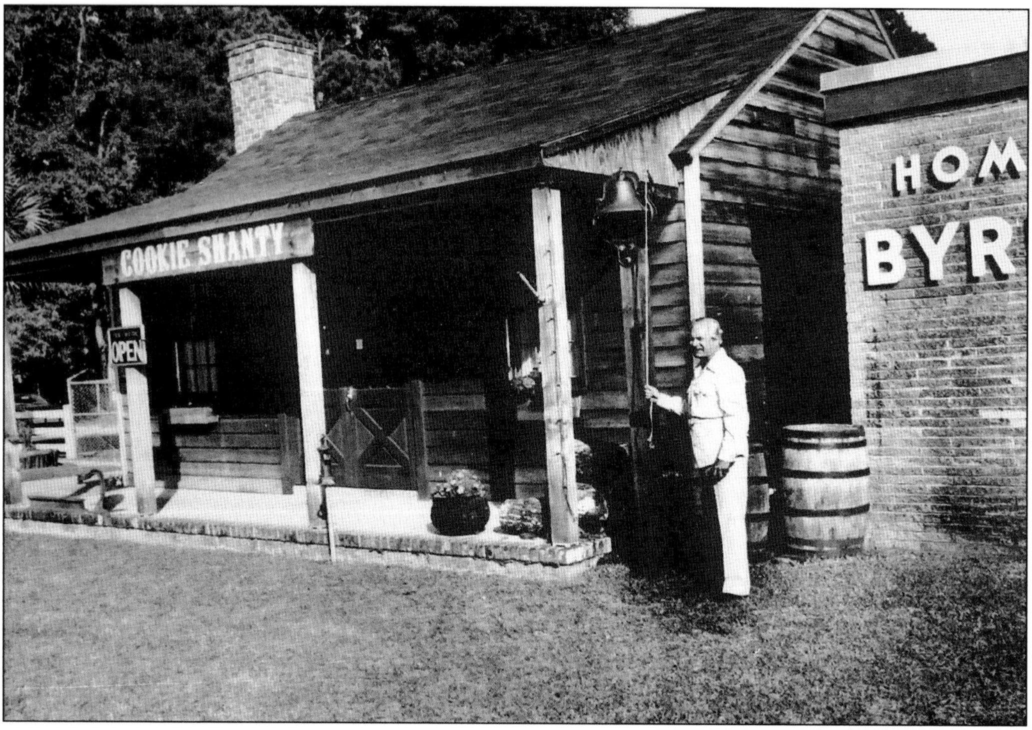

In the late 1920s, Benjamin T. "Cookie" Byrd delivered cookies and baked goods to stores in the area. His family made nine dozen cookies by hand every ten minutes, packed them into wooden boxes, and Mr. Byrd delivered them in his Model T Ford. Three years later, Mr. Byrd moved the business to Norwood Avenue. Busloads of tourists took home his famous Benne Wafers. Today, 64 years later, the expanded business, now on Waters Avenue and Eisenhower, is still run by family members. Customers love the assortment of free sample cookies.

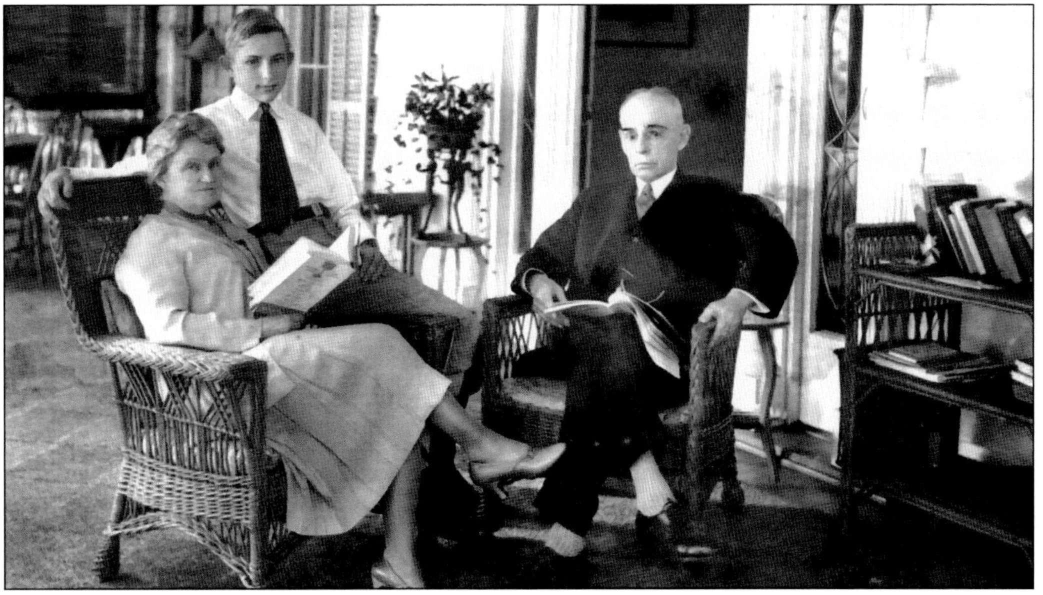

Col. Alexander Lawton, born the son of Confederate Gen. Alexander Lawton in 1858, reads with his wife, Ella, at 7 Bluff Drive. She was the daughter of Bishop Beckwith, Episcopal Bishop of the Diocese of Georgia. Colonel Lawton was the legal director of Central of Georgia Railroad, the vice-president of Ocean Steamship Co., a colonel in the Spanish-American War, and the president of the Georgia Historical Society. Ten-year-old Spencer Lawton, shown here with his grandparents, later married Sally Parker from Canton, Georgia. His son, Spencer Lawton Jr., is Savannah's district attorney.

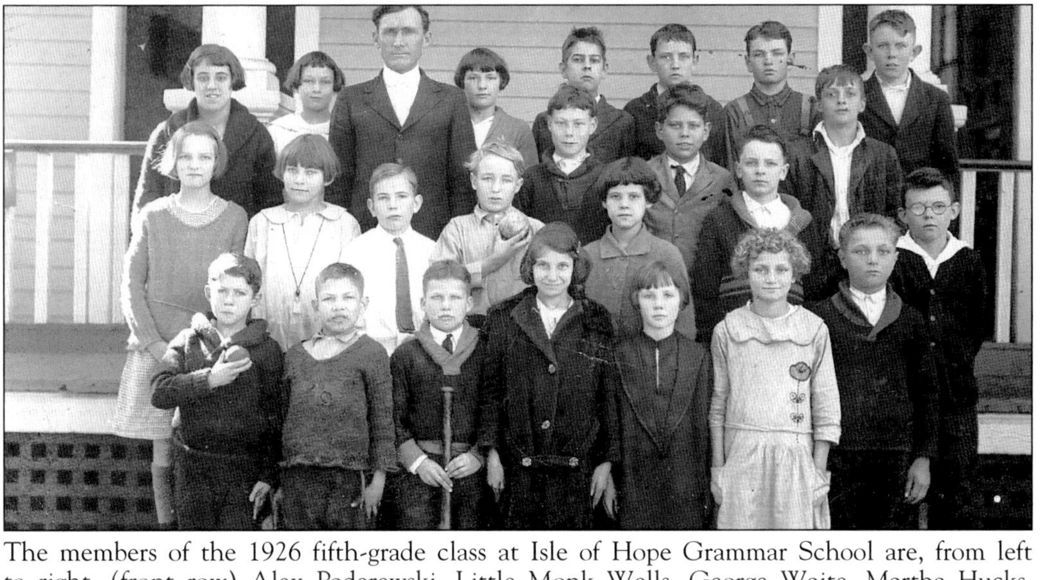

The members of the 1926 fifth-grade class at Isle of Hope Grammar School are, from left to right, (front row) Alex Paderewski, Little Monk Wells, George Waite, Martha Hucks, Elizabeth Kelly, Leila Shuman, and Arthur Shuman; (second row) ? Exley, Thelma Sharpe, Vinton Waite, Joe Mock, Irene Perry, Willis Exley, and George Coolidge; (third row) Elmore Schou, H.P. Perry, and William Roberts; (back row) Tallulah Barthelmous, Sidney Walsh, James Kelly (teacher), Isabel Waite, Trenholm Hopkins, Johnny Tiencken, Harry Hucks, and Spencer Eason.

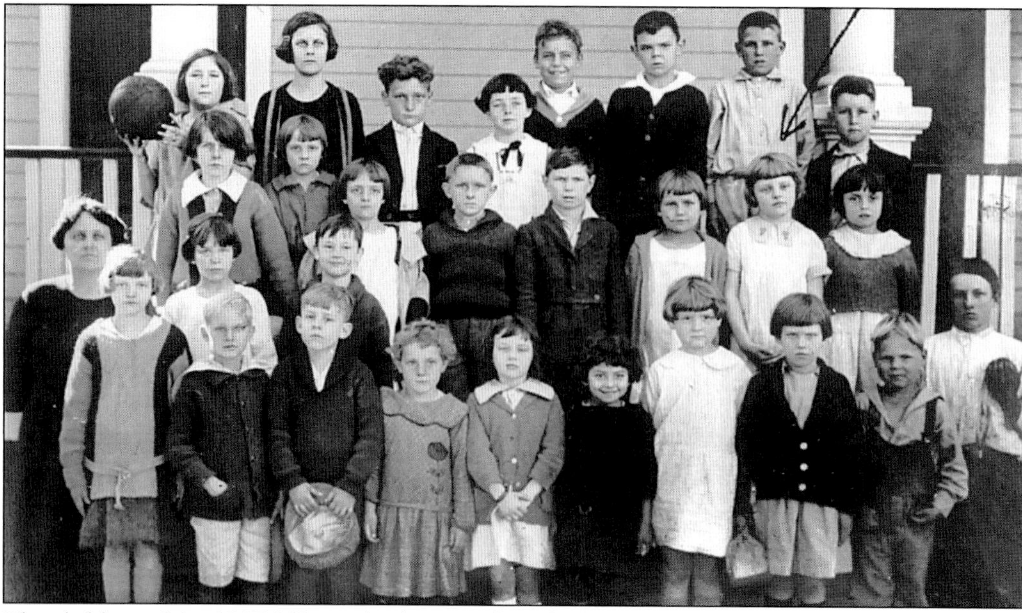

The children of the 1927 fifth-grade class are identified according to Cookie Byrd. Pictured, from left to right, are (front row) Thelma Dillard, Olin McIntosh, Robert McCreery, Doris Schuman, Ann Marie Bandy, Pearl Maltinsky Portman, Helen Rodewalt, Mary Jane Sharpe, B.J. Mock, and John Mock; (second row) Mrs. Kelly (teacher), Florence Waite Byrd, and Robert Norton; (third row) Jo Hanna Eason, Priscilla Kelly, Bessie Roberts Quante, Irwin Mock, Bennie Hucks, Ruth Rodewalt, Chappie Bragg Davis, and Violet Edwardy; (back row) Francis Sales, Amelia Clifton, Slater Schuman, Sidney Walsh, Arthur Schuman, Hermann Coolidge, Tom Mock, and Andrew Cory. Some of the girls are listed by their married names.

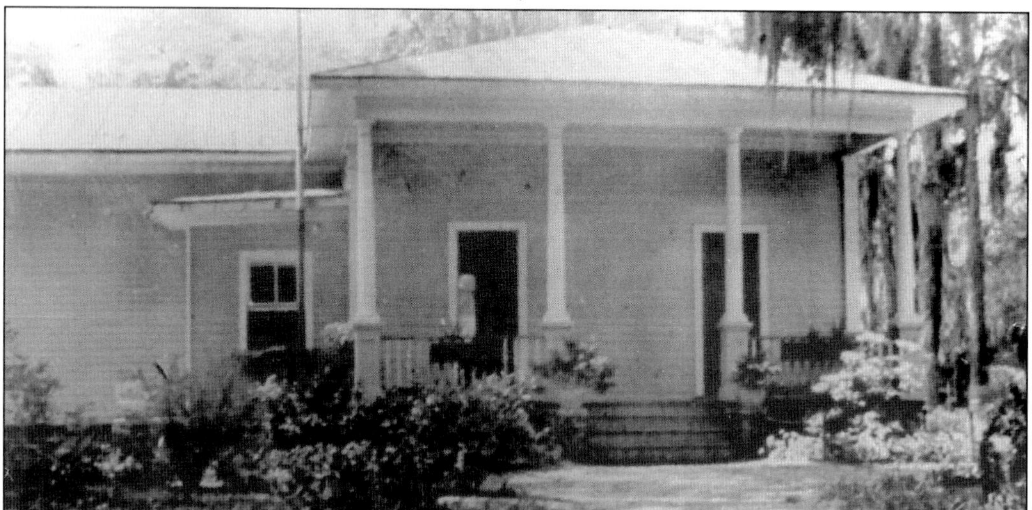

The Isle of Hope School, built in 1899, was a wooden frame building with 2 rooms on 3.2 acres. It began with 84 students. First through third grades were taught by Mrs. Elise Harmon in one room and fourth through sixth grades were taught by Mrs. Jillie Downing in the other. The heat source was a potbelly stove. Often, Bessie Roberts brought cornbread and soup to the children when rations were short. Next to the school was the Wylly Community House where PTA, 4-H, and Home Demonstration meetings were held.

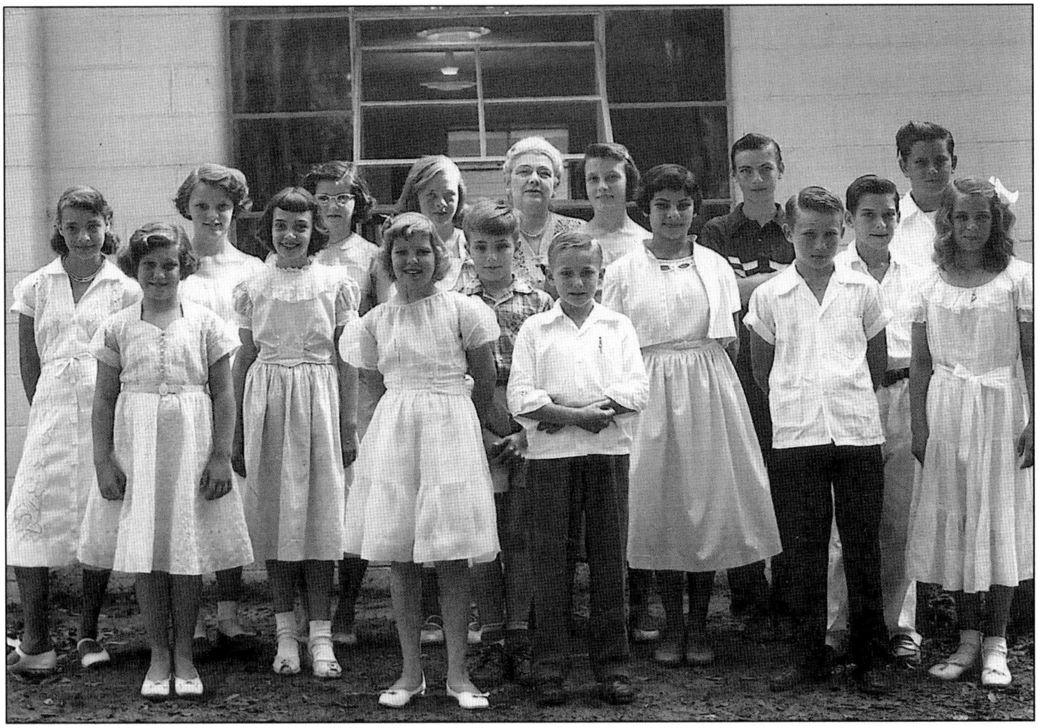

Here is the sixth-grade graduating class of 1951 in front of the new building at the Isle of Hope School. The students, from left to right, are Helen Thompson, Alva Mae Orton, Elise Youmans, Ann Thompson, Marie Skinner, Delores West, Margaret Ann Quante, Bruce Baxley, Mrs. Jillie Downing (teacher), Alfred Rahn, Clara Roebling, Barbara Ann Portman, James Williams, John Clifton, Everette Boaen, John Bowen, and Vera Mae Sharpe.

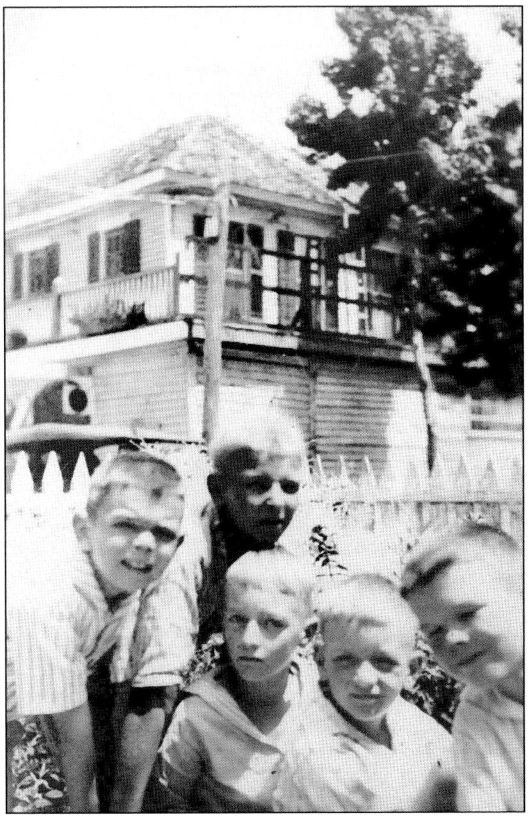

What an ideal place for young boys growing up in the 1920s. Frank and Philip are sitting in a four-wheeled wagon, which they built out of old crates and skates. A glimpse of Barbee's Pavilion is in the background. Pictured in the front row, from left to right, are brothers Francis and Philip McLaughlin and George Coolidge, and in the back row are Hermann Coolidge and Lester Hagan.

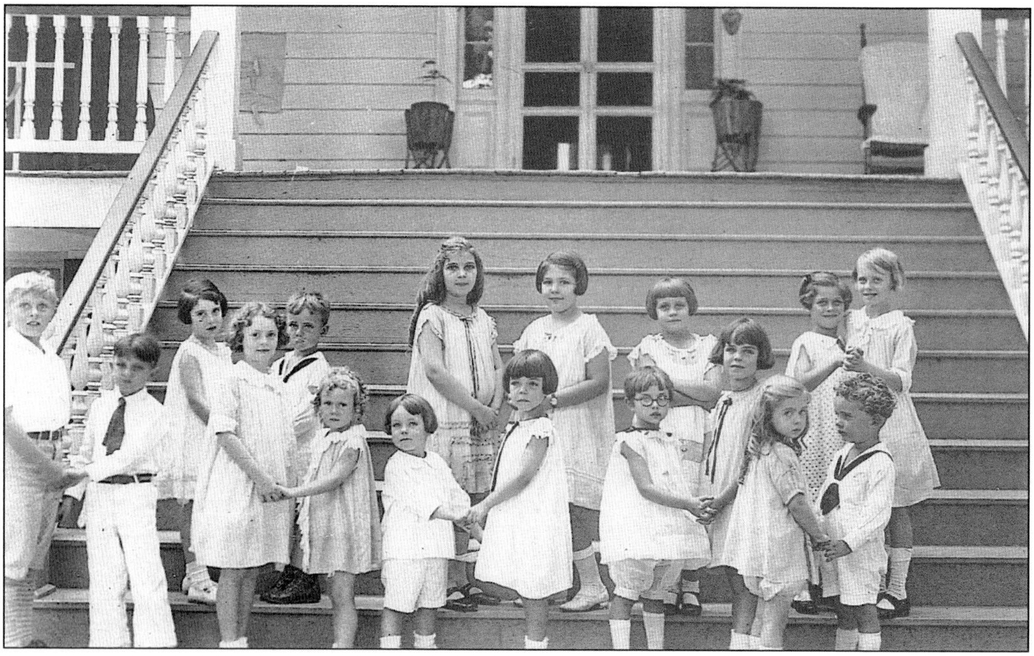

Billy Wylly invited his chums over for his 10th birthday in 1926. They are seen on the front steps of the Wylly House on the bluff. Pictured from left to right are (front row) Grover Paulsen Jr., Billy Wylly, Margaret Gilchrist (Livingston), Jean Gilchrist (Miller), Lee Mueller Jr., Lyn Mueller, Marietta Wylly, Lillian Mueller, Alberta "Bertie" Robertson (Beckwith), and Armand Ellis; (back row) Mary Moore, Charles Ellis, Electa Robertson (Hoffman), Daisy Moore (Lake) (Smith), Betty Paulsen, Muriel Friedman, and Barbara Gilchrist (Budreau).

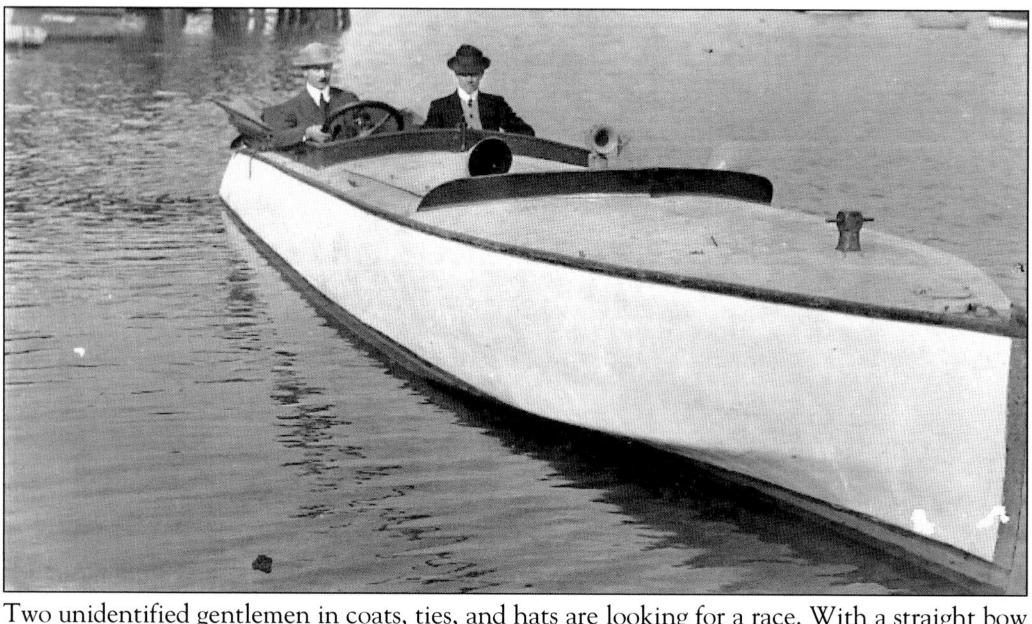

Two unidentified gentlemen in coats, ties, and hats are looking for a race. With a straight bow and deep keel, this was a classic design for speedboats in the 1930s.

Two-year-old Alex Barbee displays a good saddle seat as his mother, Rose, hovers protectively. Rose was the wife of William Barbee, who was the son of Alexander Barbee and the owner of the well-known terrapin farm at Isle of Hope. Rose could tell if it was going to rain by watching to see if the terrapins stuck their heads out of the water. Her terrapin stew had a far-reaching reputation.

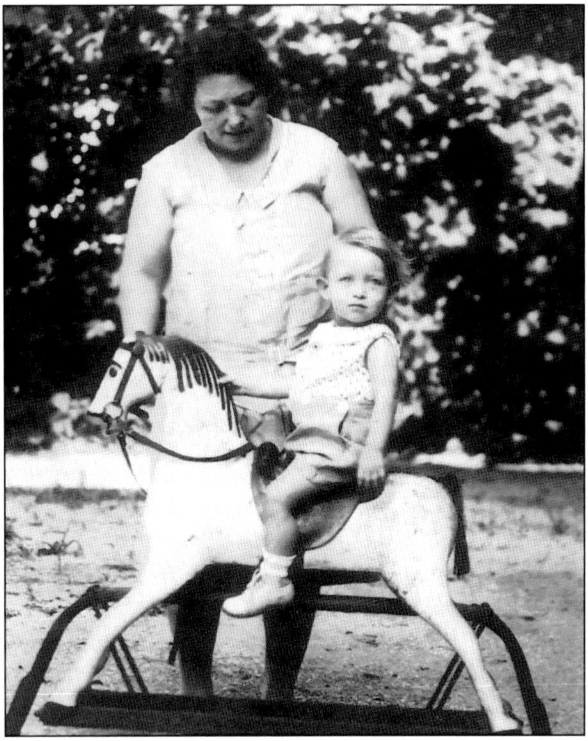

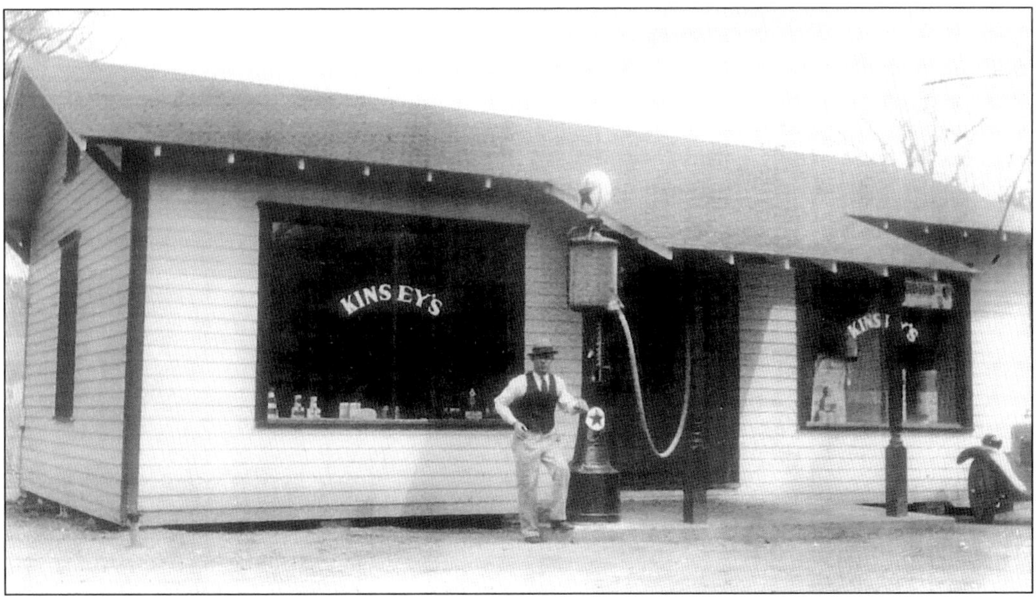

Kinsey's Store on Parkersburg Road sold meat, flour, grits, sugar, eggs, and other staples. Teens cut grass and pulled cockspurs for hotdogs and a Pepsi. Cokes were a nickel with a refund upon bottle return. In this photo, Billy Kinsey stands beside the gas pump in 1936. Billy's wife, Thelma, ran the store for years. The Kinseys bought it back and put in a post office in the 1960s. The Penn Boyds bought the store in 1947. Customers could phone in their grocery lists and have them delivered by truck with young Pennyann Boyd (Rhine) behind the wheel. The later owners of the store were the Witheringtons.

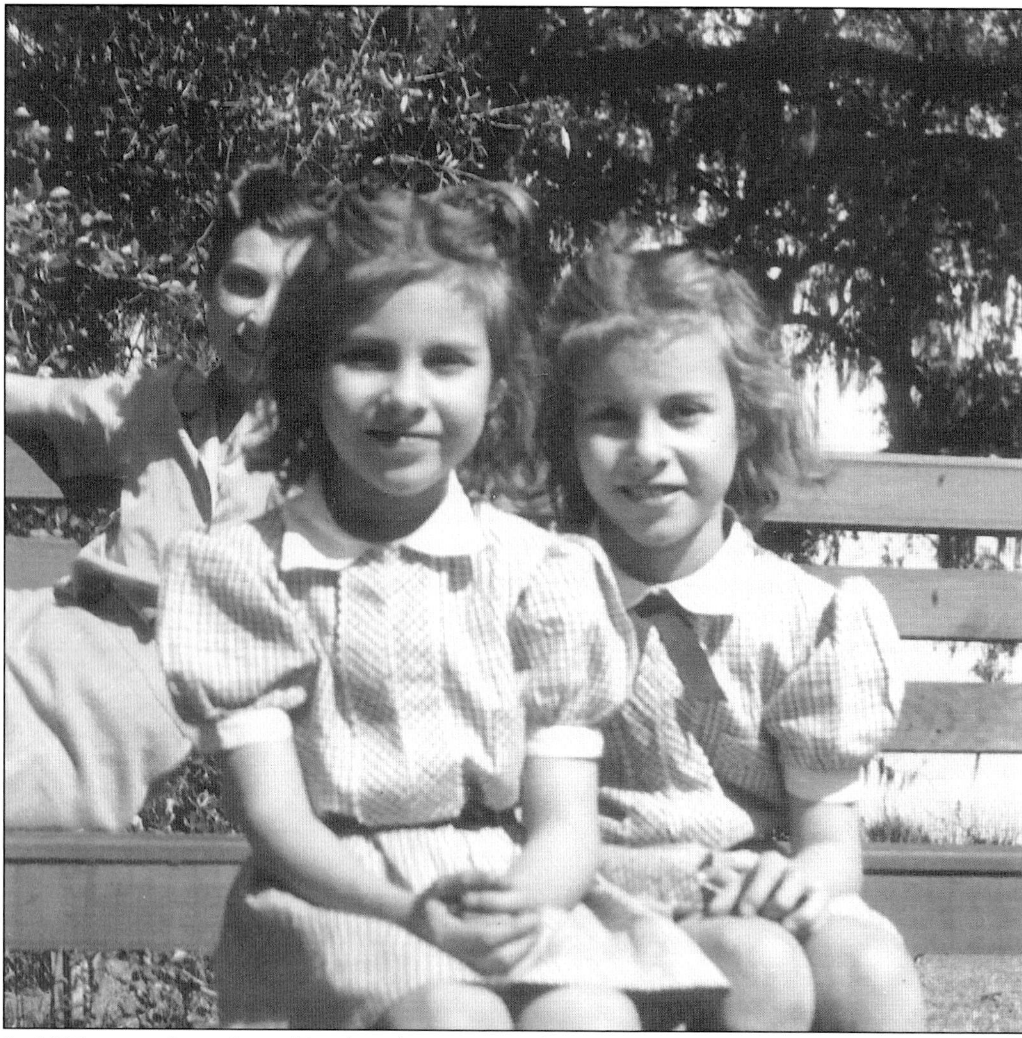

In 1936, twins Joan Cope (Paez) and Jean Cope (Ennis) relax with their cherished "Mummy" Kitty Parish (Cope) in front of their home at 67 Bluff Drive. The home was built in the 1850s and the Copes lived there for 42 years. Kate Parish, the children's grandmother, sewed the dresses that the girls are wearing. After supper, while washing dishes, Mummy would initiate her favorite song, "Alice Blue Gown." Jean and Joan sang harmony. From behind the newspaper, their father, Jack Cope, blended his lovely baritone voice into the mixture. The four-part harmony made dishwashing a pleasure.

In 1936, Bishop Gerald O'Hara saw the need to spread Catholicism to rural areas. Many children had never attended mass. On 24 acres at Grimball Point, barracks, an administration building, infirmary, mess hall, and chapel were built. After World War II, Bishop O'Hara was made archbishop and served as papal representative to Romania, Ireland, England, and Wales, while remaining Bishop of Savannah. In 1937, the Chapel of the Holy Child Jesus was dedicated and Camp Villa Marie opened its doors. (Courtesy of the Archives of the Catholic Diocese of Savannah.)

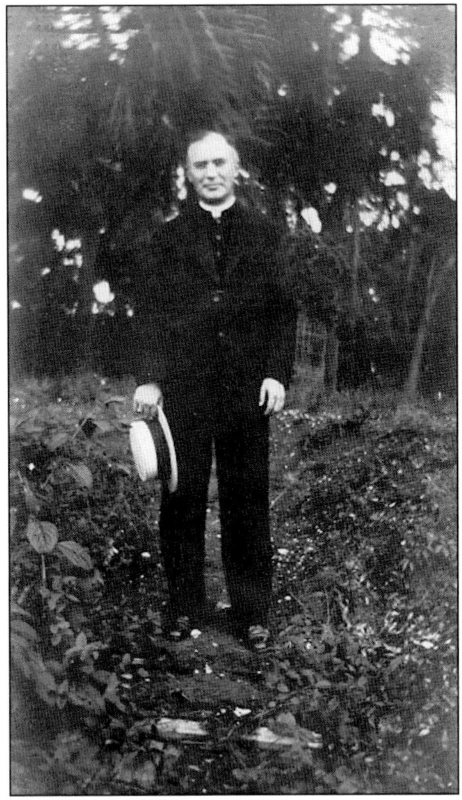

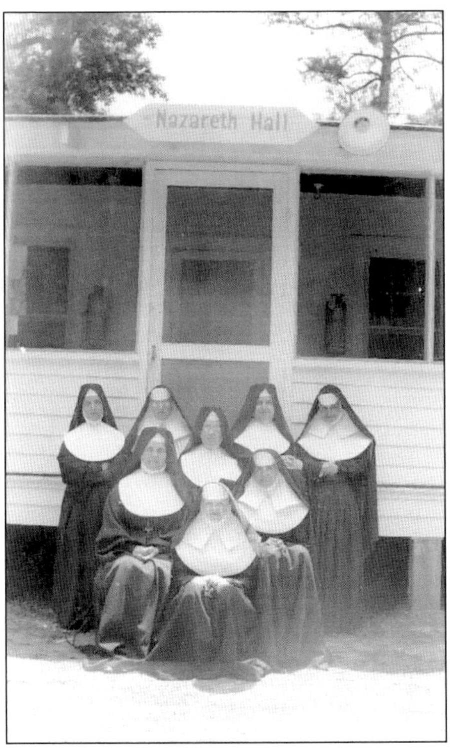

Staffing the Camp Villa Marie were the Sisters of Mercy and the Sisters of St. Joseph. Later, the Franciscan Sisters, the Vincentian Sisters of Charity, seminarians, and laypersons would join the staff. Here, a group of sisters line up in front of Nazareth Hall in the 1940s, pre-Vatican II. The heavy, hot habits were the order of the day—no matter how high the mercury sizzled on Savannah's temperature gauges.

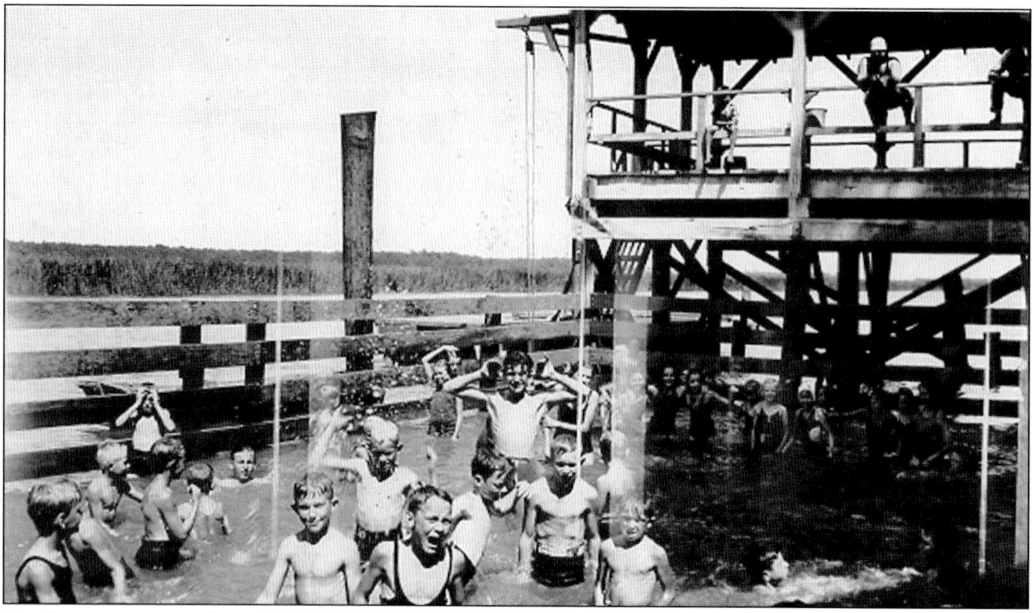

Students swam in Grimball Creek before the pool was built. Often, a dip in the creek was the only way to stay cool. The stockade fence around the swimming hole kept swimmers from floating downstream and protected them from sharks. (Courtesy of the Archives of the Catholic Diocese of Savannah.)

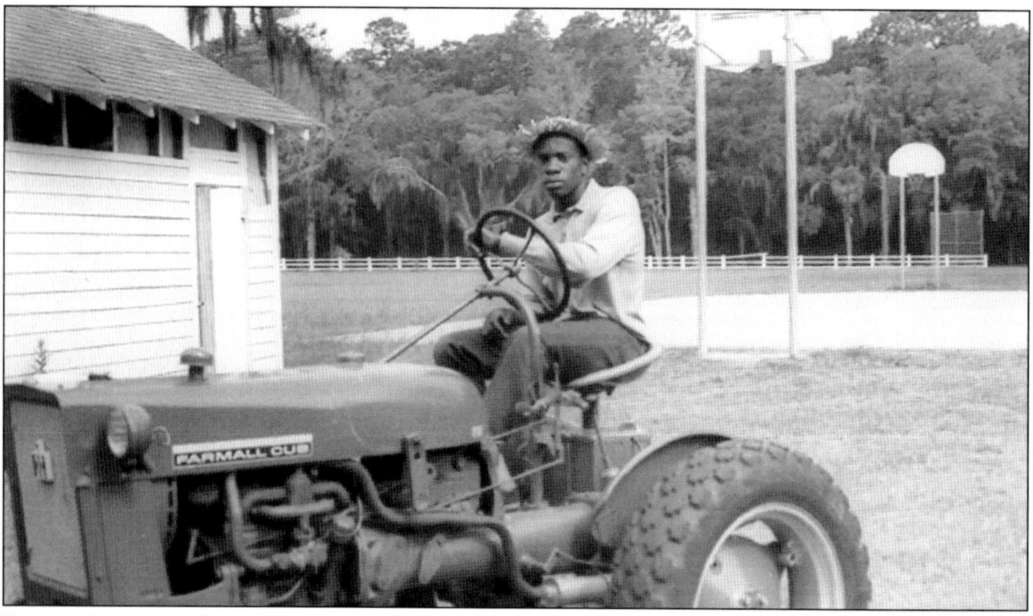

Future Supreme Court Justice Clarence Thomas enjoyed his summer job maintaining the grounds. He was a student at St. John Vianney Minor Seminary, which opened in 1959 on the same campus as Camp Villa Marie. It was a rigorous high school, which offered religion and Latin courses along with the usual curriculum. This was a structured environment for young men who might go into the priesthood. Clarence Thomas made top grades, played sports, and sang in the choir. He was also the editor of the school newspaper and the yearbook. (Courtesy of the Archives of the Catholic Diocese of Savannah.)

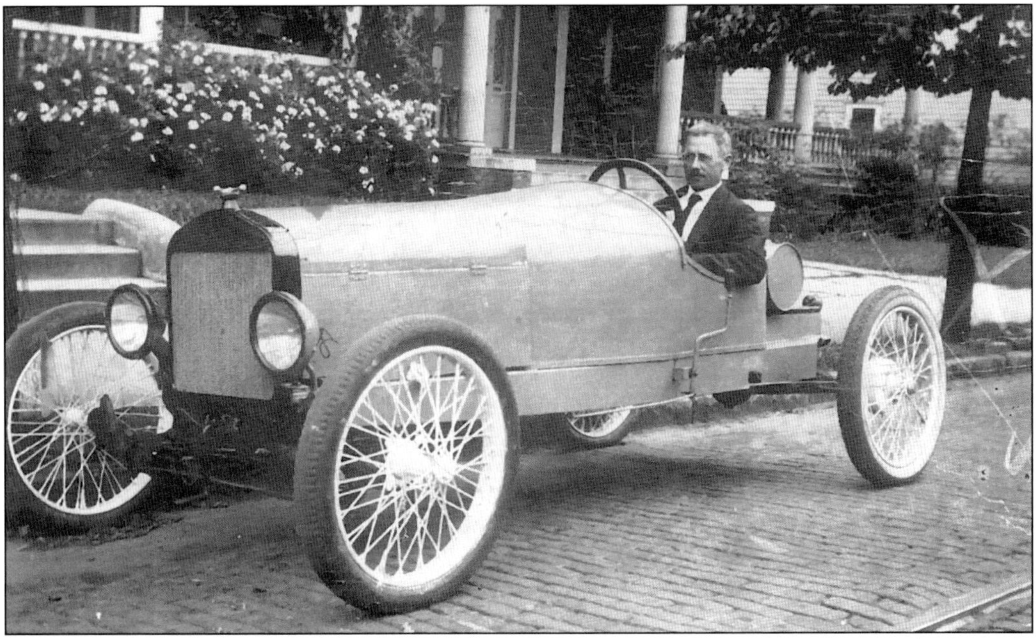

Albert "Skeet" Wylly looks dapper in the homemade hotrod that he built in a shed at Isle of Hope. He was called "Skeet" because when he was born, his father commented, "Why, the boy's no bigger than a skeeter (mosquito)!" Skeet is shown here visiting friends in the city. Many of Savannah's streets were attractively built by laying each brick by hand. Streetcar tracks are visible in the bottom right corner.

The Roeblings's schooner, *Black Douglas*, which was launched at Bath Iron Works in 1930, was fitted out for luxurious cruising and fishing. The family sailed around South America and then lived aboard the boat at their Modena Plantation dock on Skidaway Island. The Roeblings gave the schooner to the United States during World War II. Robert Roebling was the great-grandson of John Roebling, who was a designer and builder of aqueducts and bridges. Some of his constructions include the Niagara Suspension Bridge, the Brooklyn Bridge, and the Cincinatti-Covington Bridge. The Roeblings had five children—Ellin, Karl, Wainwright, Clara, and Henry. (Courtesy of Henry Roebling.)

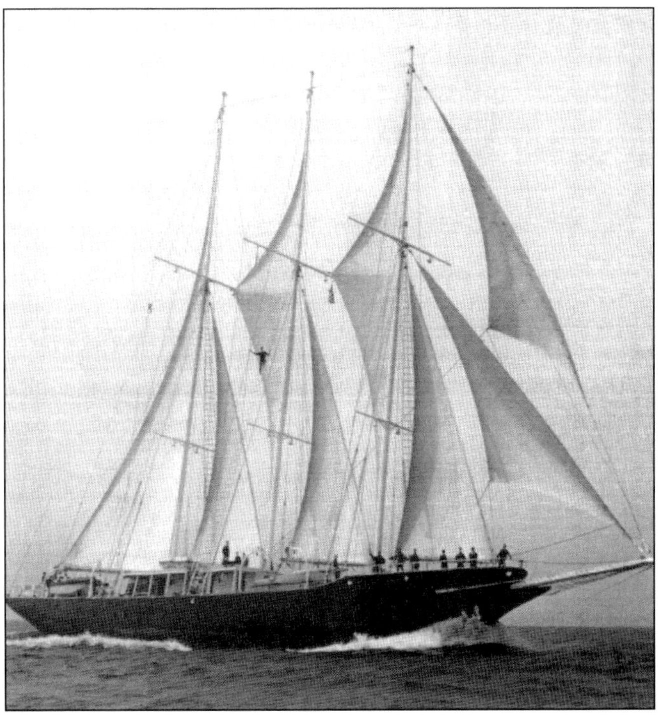

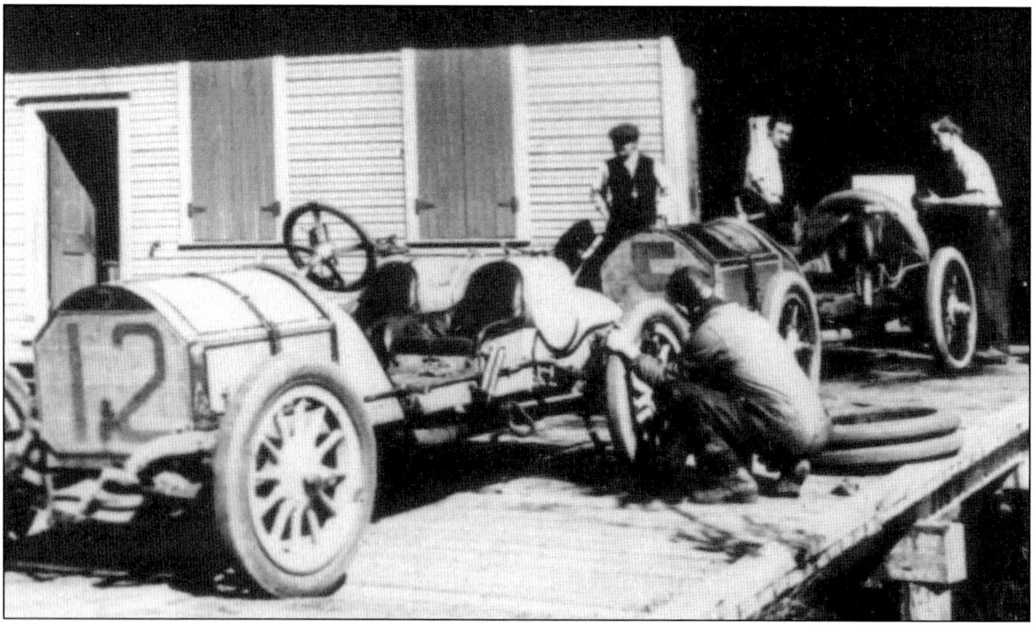

In addition to their cable business called John A. Roebling's Sons, Co., the Roeblings were partners in the Mercer Automobile Co. Washington Roebling II raced Mercer cars in The Great Savannah Automobile Races. The Mercer Camp was on Laroche Avenue. Today, the ruins can be seen opposite the entrance to Majestic Oaks Subdivision. (Courtesy of the Roebling family.)

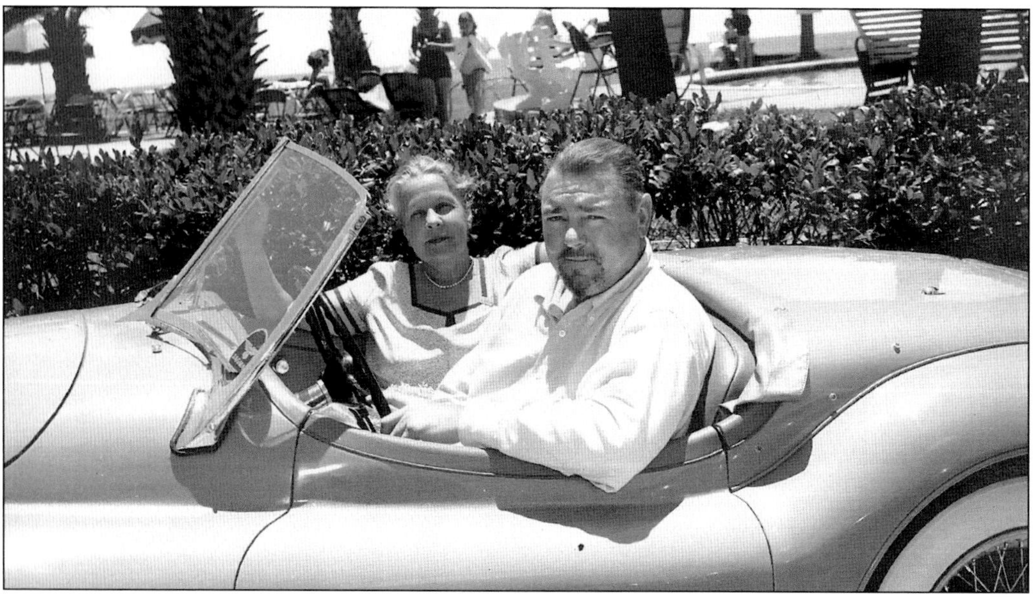

Robert Roebling had a business investment with a little sports car shop downtown owned by Ed Rehal and Johnny Reuter. When he took his investment out of business, he gave a sports car to each member of the family—"What a popular Pop!" The whole Roebling family took a trip down to the King and Prince Hotel on St. Simons Island. With the top down on the classy Jaguar, Dorothy ("Dickie") and Robert enjoy a fine spring day. (Courtesy of the Roebling family.)

Wainwright Ripley "Rip" Roebling is pictured here riding his incredibly patient (or lazy) mule, "Eatin' Trouble." Modena was named after Modena, Italy, where silkworms were successfully farmed in the Middle Ages. Modena was named by Gov. John Milledge, who was the original owner of the land. (Courtesy of the Roebling family.)

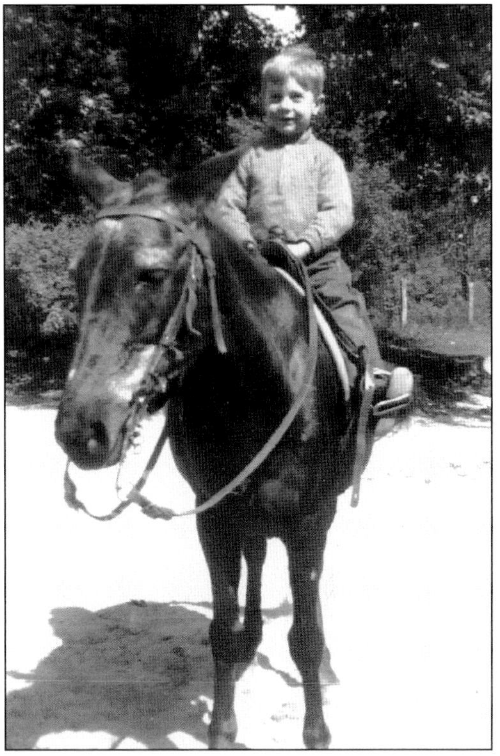

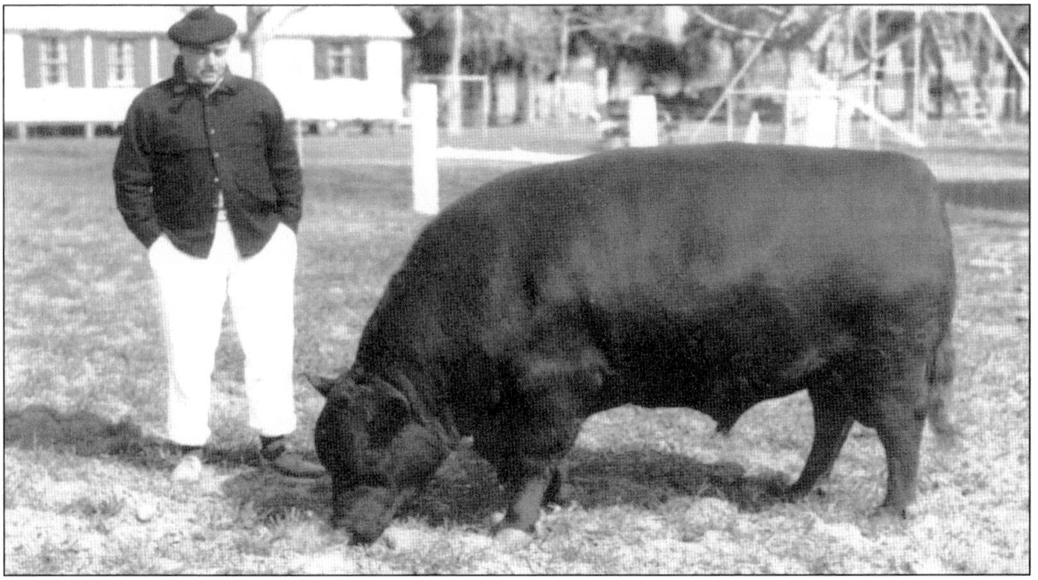

The Skidaway Institute of Oceanography began with a grant of the Roeblings' inland waterway farm, Modena Plantation, in 1967. The Roeblings had previously used the land to raise Hampshire hogs and Aberdeen Angus cattle. Modena Plantation was granted to the State of Georgia for marine research. Mr. Roebling was also an ardent supporter of the Sports Car Club of America (SCCA). He gave some of his land in Effingham County for the creation of Roebling Road for driver training and SCCA-sanctioned races. In this photo, Robert Roebling admires his prize Angus, Blackcapmere. (Courtesy of the Roebling family.)

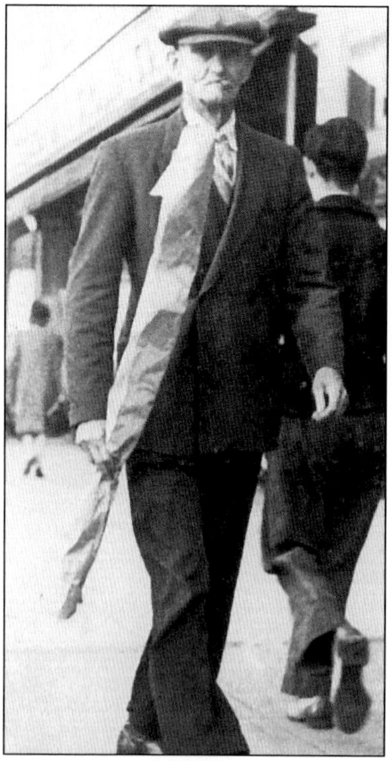

Charles Sisson (1871–1950) retired after 39 years as a lighthouse keeper. He and his wife, Ruth Ellen, raised five children in lighthouses at Amelia Island, Hilton Head, Daufuskie Island, and the Venus Point Lighthouse in the Savannah River. At his last job, he replaced George Martus, brother of Florence Martus, the famous *Waving Girl,* whose statue is on River Street. Mr. Sisson is shown here on Broughton Street with his new fishing rod. Little Charlotte (Glendye) couldn't resist sneaking it down to Barbee's Pavilion to cast for yellowtail.

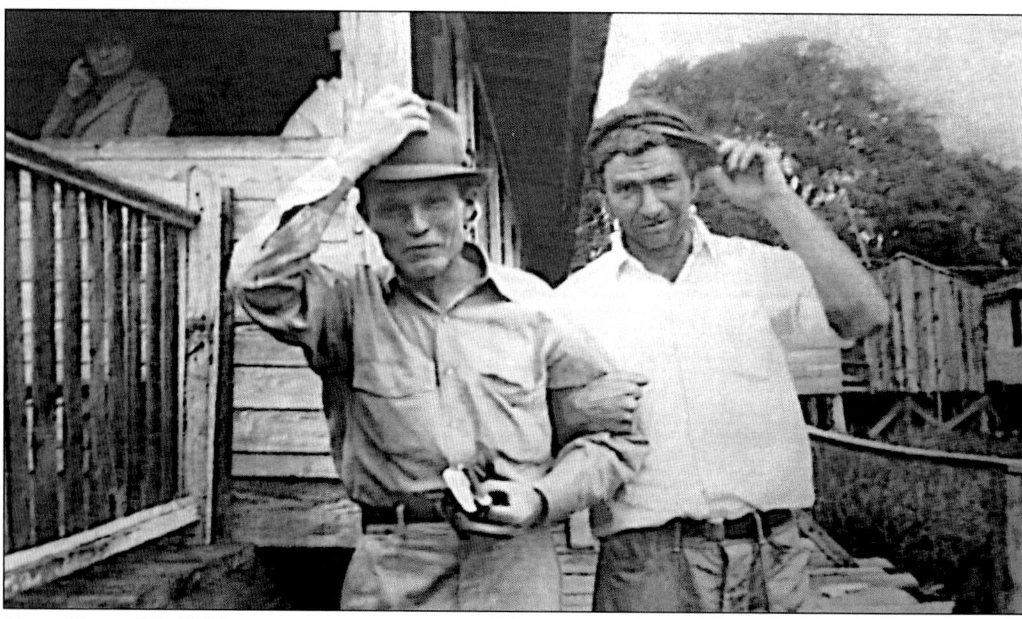

Harry Reynolds (left), a house painter, painted the cloud-piercing steeple of St. John the Baptist. He and Gertrude Sanders had five children—Adele (Zeigler), Marjorie (McDonough), the late Betty (Lockett) (Slater), Harriet (Moore) (Barras), and the late Harry Reynolds. Harry Hucks, also pictured, was a shrimper and worked for the Corps of Engineers. He and Stella Inez Mock had six children—Inez (Nelson), Leagre, Sarah (Marks), Portia (Parrish), Lula (Williams), and little Carson. Barbee's Pavilion advertised "Where the Pretty Girls Go." The two Harrys must have just spotted one.

Stella Mock must have been one of those pretty girls. Mr. Hucks married Stella Mock in 1934 at St. Thomas Church. He fished and hunted on his boat, the *Dill Pickle*, and unloaded shrimp to be canned at Barbee's shrimp factory. In 1940, the couple bought the home of his parents at 55 Henderson Avenue. They paid the $25 down payment, and the rest of the $2,000 balance, by selling coon and alligator hides, which he bagged with his 32-20 rifle.

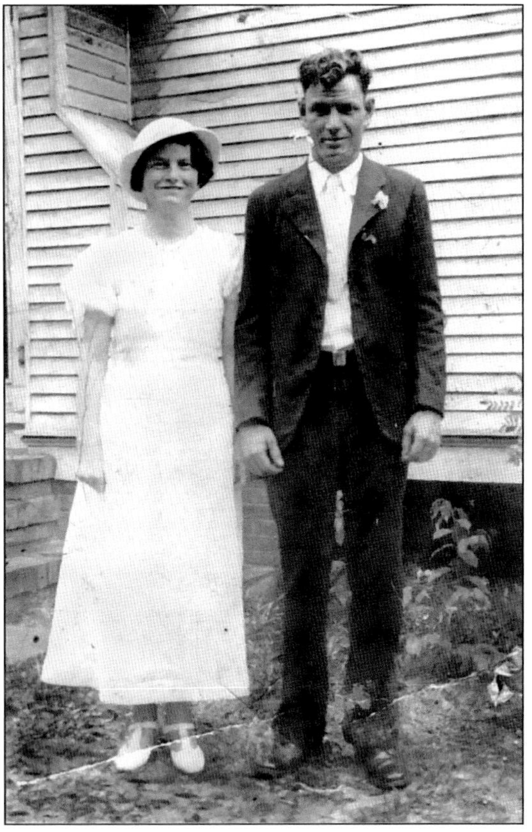

In a room full of bowed heads, Ella Lebey blesses their milk and cookies and then says the Pledge of Allegiance to the Flag with her Sunday school class at the Methodist Church.

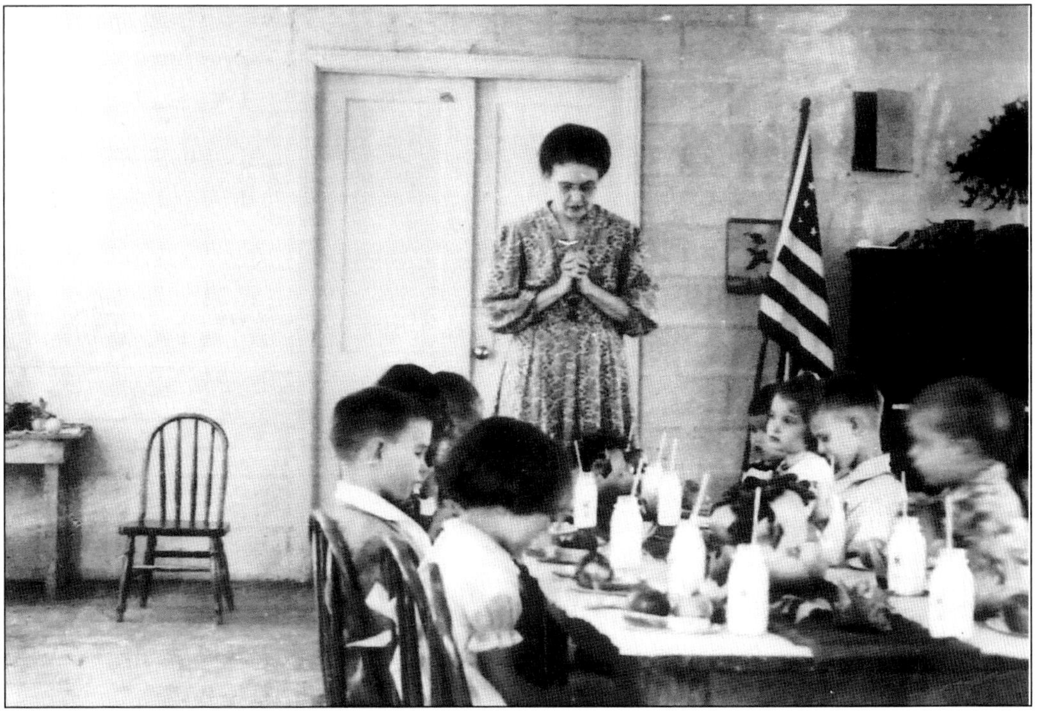

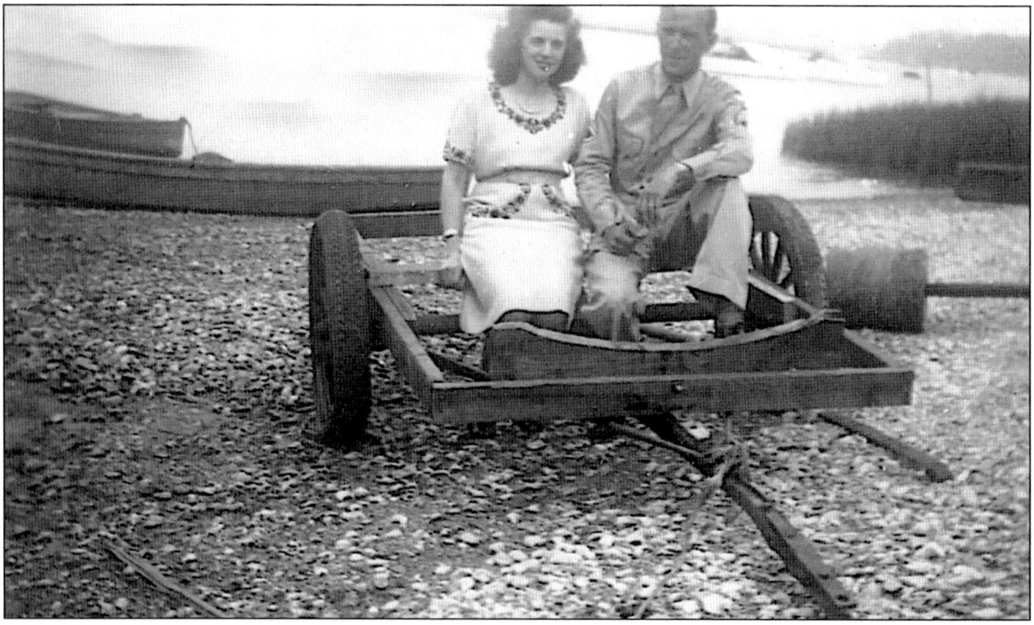

This old rusty boat trailer might as well have been a royal chariot to these young lovers clutching hands. Matthew Wilde and Rosa Mae Kessler rode the streetcar to Barbee's Pavilion for skating and dancing. He was a staff sergeant stationed at Hunter Field and she was a music teacher. They were married for 52 years and had 2 children—Julie Wilde and Lucy (Warren).

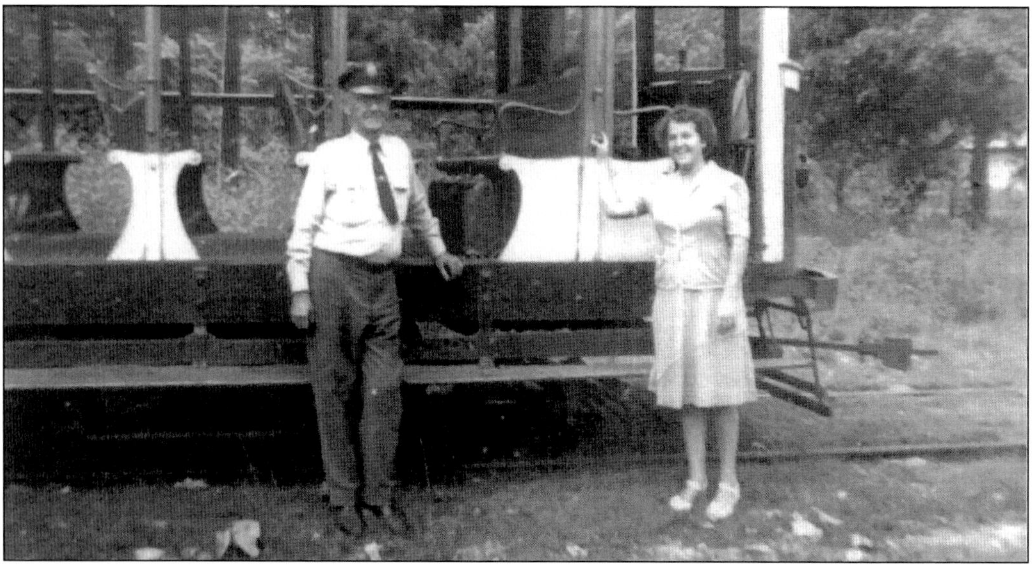

Streetcars ran to Isle of Hope from the 1870s until 1946. Here is Helen Smith (Johnson) with the motorman, Mr. Martin. The token-taker, Mr. Woods, walked along the running board to collect the fares. At the terminus, the seat backs were flipped and the motorman drove from the other end. In 1945, a streetcar braked at Helen's house on Central Avenue. To her surprise and delight, her uniformed husband, Jimmy Guy Johnson, who had been stationed in England, leapt from the streetcar. Mr. Martin yelled, "I'm not leaving 'til you kiss her!" Jimmy and his sweetheart Helen were married for 43 years.

Margaret Paxton and Philip Billac were married in 1945 in Our Lady of Good Hope chapel. Billac was in the 5th Army Air Force when he and his new bride were courting. The couple had three children—Patty (Troxell), Alma (Mills), and Jimmy Billac. They loved Isle of Hope and called it "the jewel of Georgia." Billac Vending Co. was started in 1965 and was family-owned for 36 years. Mr. Billac was instrumental in starting the Chatham County Athletic Association.

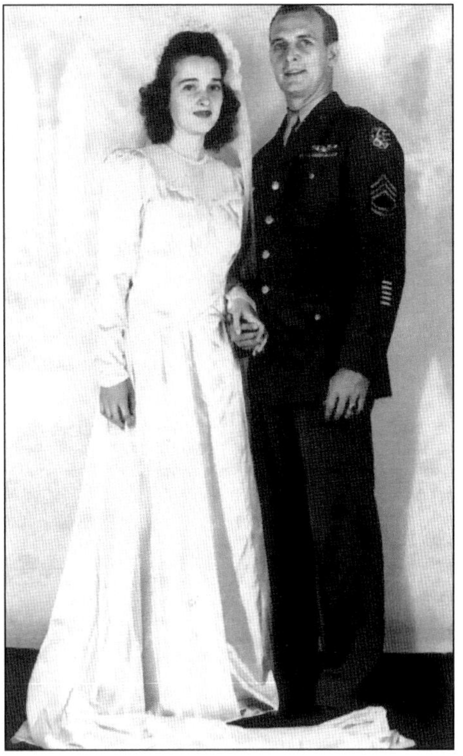

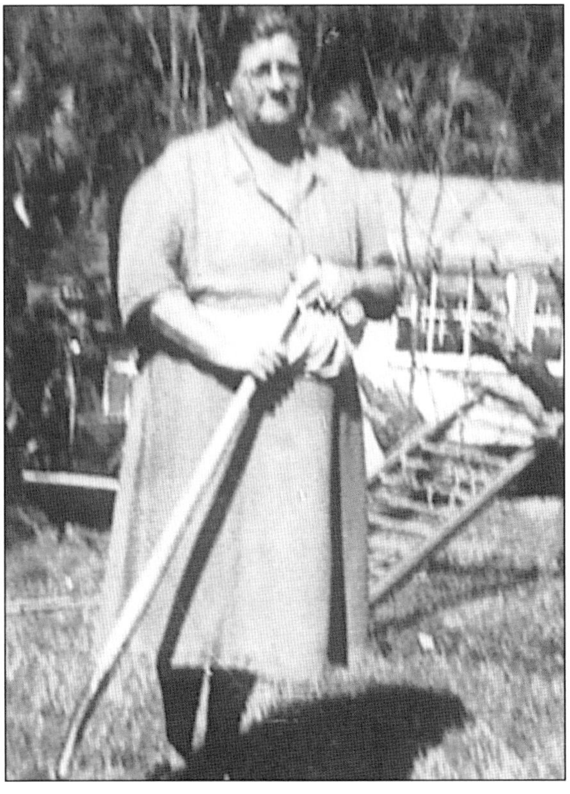

Anna Elizabeth Sharpe Roberts ("Aunt Bessie") was the mother of six children—Nanny, Bessie, Mary, Horace, Eleanor, and Tom. After the five Sisson children lost their mother, Aunt Bessie and her husband, Horace Roberts, kept them until their father could provide a home for them. She took part in the PTA of Isle of Hope School, the Home Demonstration Club, and was a pillar of St. Thomas Church, often preaching when the pastor was ill. She taught Sunday school and made memorable oyster stew for church socials.

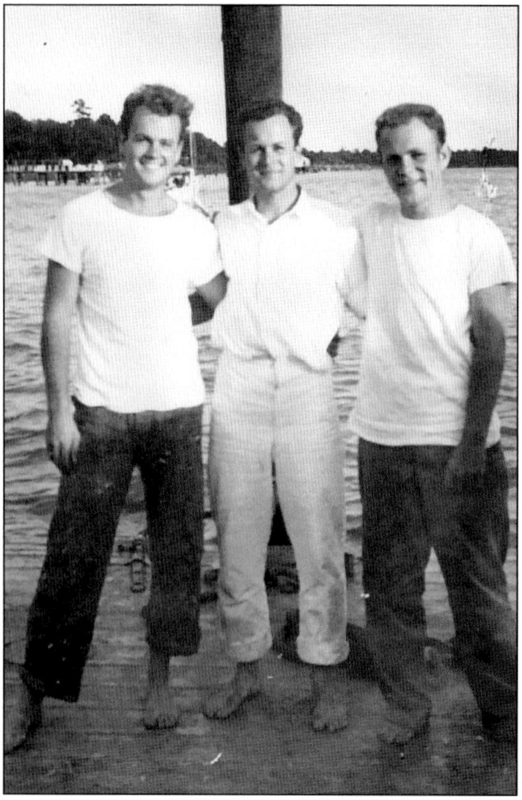

The handsome Johnson brothers, from left to right, are David, Tommy, and Bobby. Judging by their happy grins, they must have sailed a winning race in their Larks in the Skidaway River. The South Atlantic Sailing Regattas took place every summer, beginning with three days of races in Savannah. The races were also held in Beaufort, Rockville, Charleston, and Wilmington.

Remshart "Remmy" Roux (left) and Tommy Johnson relax with cold beers and discuss their day of fishing. Mr. Roux and Mr. Johnson were both members of the Shark Fishing Club—better known as The Poor Man's Tarpon Fishing Club. The sharks were planted under scuppernong arbors for potent fertilizer.

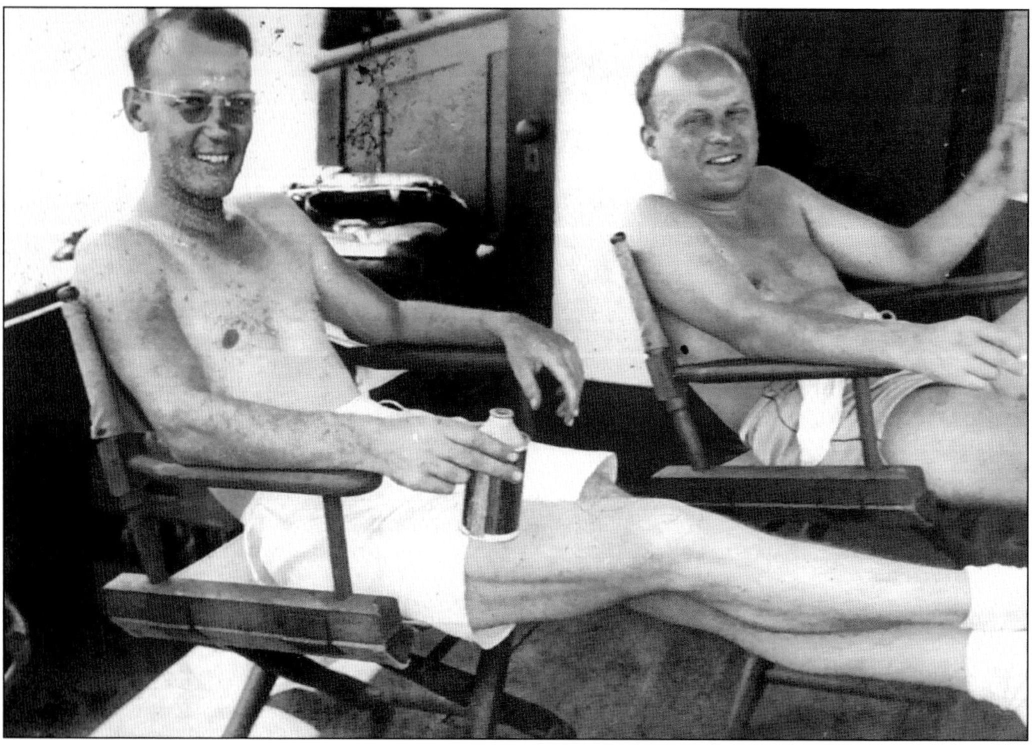

Melba Burroughs and Fred Fischer were married in 1945. They have four children—Fred, Mary (Haynes), Gary, and Kevin. Melba's brother, Clyde, started Burroughs Heating and Air Conditioning Co. in the 1940s. After spending time in the Coast Guard, Fred worked at Kennickell Printing for 32 years. Referring to their 1892 home on Rose Avenue, Melba said, "May our Heavenly Father bless those people who live here after we're gone."

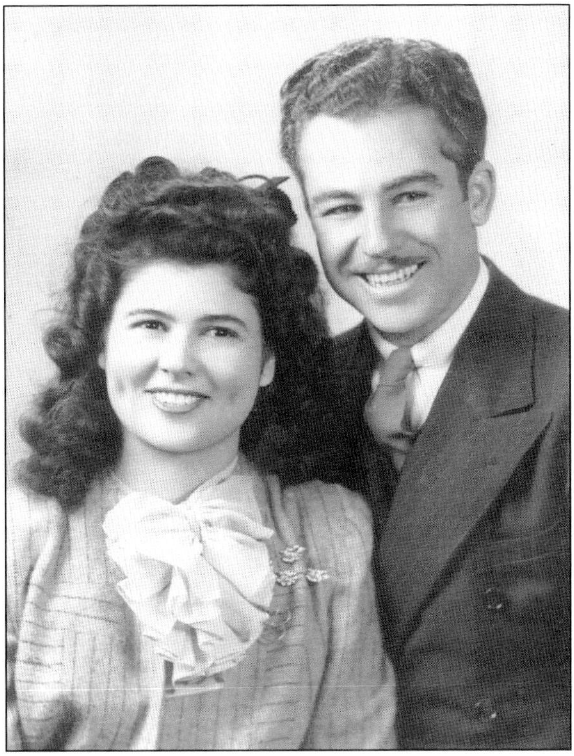

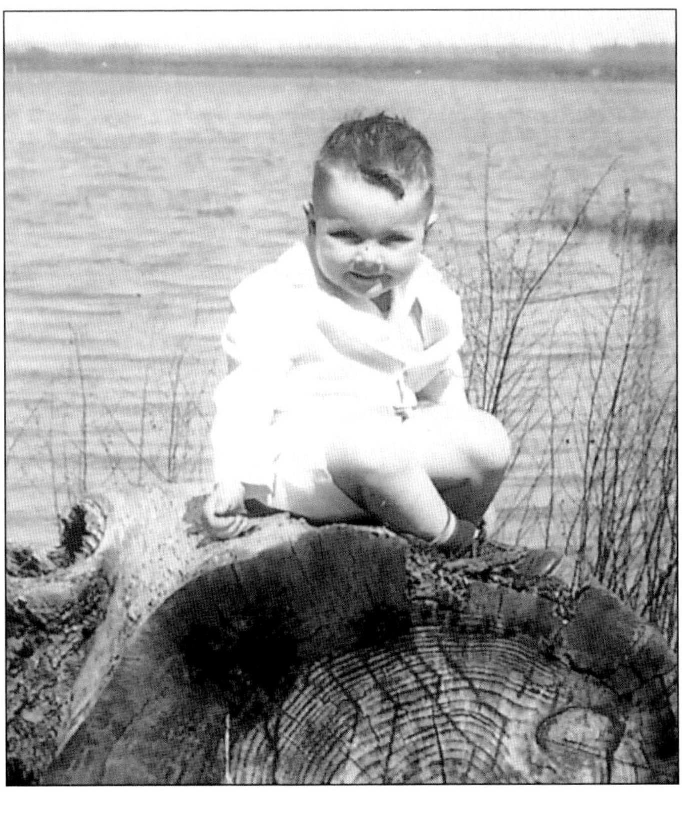

Two-year-old Harlan Hostetter beams with boyish pride as his pet crawdad crawls across his forehead. After Sunday School at the Independent Presbyterian Church in the city, the Hostetter family stopped at Leopold's for pistachio ice cream. For Sunday evening entertainment at Isle of Hope, the family piled into the Chevy with a picnic, drove to the river's edge right in front of their home, and listened to the car radio. *The Shadow*, *The Green Hornet*, and *Inner Sanctum* were favorite radio programs.

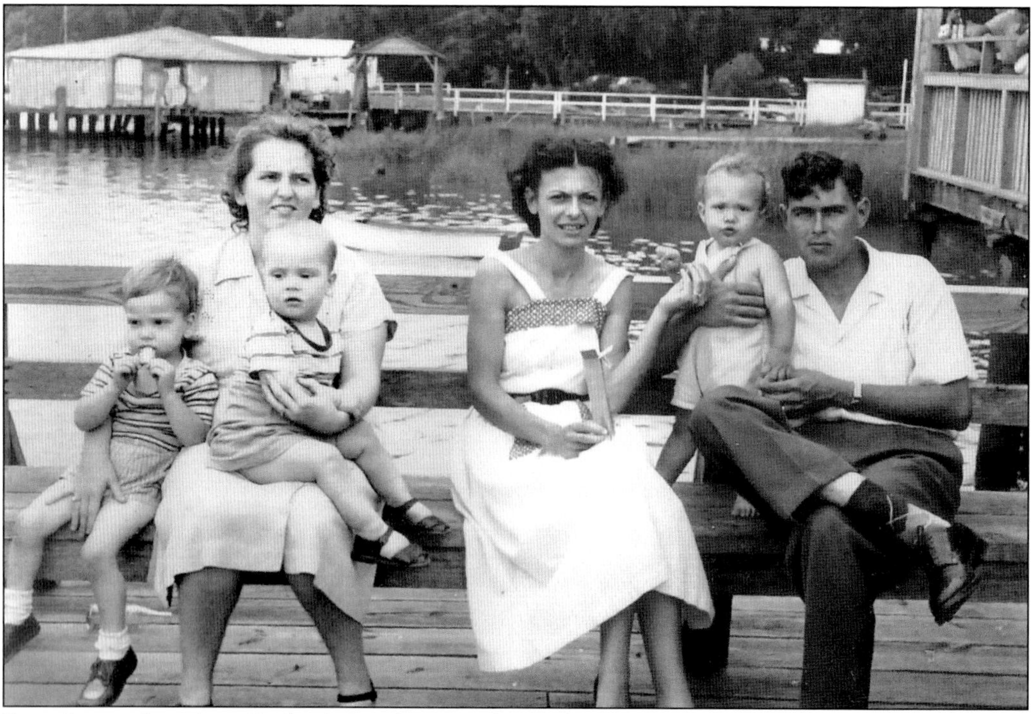

Friends met friends at Barbee's Pavilion, exchanged stories, and taught their children to fish. This photo shows Helen Smith Johnson with her two sons, Robert and Joseph, in the 1940s, visiting with Connie and Frank Falana. A portion of the pavilion is visible in the upper right corner. Brady's Boat Works is in the background. Helen met her husband, Jimmy, at the pavilion. There is no doubt that many young men proposed to their sweethearts here.

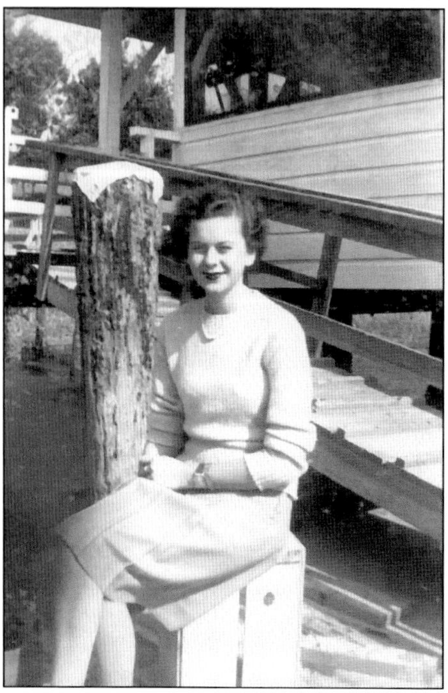

Ladies served as "spotters" in the aircraft warning system during World War II. They studied silhouettes of enemy planes and could spot a Messerschmitt or a Focke-Wulf. Mrs. Charlton Theus was chairman of the women's division of the Citizens' Defense Committee; Mrs. Horace Roberts, Red Cross and Collecting Books for Servicemen; Mrs. Clarence Cleland, knitting; Mrs. Jo Hallman, Nutrition; Mrs. Fred Sisson, Air Raid; Mrs. John Dyer, First Aid; Mrs. Julius McLaughlin, Conservation; Mrs. Georgia Bolland, Training Courses. Kathryn Johnson (Waller) takes a shift at the observation post on her family's dock.

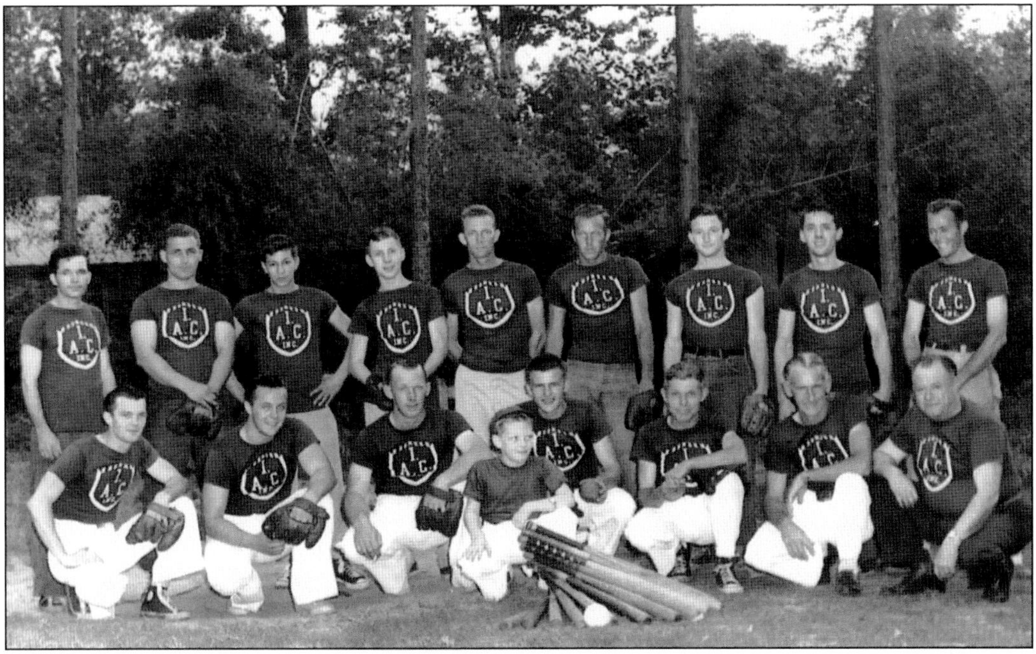

Spirited softball games were often played behind Kinsey's Store on Parkersburg Road. Members of the 1948 Isle of Hope Athletic Club, from left to right, are (front row) Frank Bandy, Bucky Lockett, Buster Elmgren, Butch Elmgren (batboy), Dennis Witherington, Harry Reynolds Sr., Bill Hardin, and Raymond Hallman; (back row) Dan O'Connell, Bubber Ziegler, Jerry Brown, Allen Strickland, Howard Norton, Ranny Lockett, Fred Yokum, Coolidge Thigpen, and Buddy Lockett.

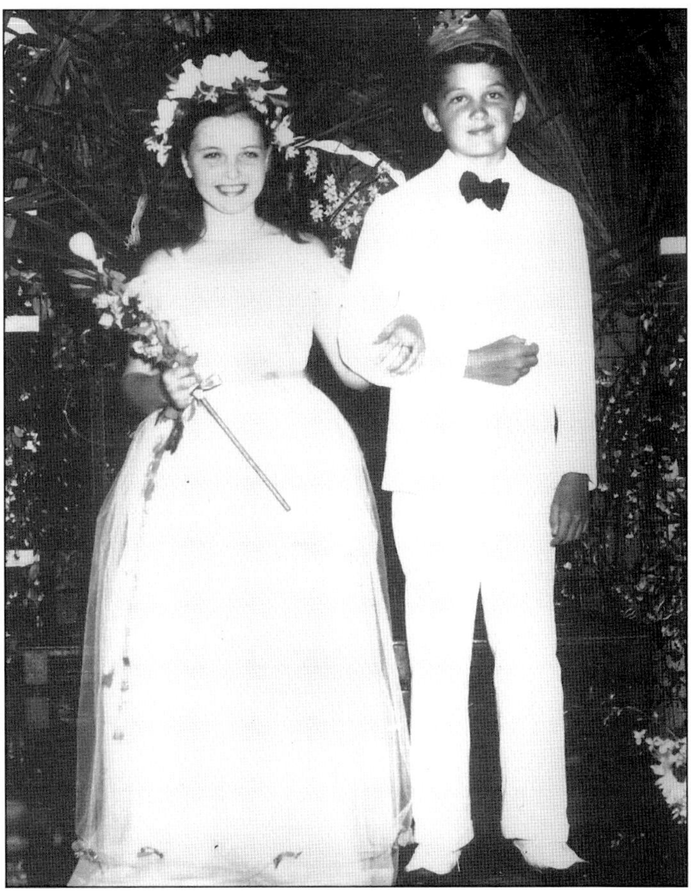

Pretty Patty Carson (Hupe) (Gignilliat), Queen of the May Court at the Isle of Hope School in 1948, regally loops her arm through the arm of His Majesty, King Nash McIntosh, whose royal bowtie is askew.

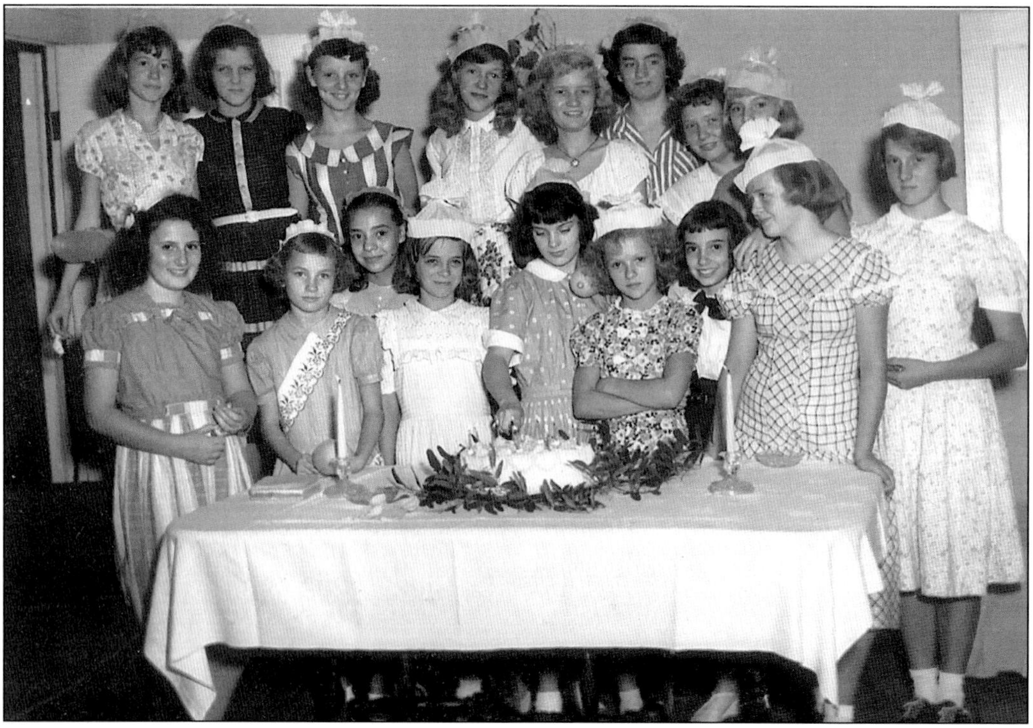

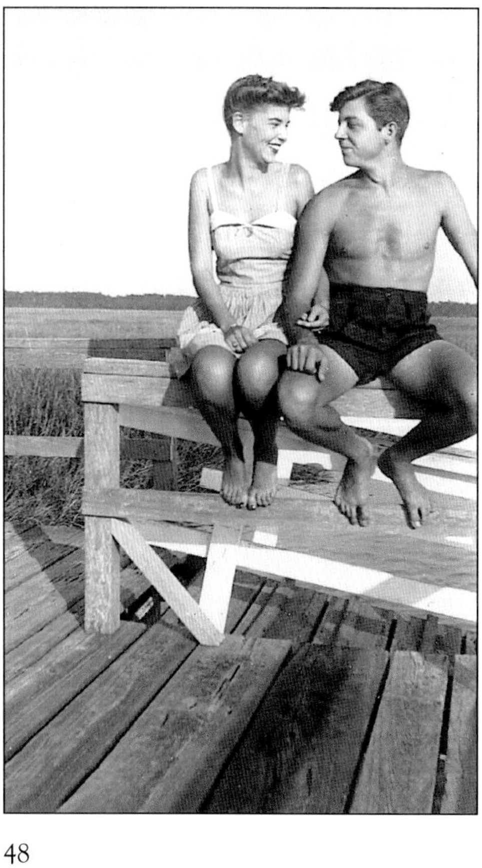

A merry group of girlfriends gathered to celebrate Sandra Kenzie's birthday in the late 1940s. From left to right, they are (front row) Marvin Graham, Sarah Hucks, Helen Thompson, Vera Mae Sharpe, Sandra Kenzie, unidentified, Ann Thompson, Margaret Ann Quante, and Clara Roebling; (back row) Joan Goss, Marie Kenner, Elise Youmans, Frances Perkins, Penny Ann Boyd, Inez Hucks, Julie McKenzie, and Margaret Williams.

Barbara Ann Neff and John McIntosh spent many hours sailing for pleasure, and in weekend sailing regattas. Barbara Ann grew up in Ardsley Park in the city, and John came from an old Isle of Hope family. Today, at the age of 78, he is still sailing and teaching his skills to youngsters on Lake Mayer and in the Wilmington River. "I enjoy teaching them to sail, repair fiberglass, and build small wooden boats," he remarked from his Wilmington Island home.

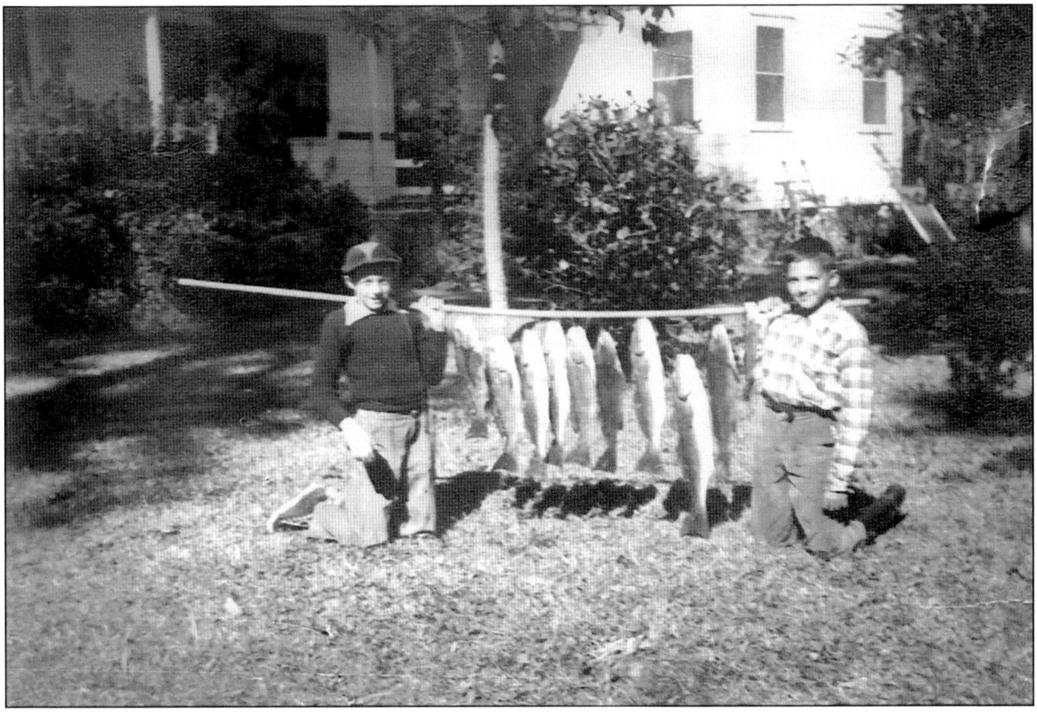

These huge bass were caught by young Carl Quante and Nash McIntosh, who used shrimp for bait. The heavy bonanza bends the pole as the boys struggle under the weight. Fish and grits was a favorite meal, even better with a few ears of fresh corn to fill in the cracks, and home-churned peach ice cream for dessert.

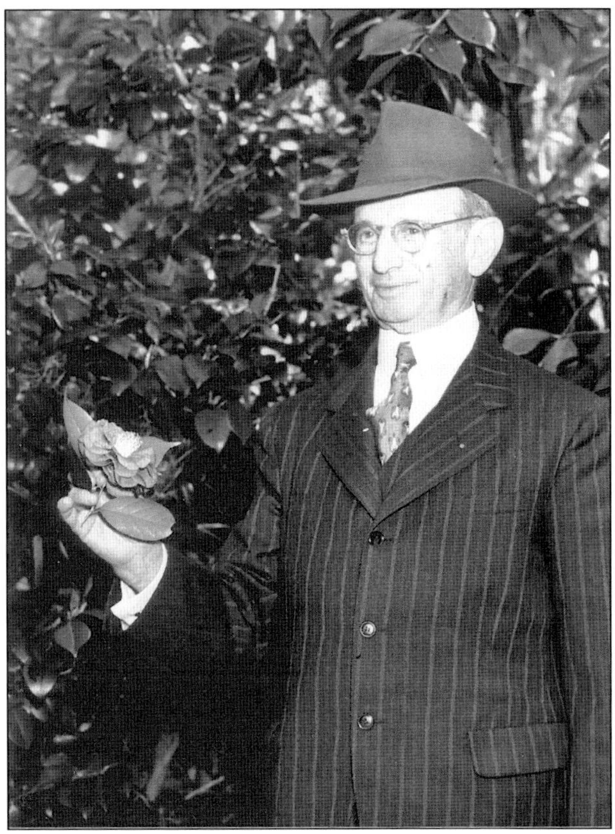

Judge Arthur Solomon admires a prized camellia in his showplace garden at Grimball Point. Judge Solomon was one of the founders of the American Camellia Society and an enthusiastic member of the Men's Garden Club. The Judge Solomon camellia is named for him. Appointed a county commissioner in 1914 for Chatham County, he continued to serve for the next four decades and was the oldest living county commissioner reflecting the most years of continuous service when he died in 1962.

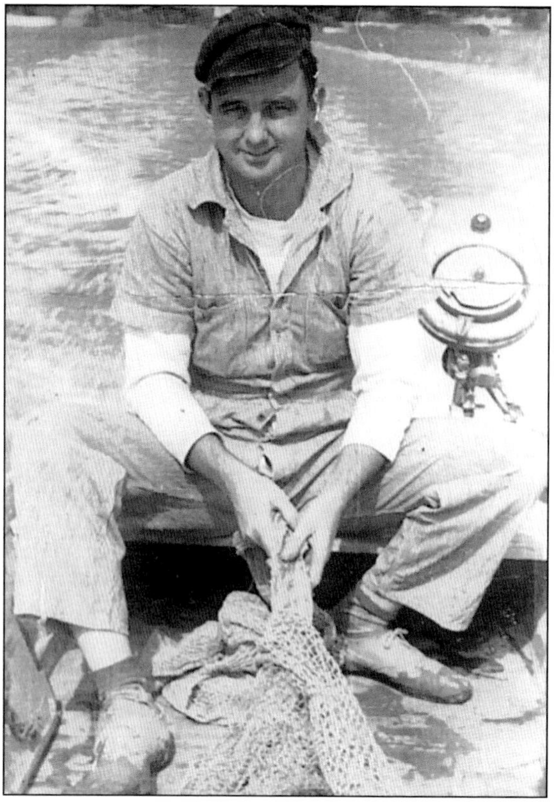

Walter "Jack" Yokum was a boilermaker and married Mary Elizabeth Todd from Atlanta. They had two children, Carolyn Jean Yokum (Bebee) and Jane Elizabeth Yokum (Gruber). Shrimp were so plentiful in the creeks during the 1940s that Jack could fill up a washtub or two with his cast net in no time. He took those fresh boiled shrimp to the pavilion for everyone to share—a real treat. Jack knitted his own shrimp nets, which was a skill requiring months of patience.

The Richmond-Bridges wedding took place in 1945. The newlyweds lived in Wymberley-on-the-Marsh when first married. Seen from left to right are Jim Richmond, Martha "Honey" Richmond, Dorothy Richmond, young Diana Richmond, Thelma Richmond (Bridges), and Jim Bridges. Jim Richmond and Max Hostetter developed Wymberley Subdivision. The Richmonds had three daughters—Diana, Nancy, and Wymberley.

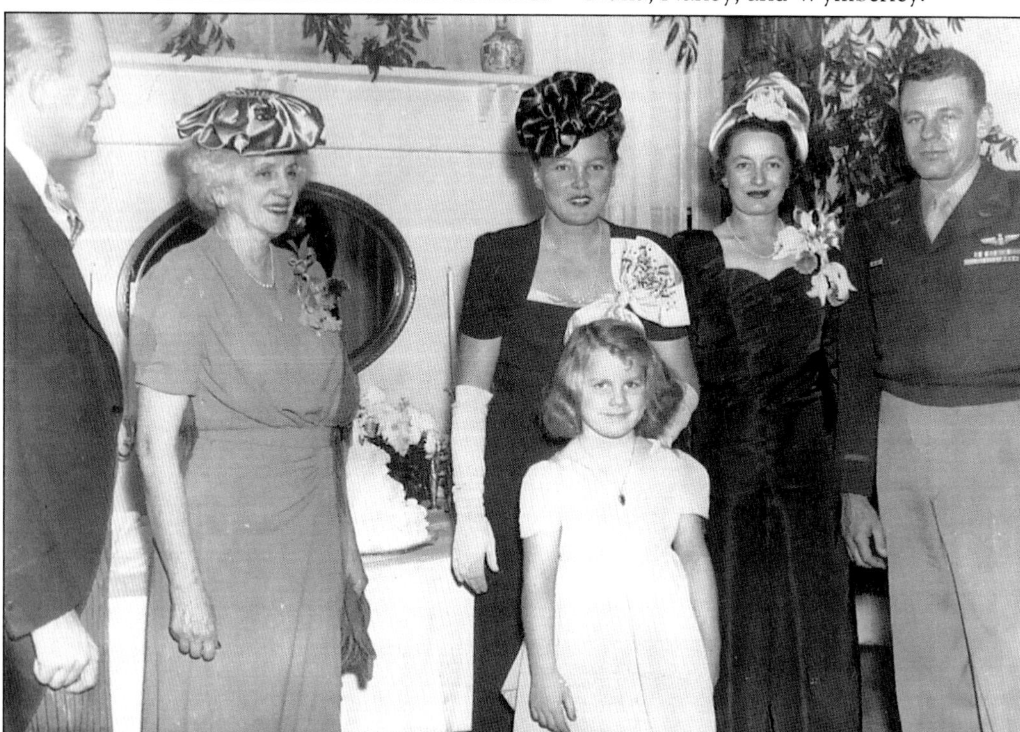

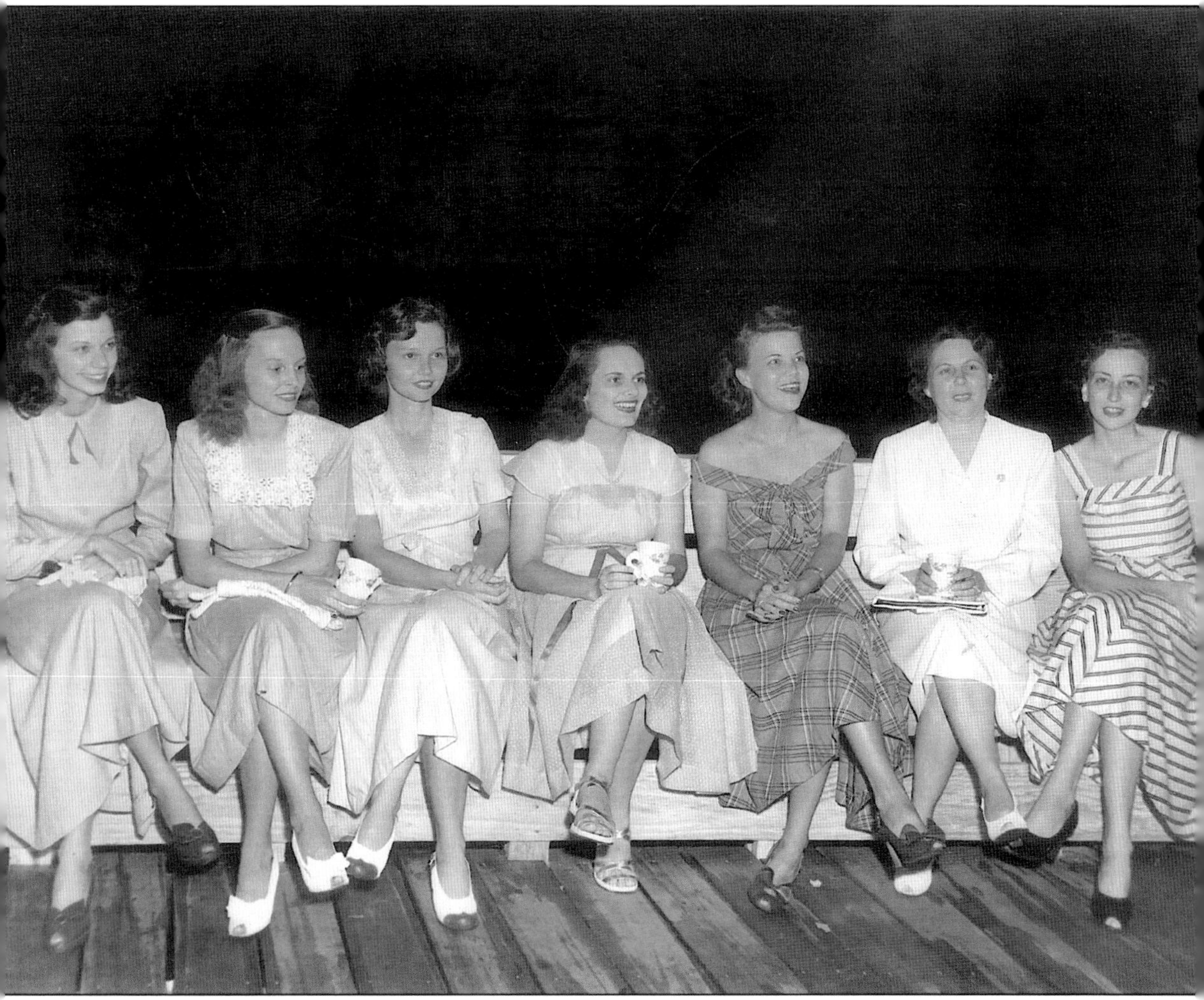

What a long line of lovely ladies! They are celebrating the opening of the Wymberley Yacht Club in the early 1950s. From left to right are unidentified, Elizabeth Waring Barrow, Freda Manley Hutchinson, Weldon Gamble Harlan, Ginny Hood, Mary Cope Sweat, and Jane McRae Schroder. Winners of the Wymberley Yacht Sailing Regatta were James Griner (1952), C.R. Nelson (1953), George Wolfe (1954), Jimmy Sweat Jr. (1955), Herman Schwalbe (1956), and Allen Sickel (1957).

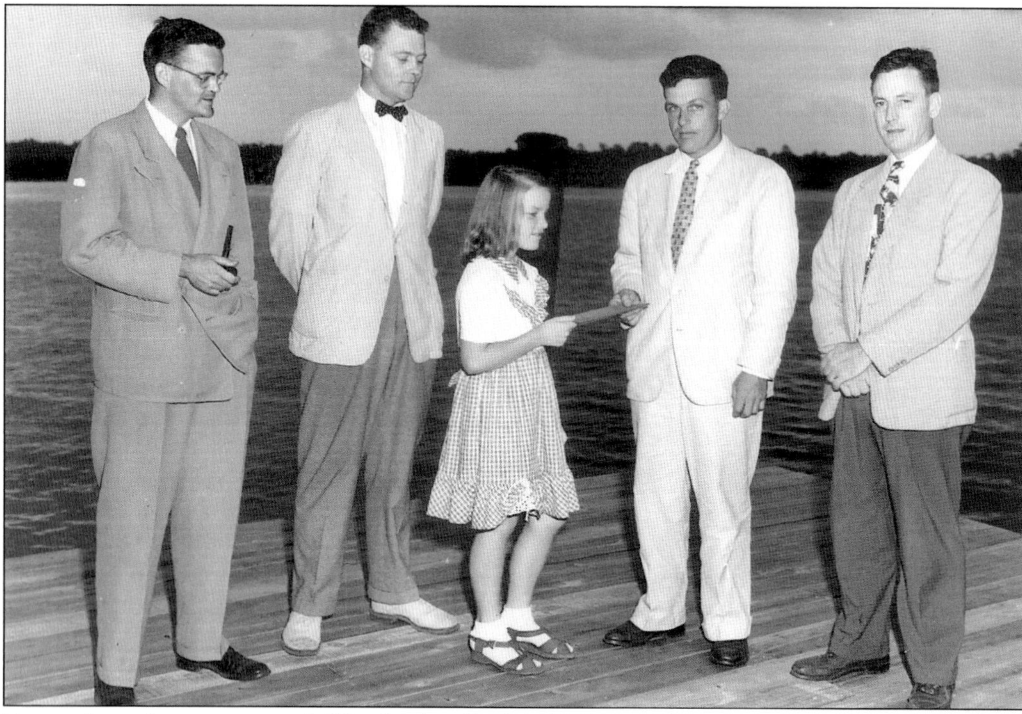

Pictured at the opening of Wymberley Yacht Club are, from left to right, Fred Ogden, unidentified, Diana Richmond, Ross Allen, and Alfred Kennickell.

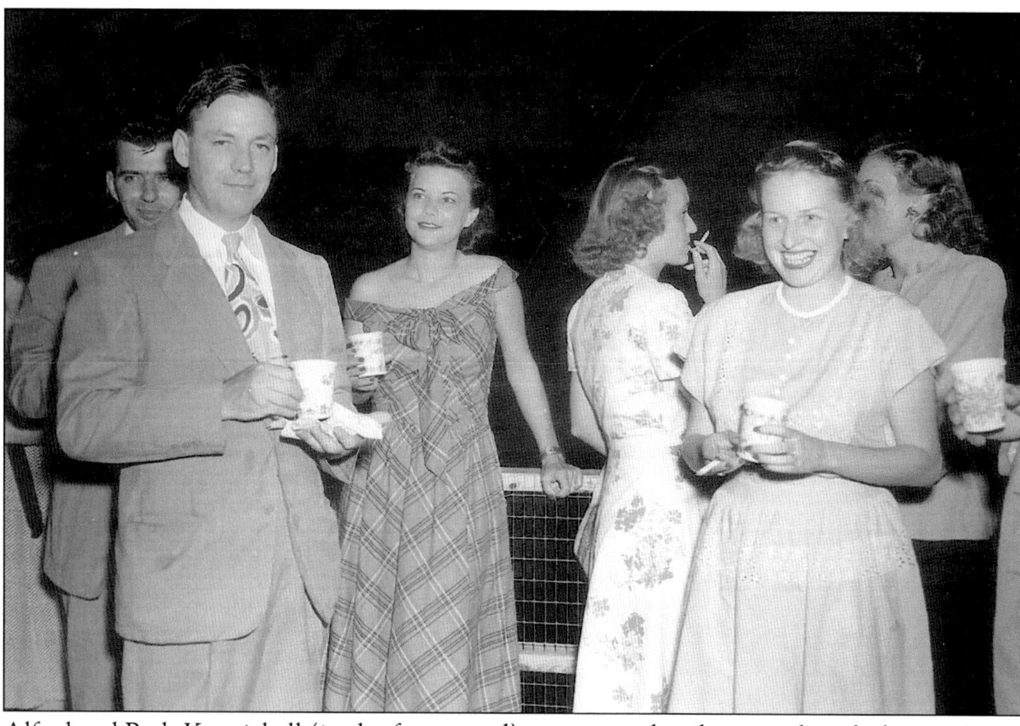

Alfred and Beth Kennickell (in the foreground) are pictured with an unidentified man, Ginny Hood, and Margaret Dawson in the background.

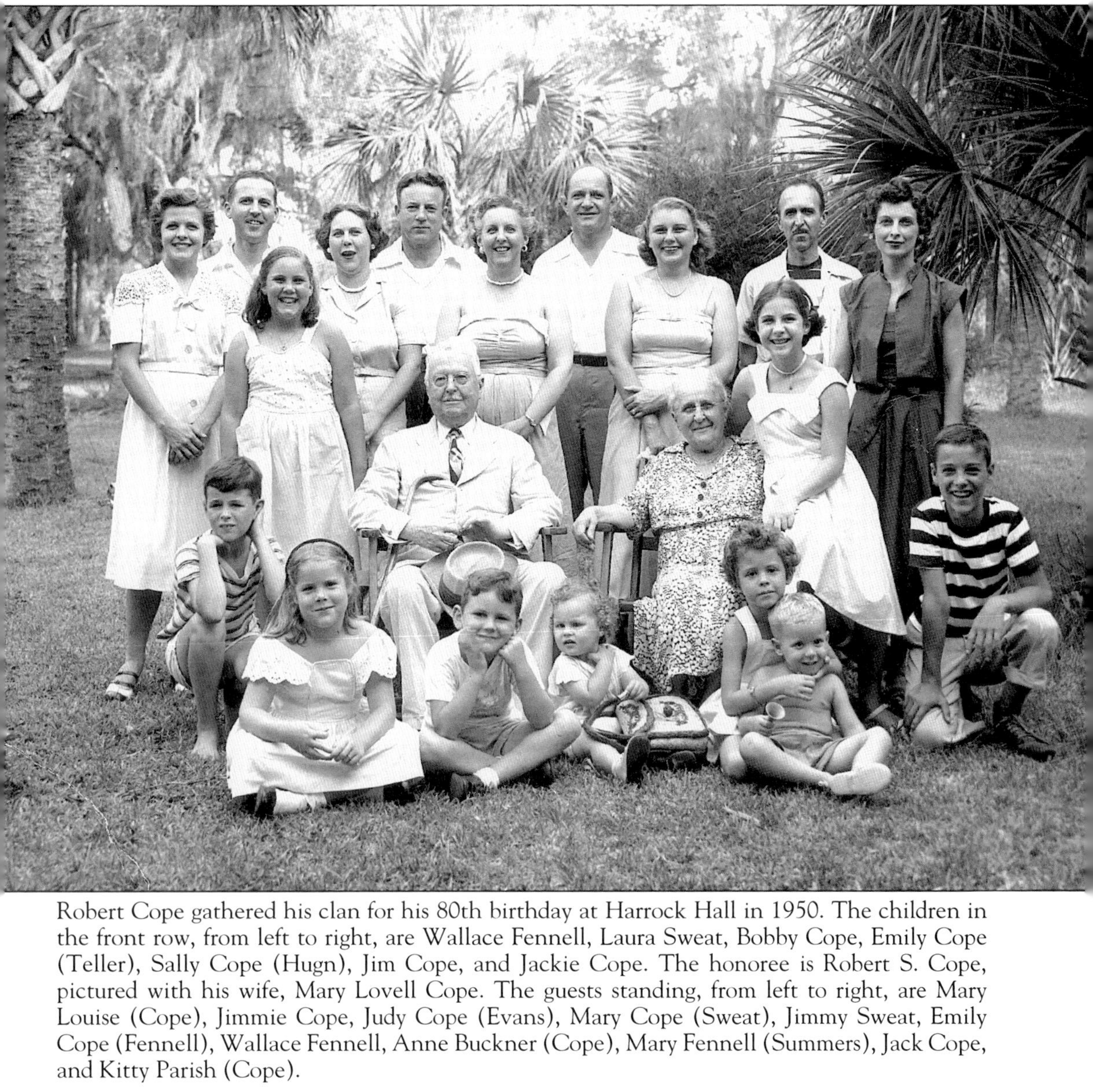

Robert Cope gathered his clan for his 80th birthday at Harrock Hall in 1950. The children in the front row, from left to right, are Wallace Fennell, Laura Sweat, Bobby Cope, Emily Cope (Teller), Sally Cope (Hugn), Jim Cope, and Jackie Cope. The honoree is Robert S. Cope, pictured with his wife, Mary Lovell Cope. The guests standing, from left to right, are Mary Louise (Cope), Jimmie Cope, Judy Cope (Evans), Mary Cope (Sweat), Jimmy Sweat, Emily Cope (Fennell), Wallace Fennell, Anne Buckner (Cope), Mary Fennell (Summers), Jack Cope, and Kitty Parish (Cope).

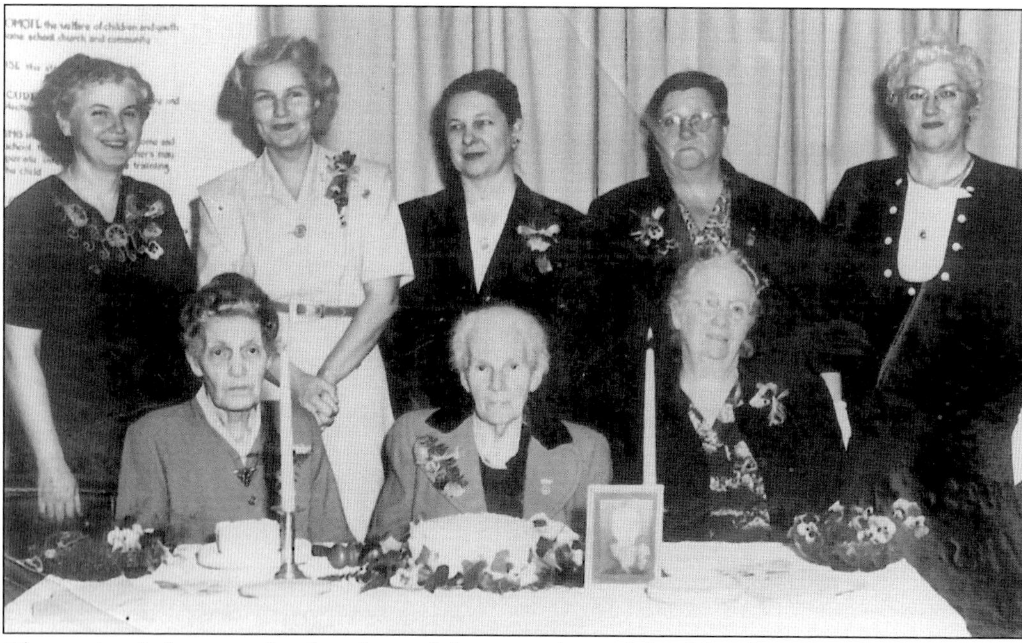

Clementine Lebey was the founder and first president of the Isle of Hope School PTA. She served as president from 1915 to 1919. In 1950, the club celebrated its 35th anniversary. Charter members, from left to right, are (sitting) Clementine Lebey, Mable Reynolds, and Mary McKenzie. Past presidents, from left to right, are (standing) Eddie Lou Stanley (1942–1944), Betsy Jackson (1947–1948), Myrtle Strickland (1940–1942), Bessie Roberts (1929–1931), and Inez Jenkins (1933–1935).

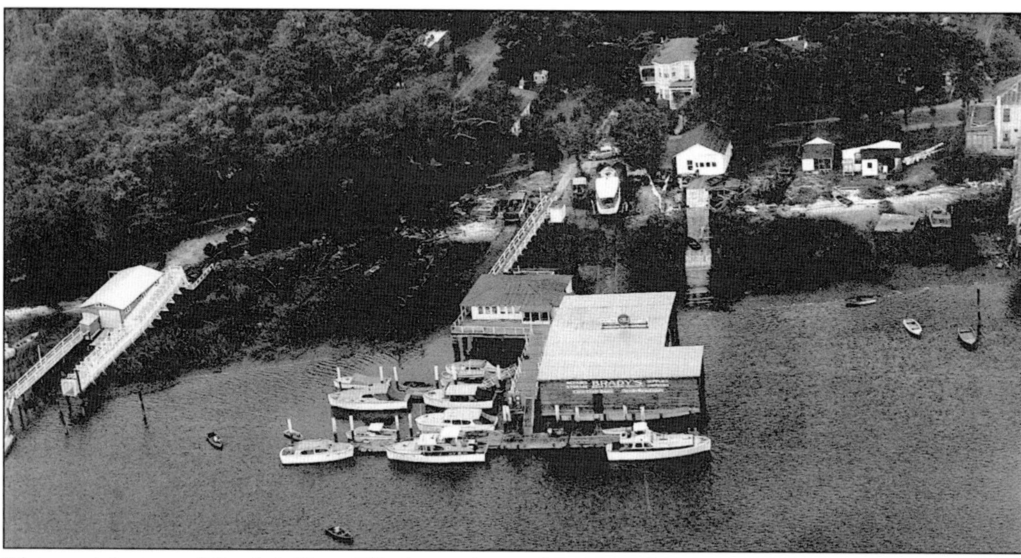

This aerial view of Brady's Boat Works in the early 1950s shows a yacht up on the (rail) ways having pesky barnacles scraped off its hull. The view of the Modena dock on the left shows the cattle chute. Also visible in the background is the home owned today by Sam McCatchern, which was the former home of Bill Brady. Neil Mingledorf owned the marina until the late 1950s. He called it the Isle of Hope Marina. It was later sold to David Johnson and then to Charlie Waller.

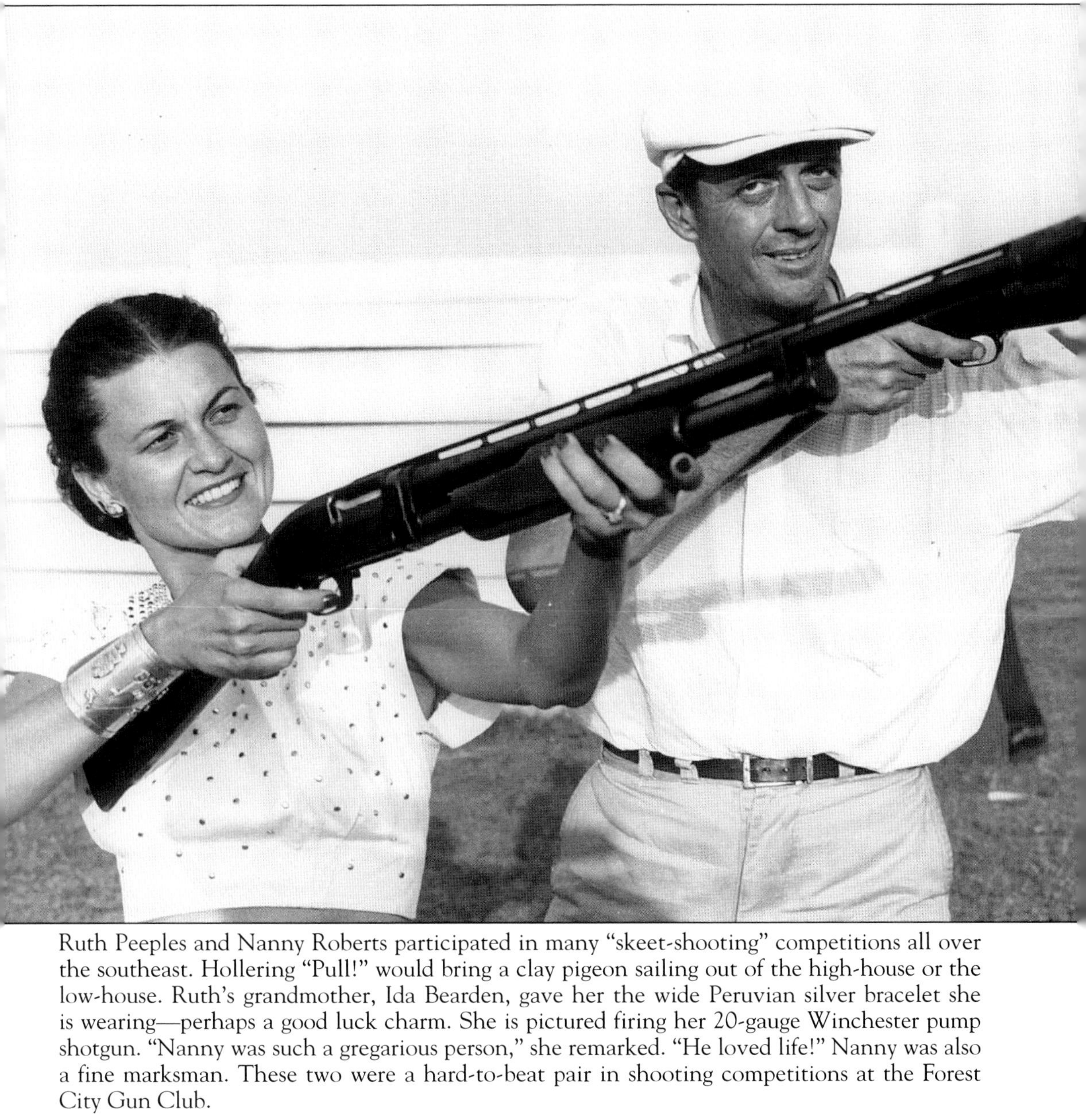

Ruth Peeples and Nanny Roberts participated in many "skeet-shooting" competitions all over the southeast. Hollering "Pull!" would bring a clay pigeon sailing out of the high-house or the low-house. Ruth's grandmother, Ida Bearden, gave her the wide Peruvian silver bracelet she is wearing—perhaps a good luck charm. She is pictured firing her 20-gauge Winchester pump shotgun. "Nanny was such a gregarious person," she remarked. "He loved life!" Nanny was also a fine marksman. These two were a hard-to-beat pair in shooting competitions at the Forest City Gun Club.

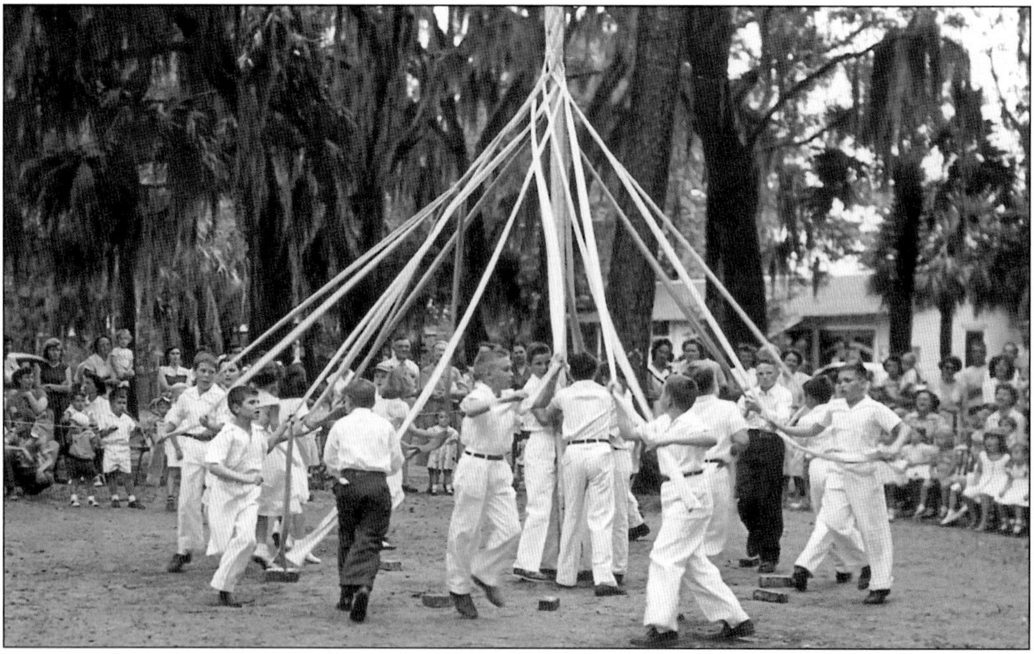

Evidence from the 16th century suggests a widespread celebration of spring with exuberant May games. The raising of Maypoles and general merrymaking were overseen by a May king and queen, who were often identified with Robin Hood and Maid Marion. Children from the Isle of Hope School welcome the arrival of spring.

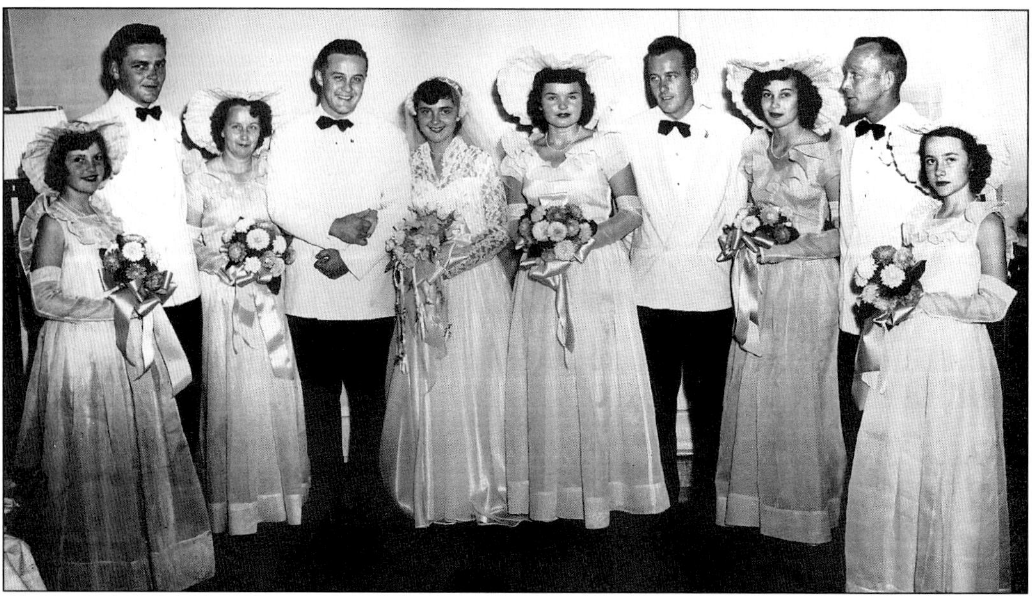

Our Lady of Good Hope Catholic Chapel has been the scene of many weddings at Isle of Hope. The Lockett-Rodewolt wedding took place here in 1951. Members of the wedding party, from left to right, are Ann Rodewolt (Farrar), Andrew Rodewolt, Martha Anne Lockett (Lewis), Frederick "Bucky" Lockett, Josephine Rodewolt (Lockett), Betty Reynolds (Lockett), Randolph "Ranny" Lockett, Lorraine Tuten (Rodewolt), Fred "Buster" Elmgren, and Jane Rogers (Quante). The couple celebrated their 50th anniversary in 2001!

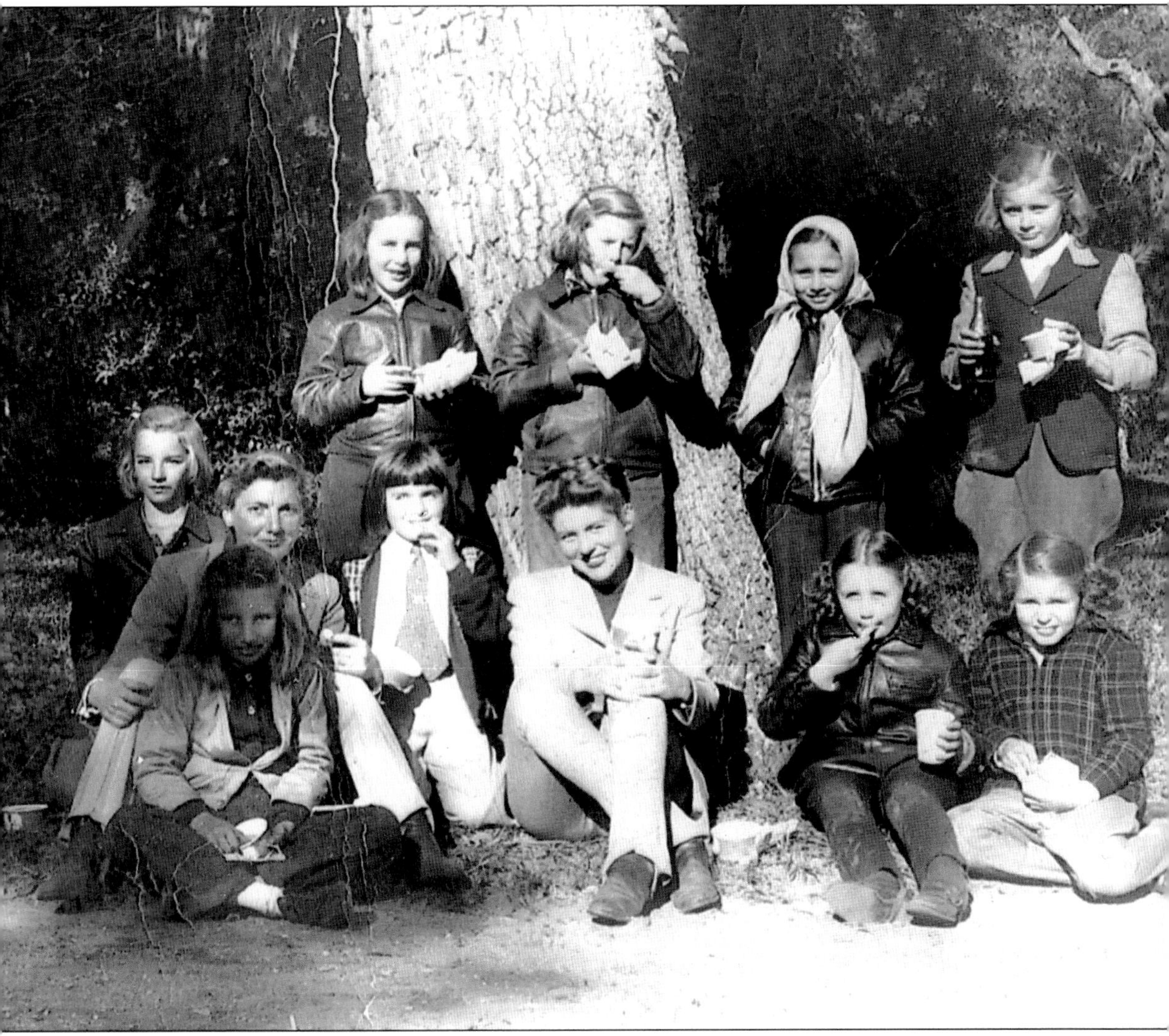

In 1950, Elfrida De Renne Barrow had her 10th birthday. Each lucky child mounted her favorite horse at SAHI Stable and rode along Skidaway Road to Wormsloe Plantation where Mrs. Craig "Dolly" Barrow waited with a picnic. Pictured from left to right are (sitting) Polly Wylly (Cooper), Instructor Jane Bulcken (King), Dale Gabriel (Thorpe), Elfrida Barrow (Moore), Instructor Pat Waters (Brannen), Martha Lee Oliver (Vaught), and Phyllis Clay (Steinbeck); (standing) Comer Varnedoe (Meadows), Ginger Clarke (Norsworthy), Dee Sharpley (Yates), and Pam Sharpley (Trosdal).

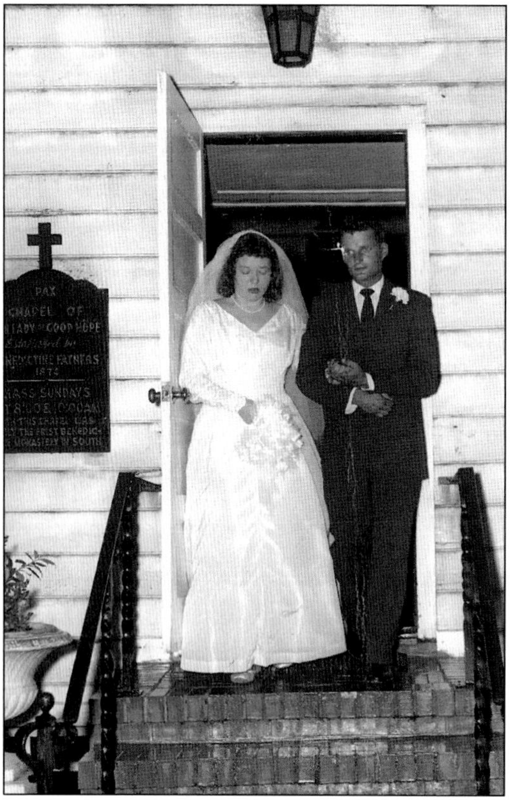

Julie McKenzie and Bob Workmon leave the chapel of Our Lady of Good Hope after being married in 1956. He was still in the Air Force and was sent to North Africa soon afterwards, reluctantly giving up a music scholarship to Oklahoma University. Julie taught at the Hebrew Community School on Abercorn Street and Bob worked in electronics. The Workmons had four sons—Bobby, Bud, Tom, and Patrick. Julie's parents, Tom and Betty McKenzie, lived on the island for years.

Lightenings were popular sailboats in the 1950s. According to Nash McIntosh, the most famous and outrageous race was the Burntpot Regatta. The trophy was a charred cast-iron pot. Rules were simple: have a sailboat; start at the Yacht Club; sail to the marker off Burntpot Island; try not to "tump" over; finish at the Isle of Hope dock where the party was already hopping. Paddling and drinking were allowed and no rules of right-of-way applied. What a blast! With spinnakers up, the boats sail before the wind—a pretty sight!

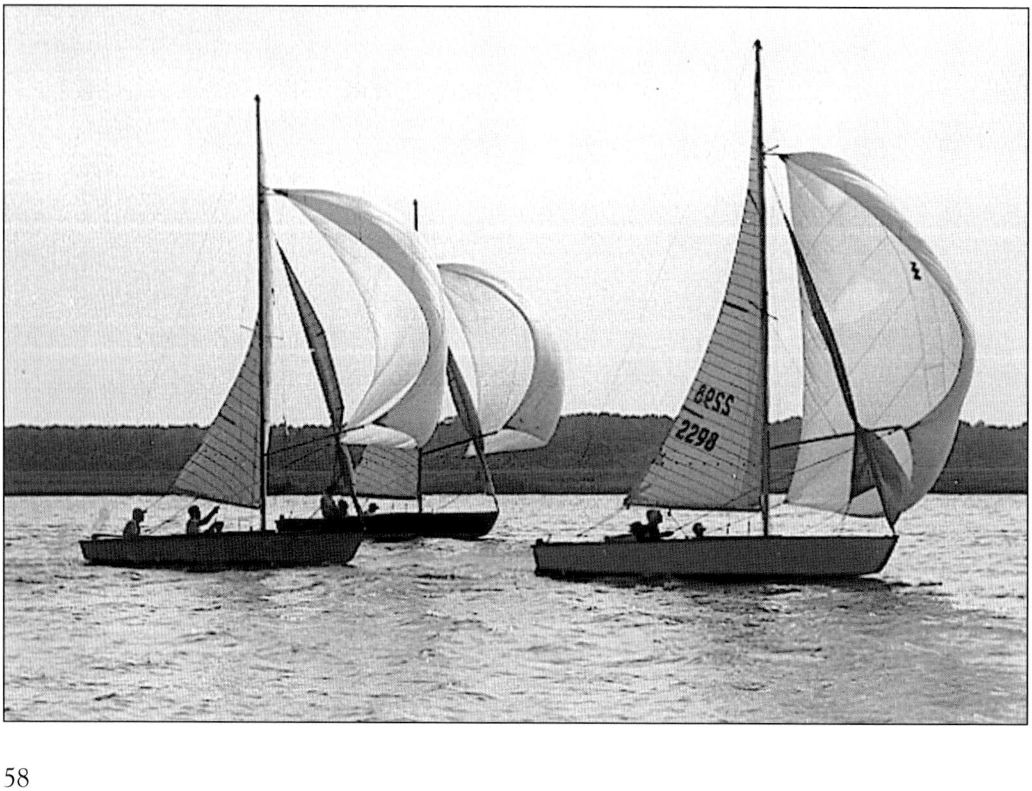

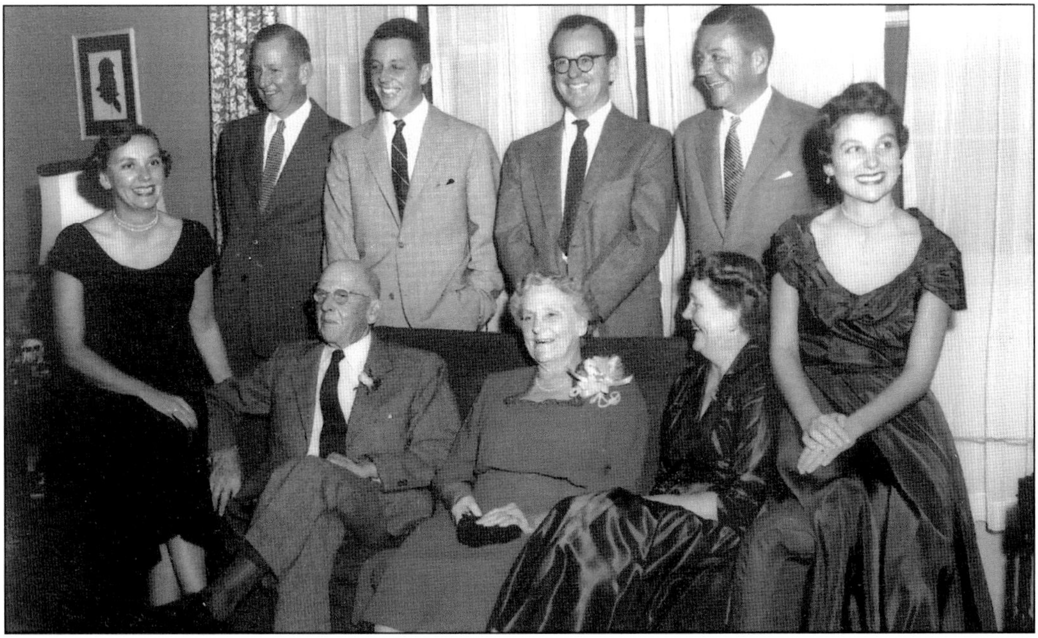

Residents of the island for years, Olin Talley McIntosh and Jane Lawton McIntosh proudly pose for their 50th wedding anniversary photo. They were married in 1905, which was the same year as the St. Louis World's Fair. Family members, from left to right, are (front row) Olin, Jane, and Annie; (back row) Jane, Billy, John, Jimmy, Olin, and Betty.

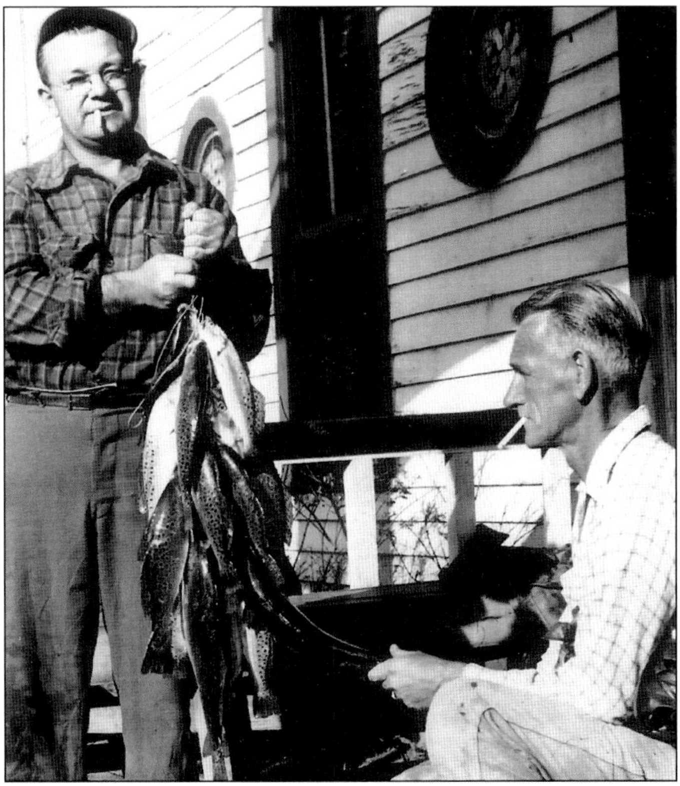

W.E "Euell" Lewis (left) holds up a nice string of summer trout which he and Bill Hardin caught using live shrimp as bait. Children learned fishing with hand-lines. No rod and reel were needed. Bait was usually a feisty fiddler crab on a hook tied to string with a sinker. The fiddler was lowered to the bottom of the river next to a piling covered in barnacles. Slight tension and the line looped over a sensitive finger could detect a sheephead or a drum nibbling the bait.

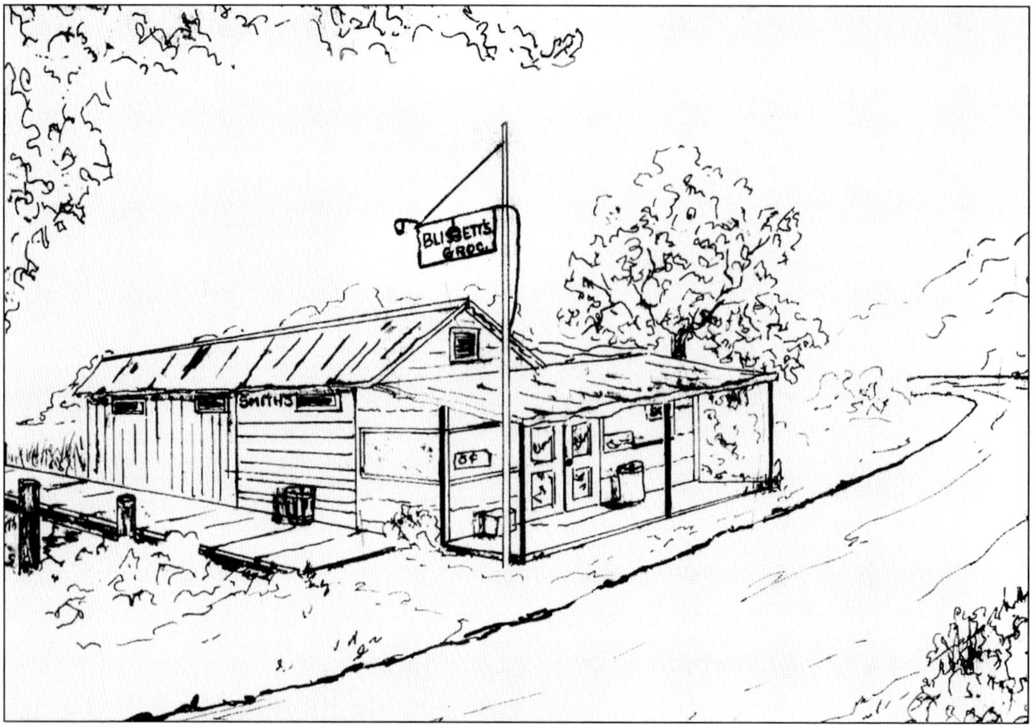

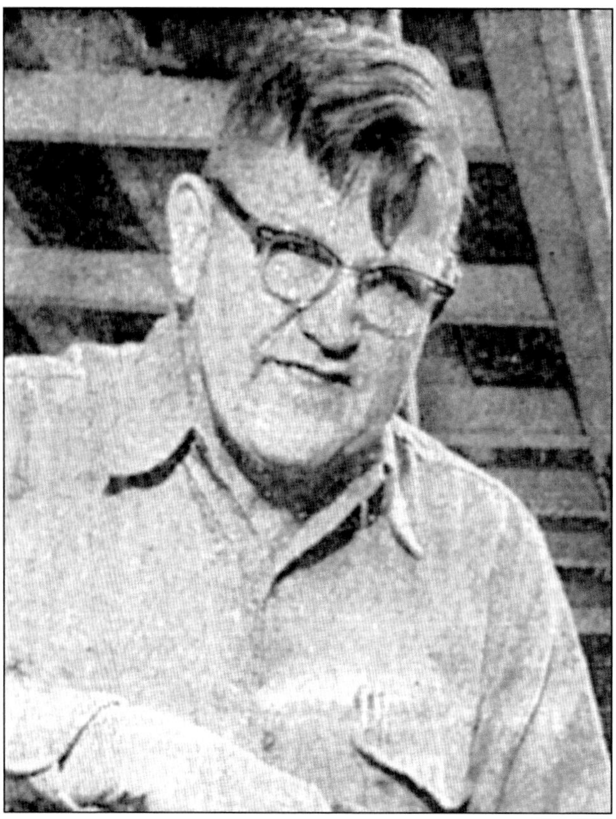

Blissett's Market, formerly Smith's Store, was in business on the bluff for years. Oliver and Ottie Blissett sold hooks, sinkers, and chicken necks for crabbing, picnic fixings, hot dogs, and Orange Crush. Mr. Blissett, or simply "Mr. B," shopped weekly for supplies in the city and brought groceries back on the streetcar for his customers. They were generous with cookies and candy treats for young "drop-ins." When a child was late for supper, mothers would often call the store to have the child sent home. This is a delightful pen and ink sketch by Barbara Strictland, a talented Savannah artist.

Oliver Blissett and his wife, Ottie, had a genuine love of children. They were special folks who, over the years, were foster parents to 33 children, ranging in age from 1 day to 18 years. This is a newspaper clipping of "Mr. B." The market was torn down in the 1960s.

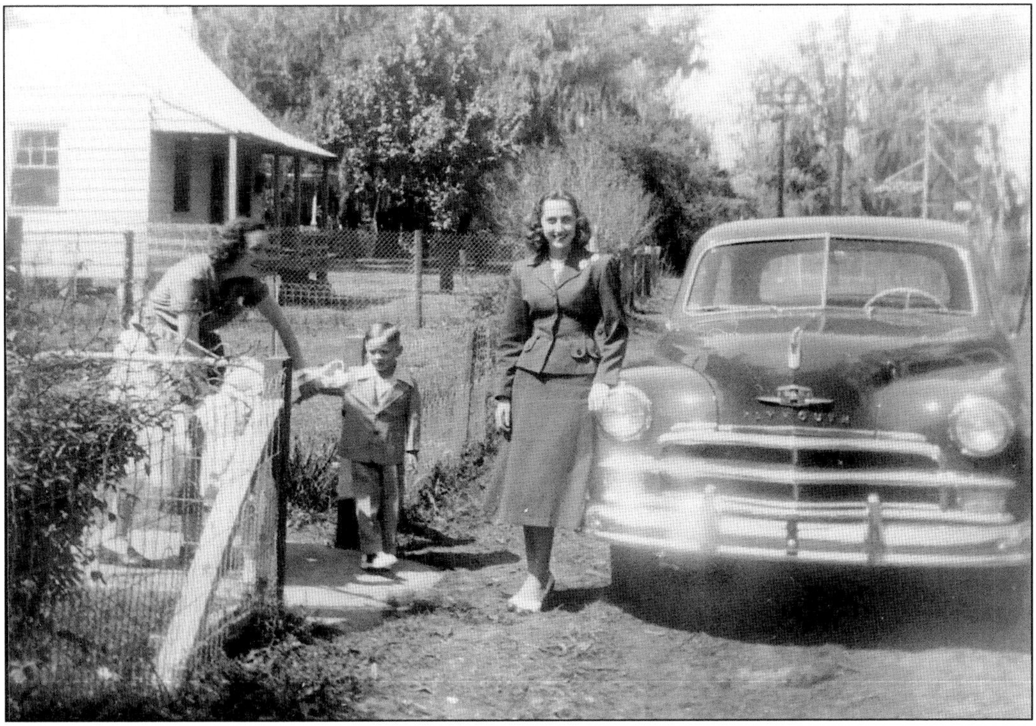

Theresa Douglas, leaning on her Plymouth, chats with Margaret Billac and her son, Jimmy, on Rosenbrook Avenue in 1953. The Hucks family rented the Wylly house (in the background) until 1944. In the fierce hurricane of 1942, an old mulberry tree crashed over in the high winds and nearly demolished the house. The house was donated to the Isle of Hope Community Association in 1952 by the Wylly family. It no longer stands, but the association still owns the land.

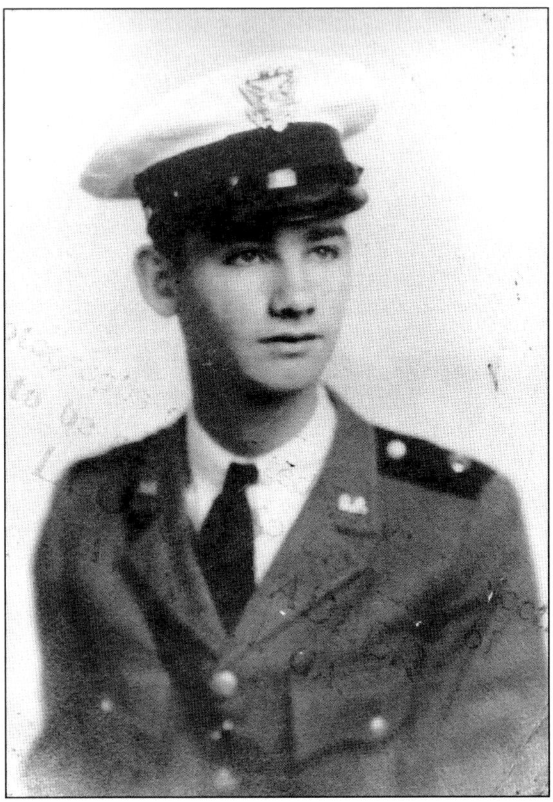

Ebbie Paxton graduated from the Benedictine Military Academy in 1936. In 1945, he was killed in World War II on Ie Shima in the Pacific. He was highly decorated for bravery and good conduct. The funeral service was at Our Lady of Good Hope and the burial was at Bonaventure Cemetery. In 1954, friends gathered to unveil a monument in his memory at the Ebbie Paxton Memorial Park. The park was given to the community by William Barbee.

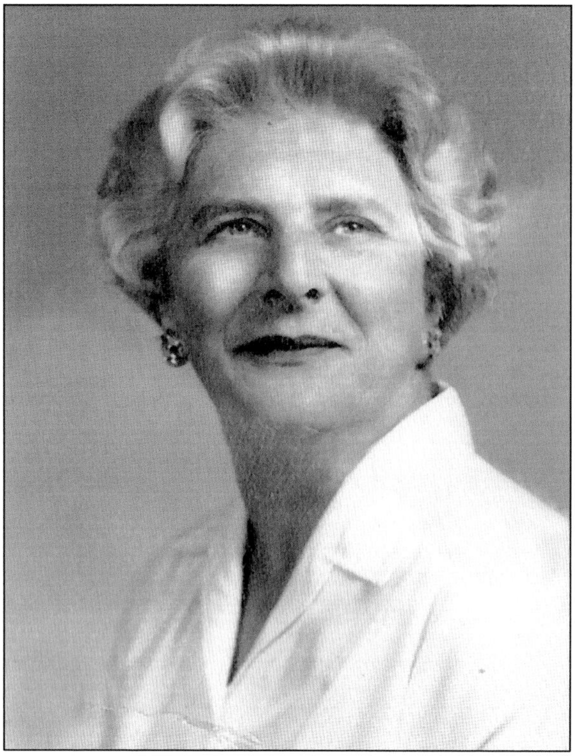

Anna Beckmann started the popular Chickadee School in the barn behind her house on Rose Avenue. The school operated from 1949 to 1967. This photo was taken in 1950. She took them on picnics, hiking trips, and taught them wonderful songs. Winning the hearts of all of her "chickadees" with kindness, she had no problem managing 20 youngsters by herself.

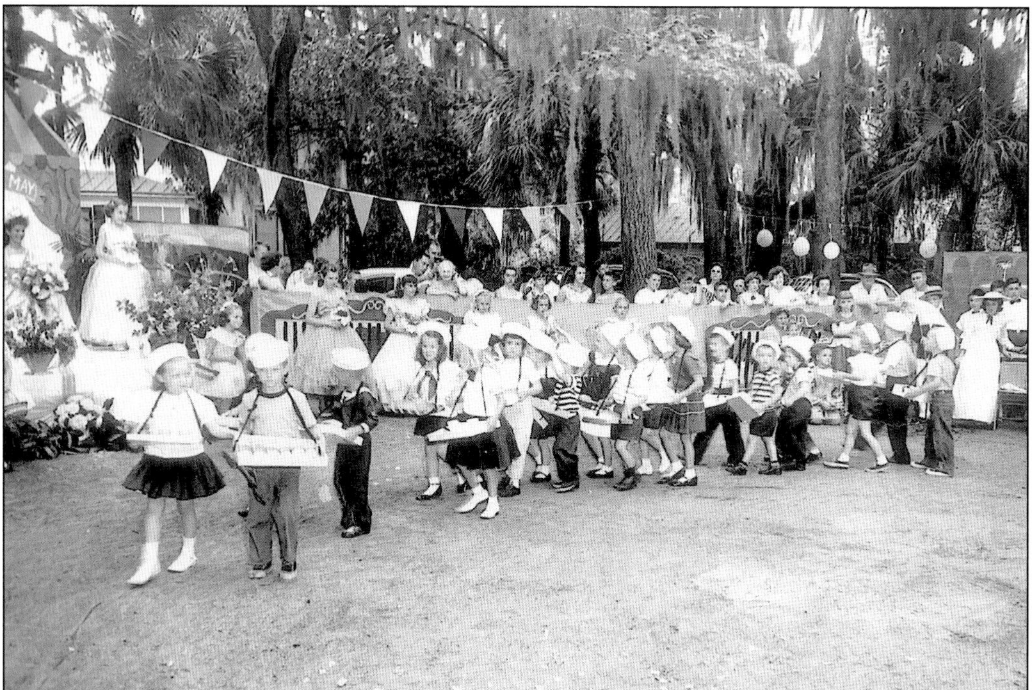

Kathy Barbee and Bubby Sorrenson lead the procession at the May Day celebrations at the Chickadee School in 1955. The queen and a member of her court can be seen on the left.

Three-year-old Tommy Norton looks as though someone took away his pink junket, a favorite dessert for children. His mother, Leila Norton, explains that their address was once Route 6, Box 172. She and her husband had furnished the dogwood trees on their road and named it Dogwood Lane. Judge Solomon said that the name would have to be changed because there was already a Dogwood Avenue at Thunderbolt. Mrs. Norton and her neighbor, Mrs. Caphton, decided to get around this by using the botanical name for dogwood—Cornus florida. The name was changed to Cornus and remains so today.

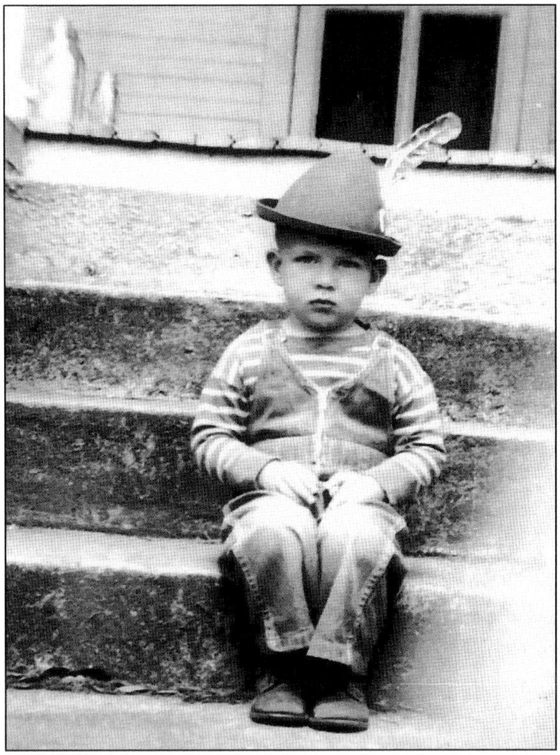

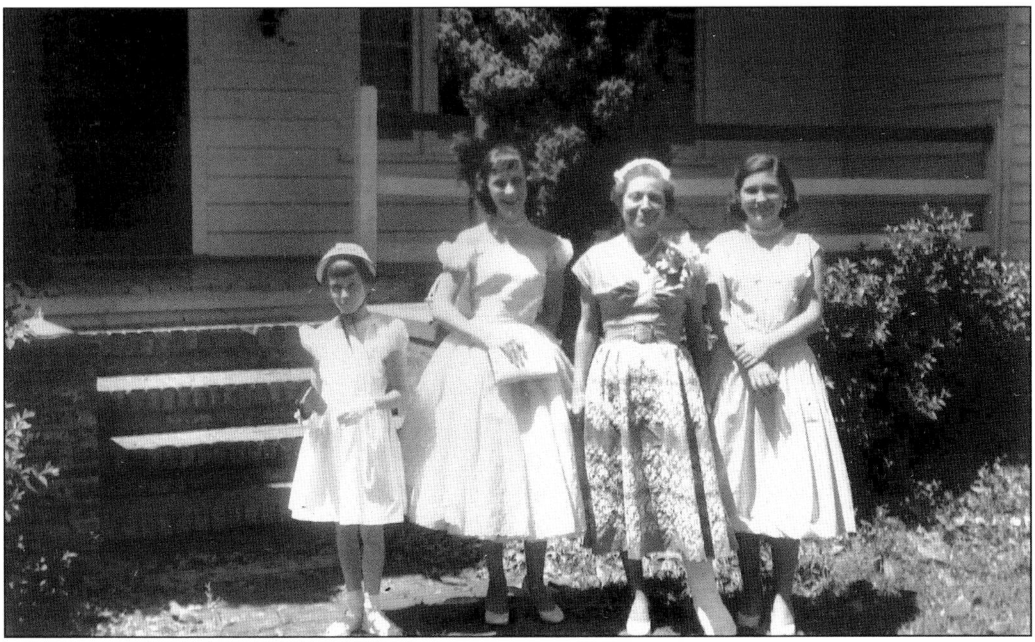

On a fine spring day in 1952, the Hancock girls and their mother visited the McIntoshes for dinner after church. Pictured, from left to right, are Janie (Long), Annie (Hammond), Tucker Tison Hancock, and Caroline Hancock. Dinner at noon was fried chicken, coleslaw, gumbo, butterbeans, cornbread, and hand-churned peach ice cream. After dinner, they took long naps under the ceiling fans and read Little Lulu comic books.

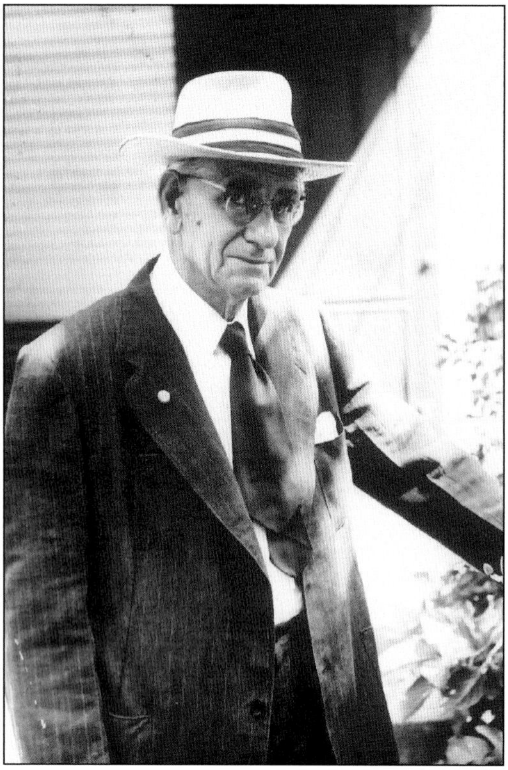

William Eugene Smith of Parkersburg Road started the "Mysterious Santa Claus" tradition, which continues to bring joy to the sick every Christmas. In 1902, he lay ill and lonely in a hospital bed while the rest of the world went about Christmas merrymaking. At that time, he vowed that he would never let anyone spend Christmas in a hospital alone without a cheerful visit from Santa. As a C&C Bank employee in charge of the vaults, he collected toys all year in the bank's basement.

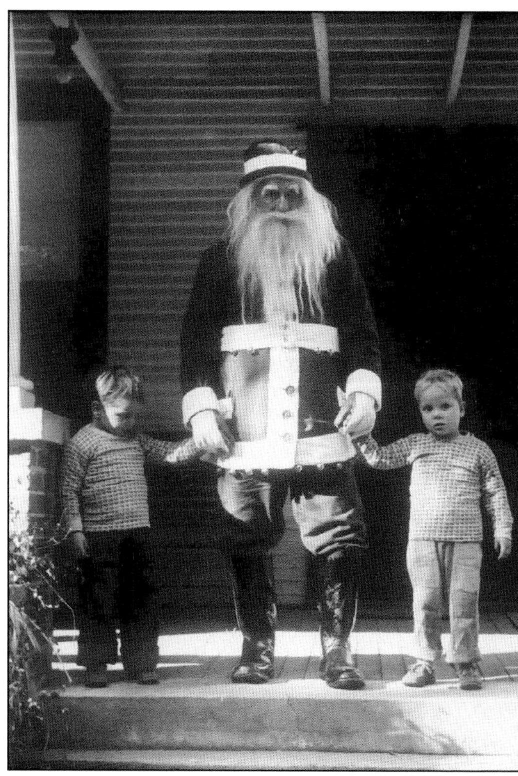

For 50 years, Mr. Smith visited hospitals and nursing homes spreading his special cheer. Today, this fine tradition continues. Many volunteers help the modern "Mysterious Santa Claus" carry out the promise of William Eugene Smith. He is pictured here in 1950 with his great-grandsons, Robert (left) and Joseph Johnson, who adore their good-hearted great-grandpa.

Jane Rogers (Quante) strikes a fetching pose on board Buster Elmgren's cabin cruiser, *The Chicken*. The Skidaway River was always full of activity with sailing, water skiing, aqua-planing, fishing, crabbing, and shrimping. Sunbathing with baby oil and iodine produced a good tan and a little lemon juice in the hair created trendy sun streaks. These were the carefree days before sunscreen came on the market.

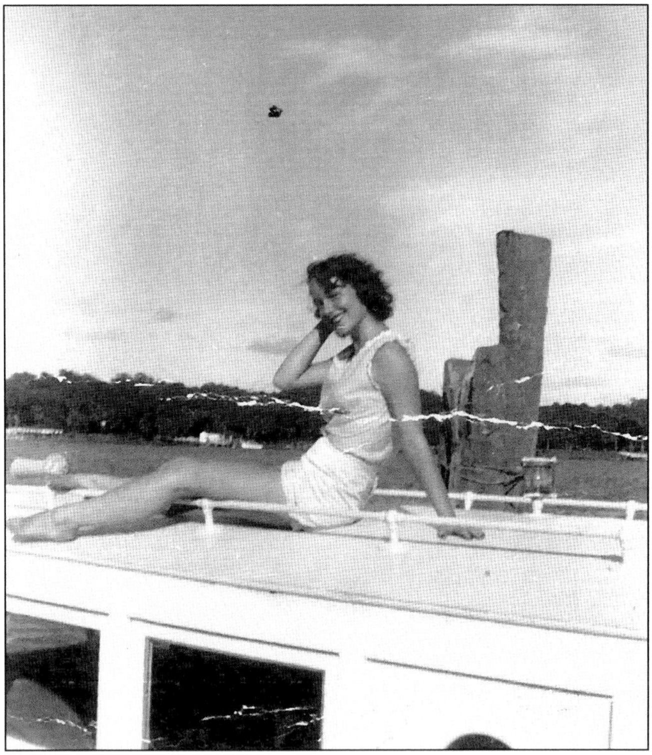

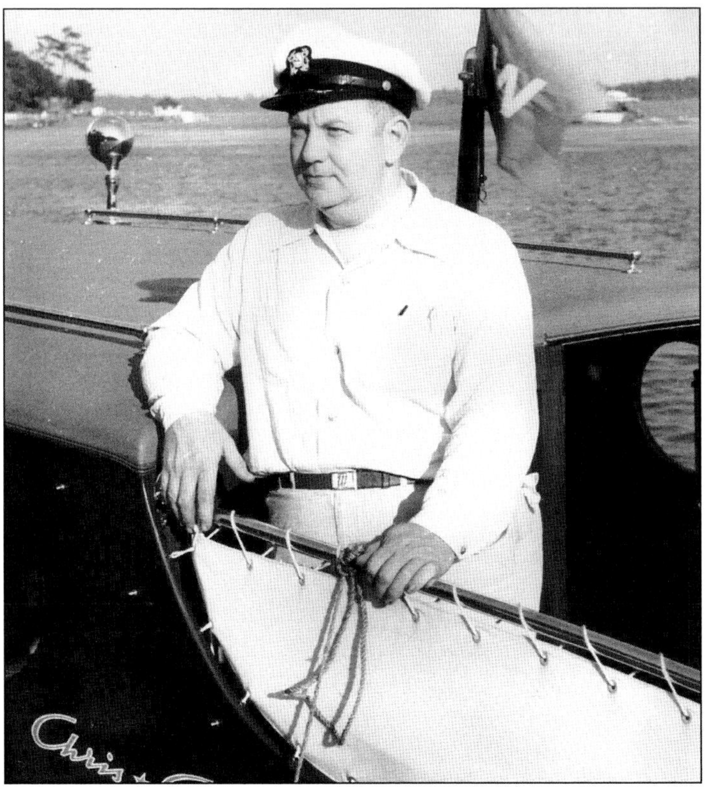

Ralston Wylly waits with waning patience for his tardy guests, Camille and Judge B.B. Heery and Betty and Perry Brannen to arrive for a spin in his new mahogany Chris Craft. Ralston spent a lot of time at the marina buying a boat and then trading it in for another boat several times before he was satisfied. He was married to May Patterson and had two children, Betty (Collins) and Ralston "Bud." He was the president of the Industrial Bank on Johnson Square in the city.

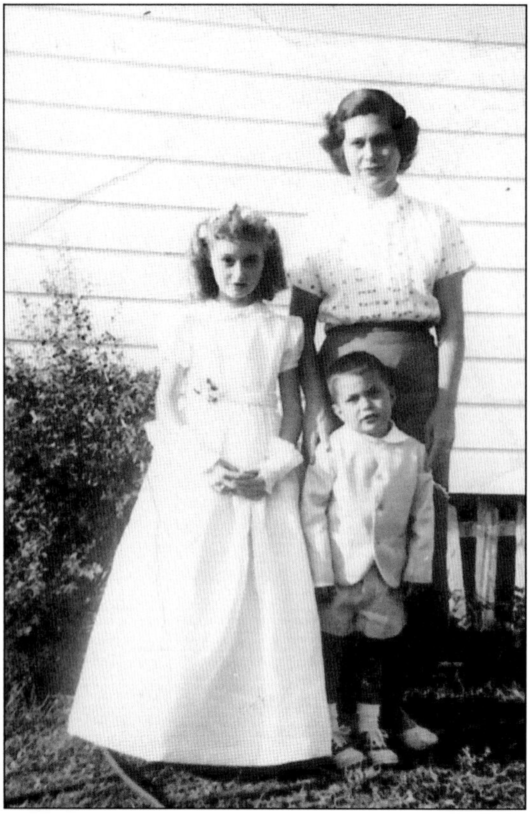

Charlotte Sisson (Glendye) has her two children all gussied up in their best finery for the May Day festivities. Her daughter, Sharon (Varn), lives with her husband, Algernon, in a restored house next to the old crab factory at Pinpoint. Her son Richard is married to the former Patricia Stephens.

Curtis "Curtie" Lewis Jr. (left) invited a few friends over to make a fuss of his important third birthday. Digging into the ice cream is Butch Goldenstar. Helen Artley (Duffy) is watching him closely. Helen's parents Jim and Helen Artley built their home on the foundation of the mansion called Wymberley at the south end of the bluff. The Wymberley mansion burned in 1933. The cannon displayed on their lawn was made in Boston and placed there in 1903. The inscription says "Under the Colonial and Revolutionary Forces."

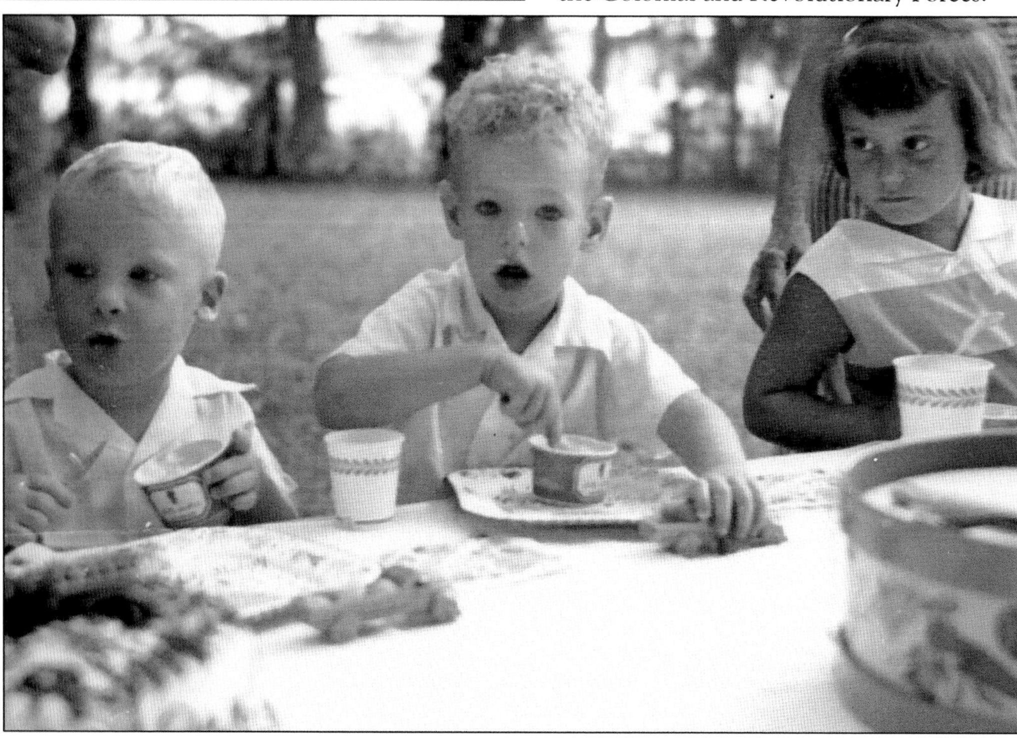

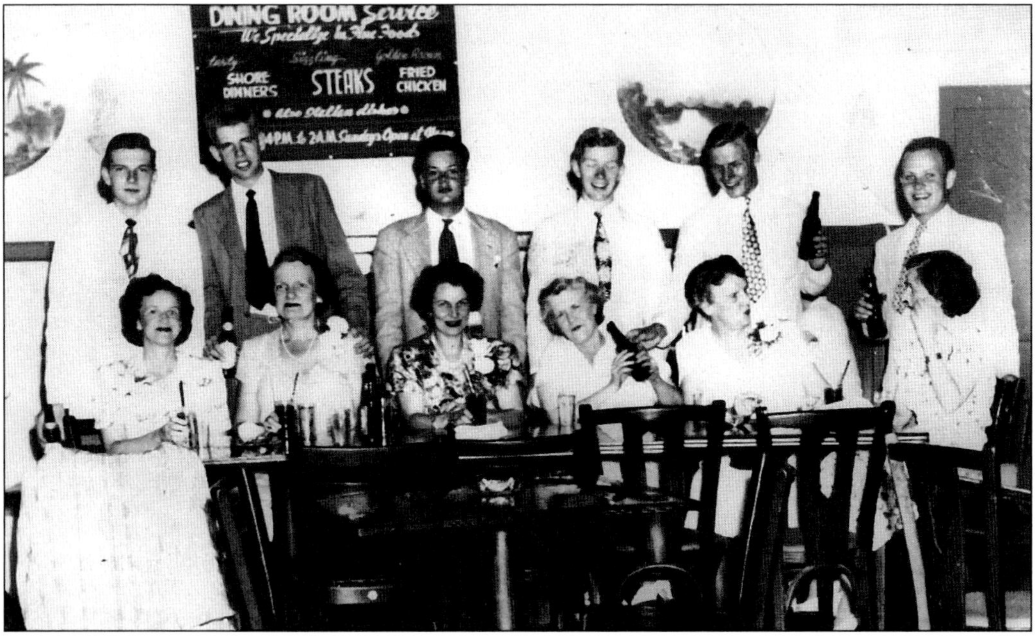

Six devoted sons took their mothers out for a special lunch at the Sapphire Room in the old DeSoto Hotel. The mothers, from left to right, are Retta Jelks, Josephine Demere, Kathryn Johnson, Hannay Rankin, Elizabeth Ellis, and Mary Bond Johnson. Their sons, from left to right, are Billy Rankin, Inman Ellis, Bradley Johnson, Freeman Jelks, Charlie Demere, and Bobby Johnson.

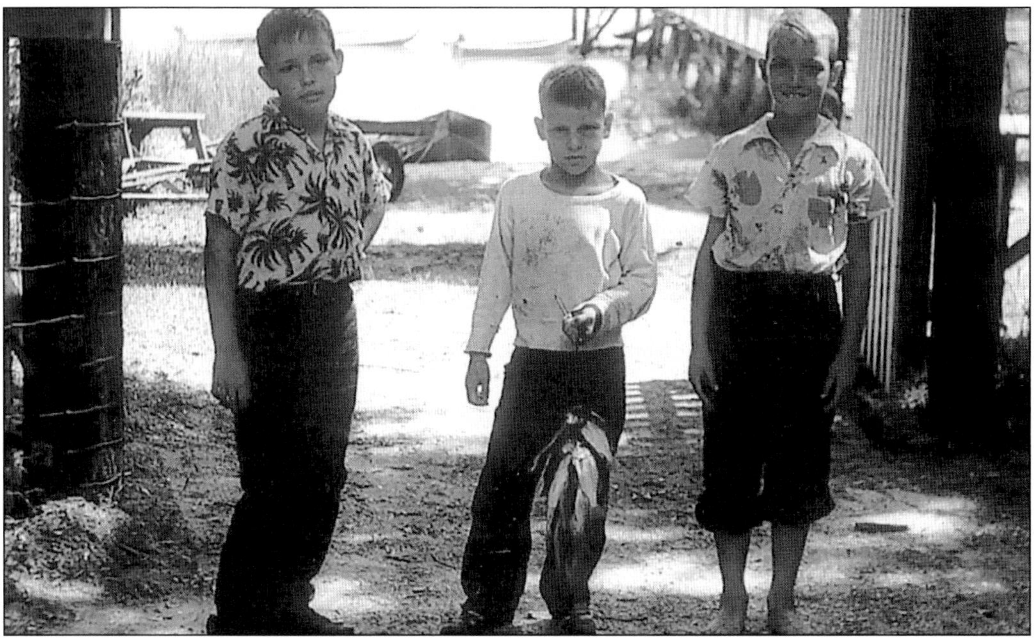

In this photo, from left to right, are Allen Sickel, Peter Hellstrom, and James Sickel. The three have just come up from the dock at the Wymberley Yacht Club with their catch. These little yellowtails won't make much of a meal, but the thrill of the catch was fun. Wymberley residents can join the club for a small fee, which includes the use of the dock and the picnic area all year.

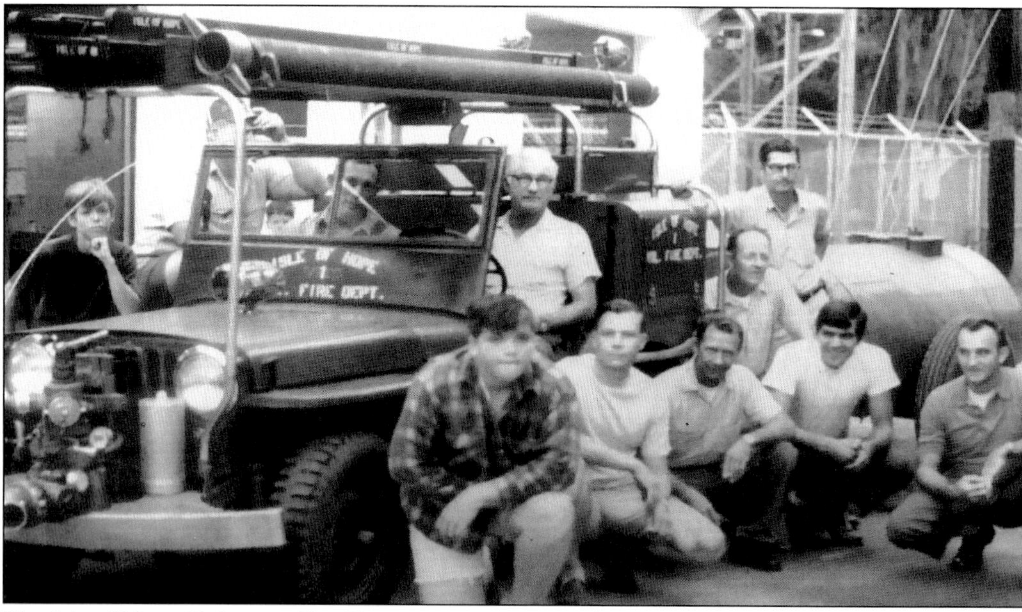

The Isle of Hope Volunteer Fire Department was started in 1948. Before that, there was a button in "Beanie" Barbee's kitchen that alerted the neighborhood of a fire. In 1956, a fire station was built on Parkersburg Road. Chief John Rodewolt led an effort to recruit more volunteers. Pictured in 1966 with a jeep pulling a water wagon are, from left to right, Randy Lockett, Kelly Wilson, Steve Cottrell, George Paxton (driving), Allen Harrelson, Al Quante, George Christiansen, Mickey Adair, Bill Roberts, and Leroy Coxwell.

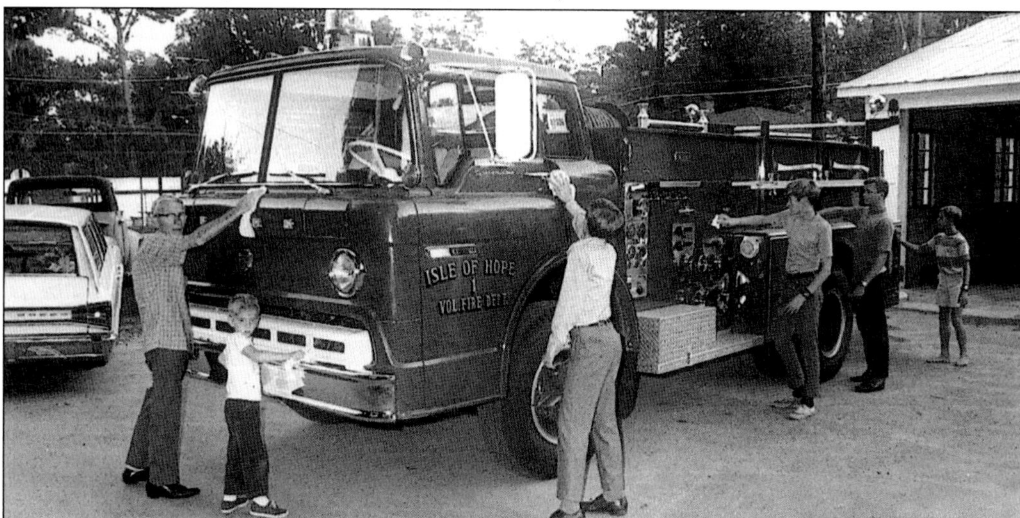

This 1970 fire truck is pictured with Skipper Hardy (left) and Jay Estill. The first female fire fighters were Lucille Christiansen, Anita Adair, Regina Wilson, and Suzanne Jonas. Today, a first response team is on constant stand-by and up-to-date fire fighting equipment is utilized. Volunteers are led by Fire Chief Tom Christiansen and assistant Jim McClain. Some local boys, such as Thad Dixon, began spending time at the station at 11 years of age, becoming junior firemen in their teens. Seen from left to right are Clarence "Skipper" Hardy, Jay Estill, Ranny Lockett, unidentified, Tom Christiansen, and Steven Christiansen.

Dr. Julian Quattlebaum Jr. stands beside his partner-in-speed, pit crew chief Berman Tucker. Brother Byron Tucker was his first pit crew chief. His mechanic was Kruger Johnson, who had a shop on Maupas Avenue. Like his father, Dr. Julian K. Quattlebaum, author of *The Great Savannah Races*, Julian Jr. loved racing cars. He raced all over the southeast including Miami, Sebring, and Daytona. In this race, he drove an Alcott special, built in Sam Allen's garage. Erica and Robert Rollings now own the Allen home on the bluff.

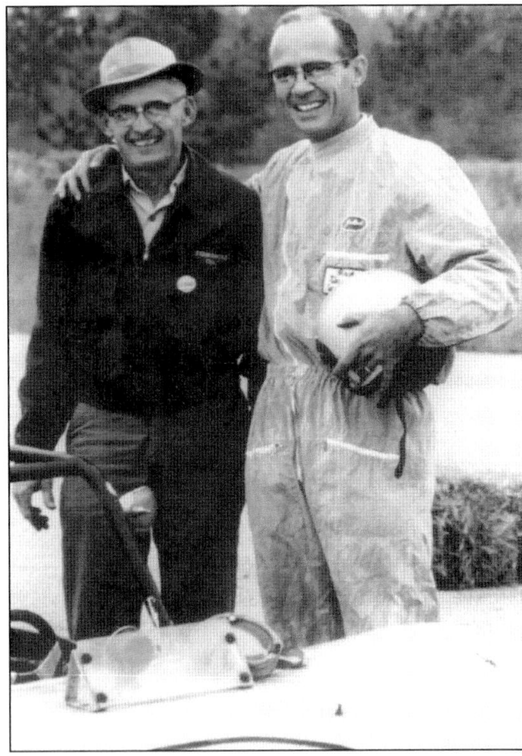

On Easter Sunday in 1960, four generations of Roberts and Quantes are dressed up for the Easter parade. Pictured, from left to right, are Carl William Quante Jr., Carl William "Bill" Quante III, Anna Elizabeth Roberts, and Bessie Roberts Quante.

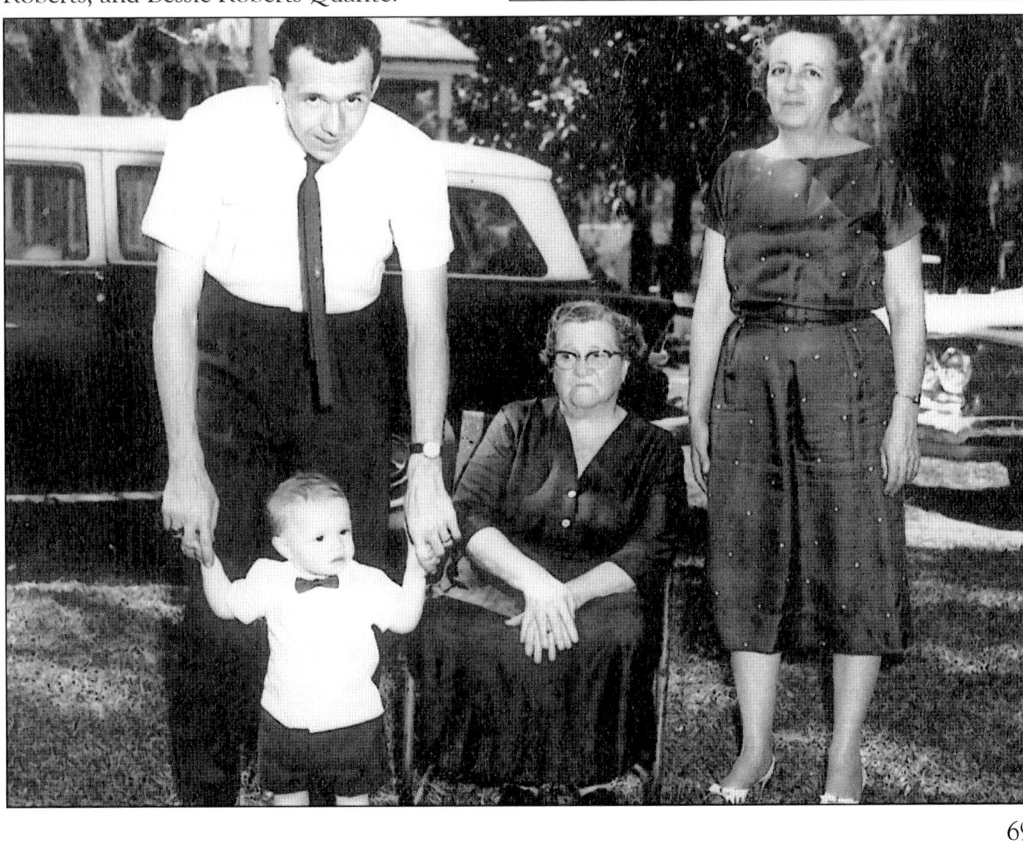

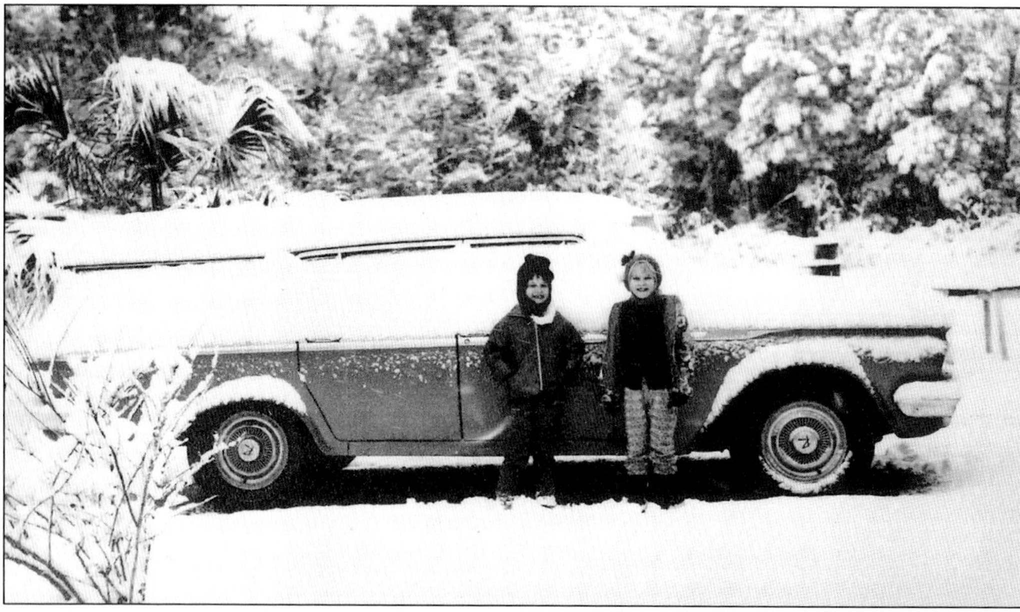

Experiencing snow, icicles, and cold temperatures in Isle of Hope is a rare thing indeed. To everyone's delight, that is exactly what happened in 1968. Phone wires were hot with people calling to tell friends and relatives to look out the window. Linda Johnson (Levangie), who lived on Central Avenue, and Cindy Allen of Paxton Road shiver in this sparkling winter wonderland. Of course, school was closed for the day!

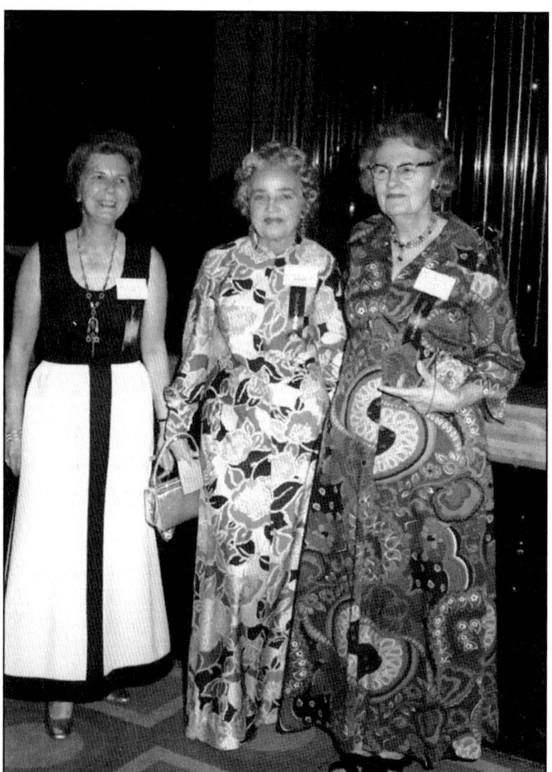

Mrs. Jeff (Ann) Tatum, on the right, was the first president of the Wymberley Garden Club in the late 1960s. The club had a garden room in the basement of the Owens Thomas House in Savannah, where they grew and gave plantings to this historic garden. Ann and her husband lived on Flynn Drive. Mrs. Harry (Dotty) Baxley is pictured on the left. The Baxleys lived at Isle of Hope for 50 years. The lovely lady in the center of the photograph is Hester Forshaw Constantine.

Officerettes in the Wymberley Garden Club in 1961 included, from left to right, (front row) Angela Dearing, Frances Quattlebaum, and Genevieve Rhoads; (middle row) Maggie Stubbs and Sybil Ellington; (back row) Eleanor Hohenstein and Hanna Rives.

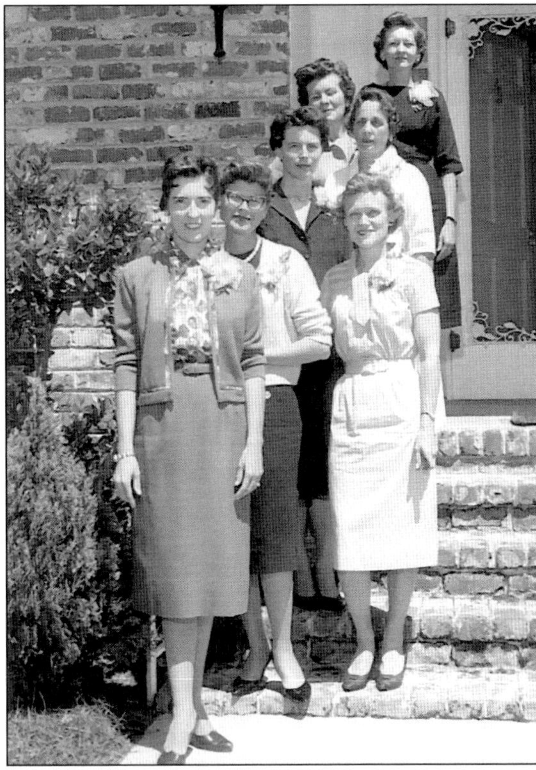

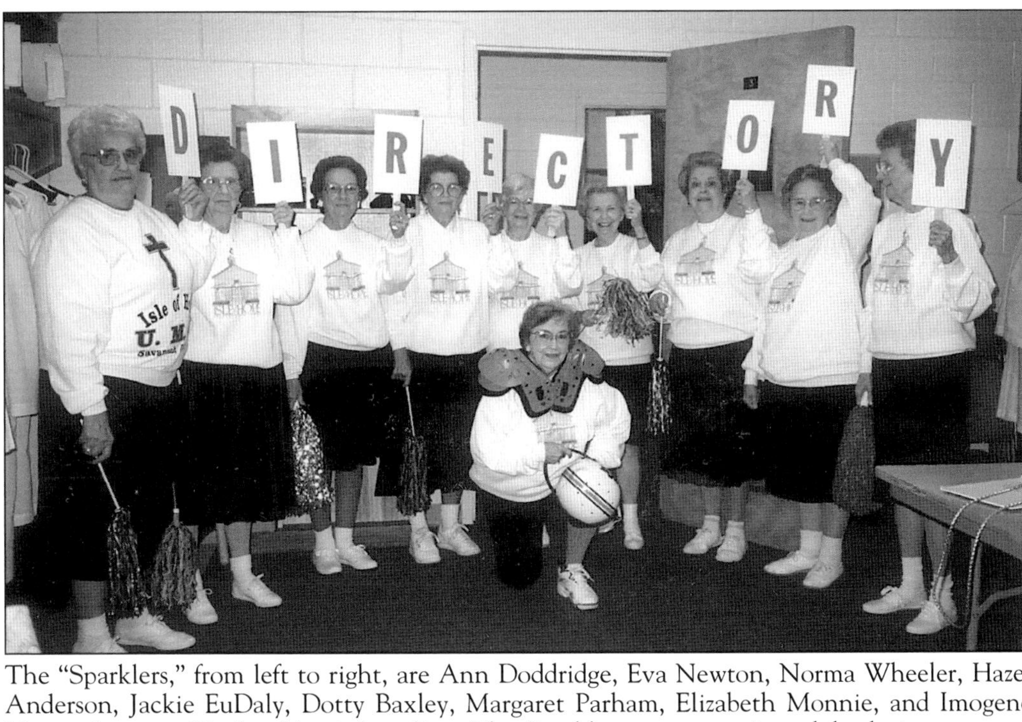

The "Sparklers," from left to right, are Ann Doddridge, Eva Newton, Norma Wheeler, Hazel Anderson, Jackie EuDaly, Dotty Baxley, Margaret Parham, Elizabeth Monnie, and Imogene Horan. Jeanette Blackwelder is kneeling. The Sparklers were a senior adult choir group and posed here for the church directory.

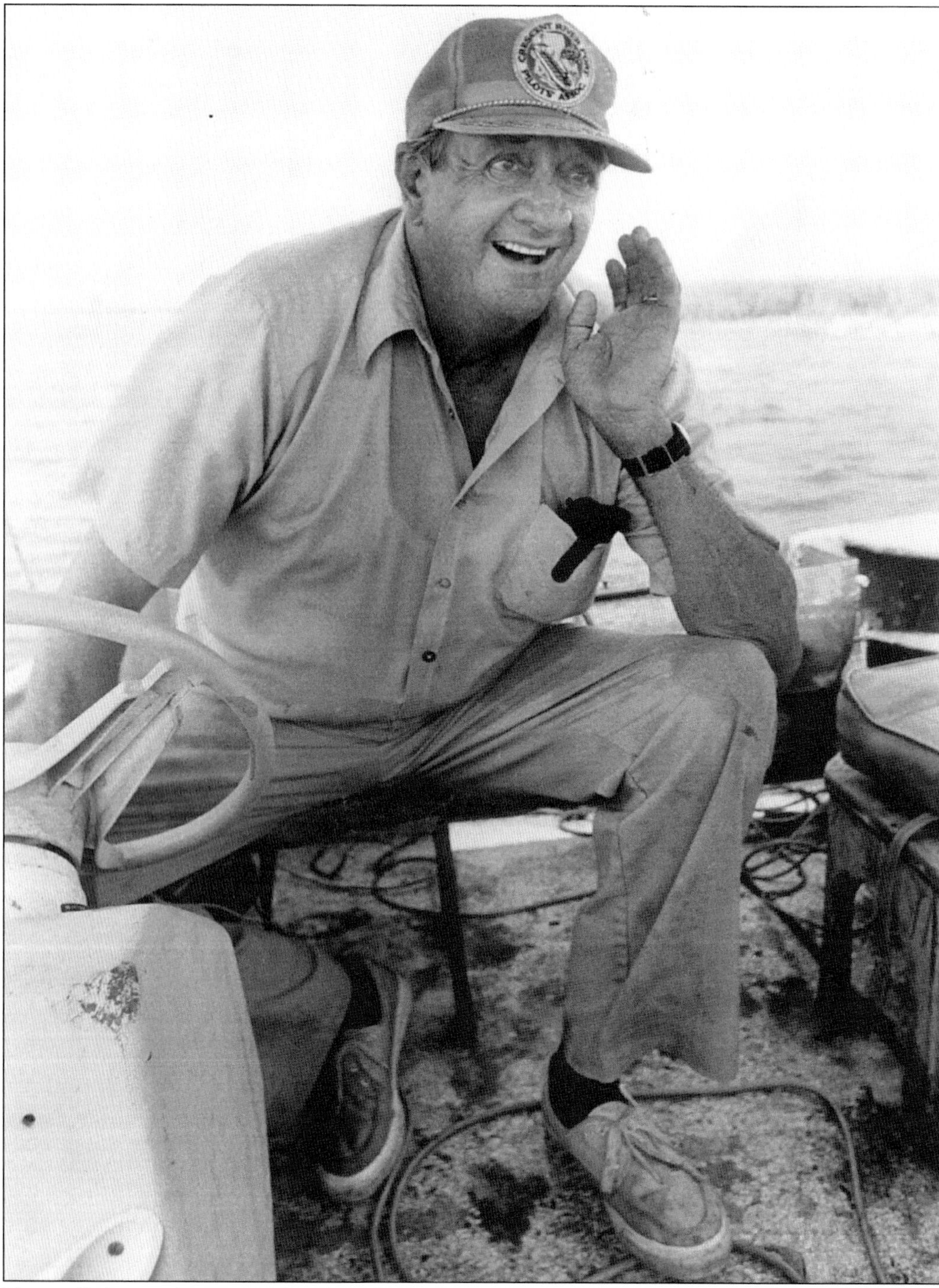

Nanny Roberts, always jovial and ready for fun, was one of the island's great characters. Nanny owned a pile-driving business and set the pilings for many docks in the area. He owned a bird dog named Richard who had his own driver's license with his picture on it. When Nanny stayed inside a friend's house too long, Richard blew the truck horn! Nanny and his wife, Sara, had one son, Bill.

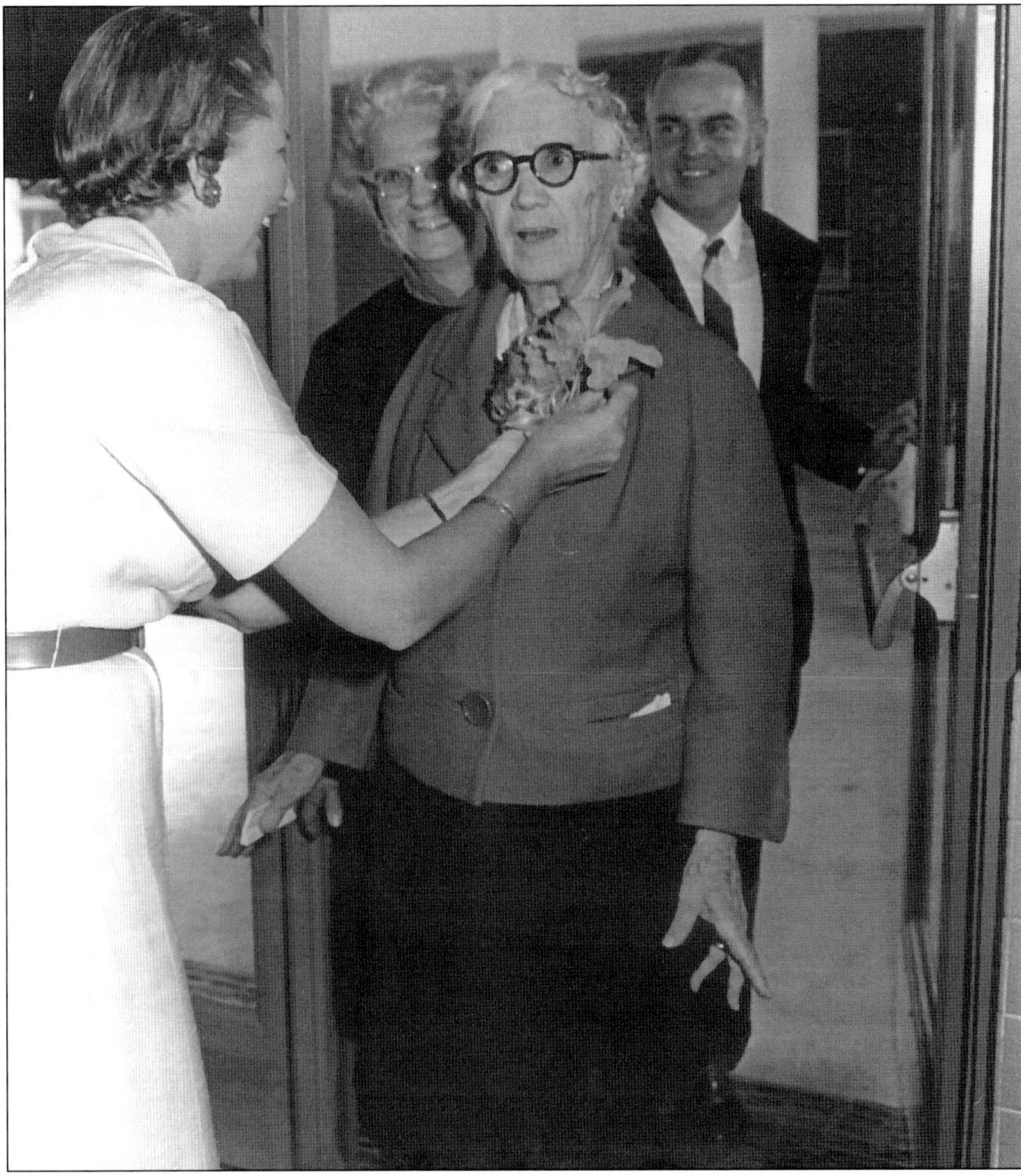

Sadie Wannamaker Cramer is remembered by the older set as the Mother Theresa of Isle of Hope. When her husband, a Methodist minister 30 years her senior, passed away, Sadie baby-sat to earn money. When the average pay for sitters was 50¢ an hour, she charged only 35¢. This simple soul, with her gray hair and sweet smile, walked all over the island to her sitting engagements. She prepared communion at the Methodist church, carefully washing the cups and linen. When new babies were born, she knitted booties and gave ladyfingers to the parents. When the children she had cared for got married, she sewed them pillowcases on an ancient, treadle sewing machine. Her pastor, Dr. Bill Hinson, said, "When Mrs. Cramer gets to heaven, Gabriel will stand up and blow his trumpet, and the saints will come greet her." In this 1969 photograph, Barbara Sowell pins an orchid on Sadie Cramer at "Cramer Day," as Marie Estes and Joe Solana look on. Five hundred people came to honor her.

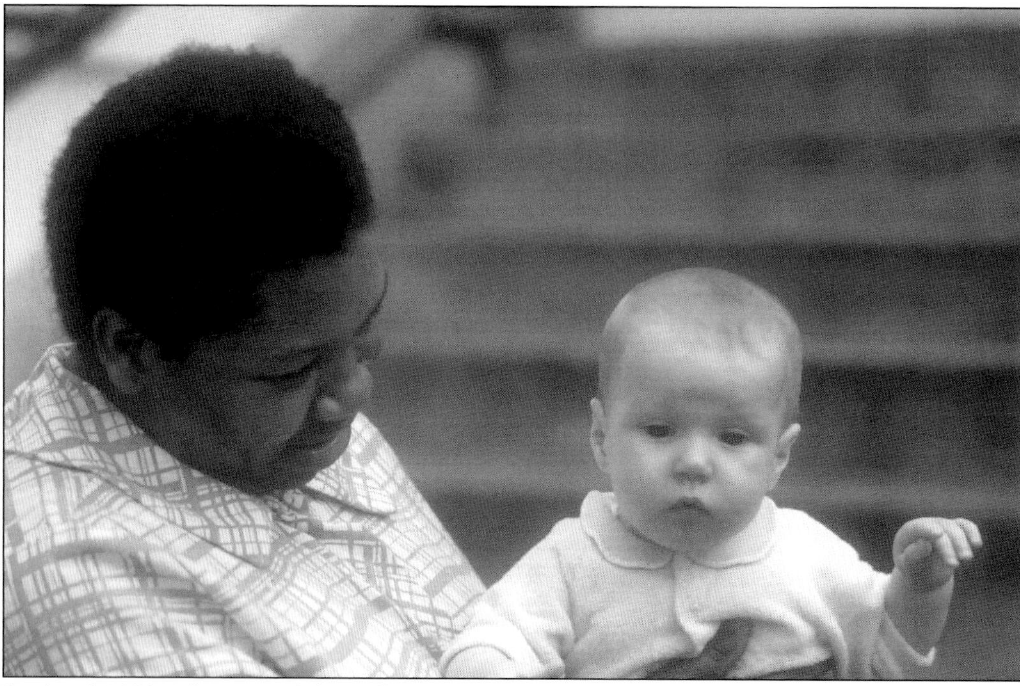

In April 1973, *The Last of the Belles* was filmed at Julian and Linda Kelly's home (pictured below) and the Solana home. This little bouncing bundle is none other than actress Gwyneth Paltrow. Her mother, actress Blythe Danner, played the part of Zelda in *The Last of the Belles*. The woman holding Gwyneth is unidentified.

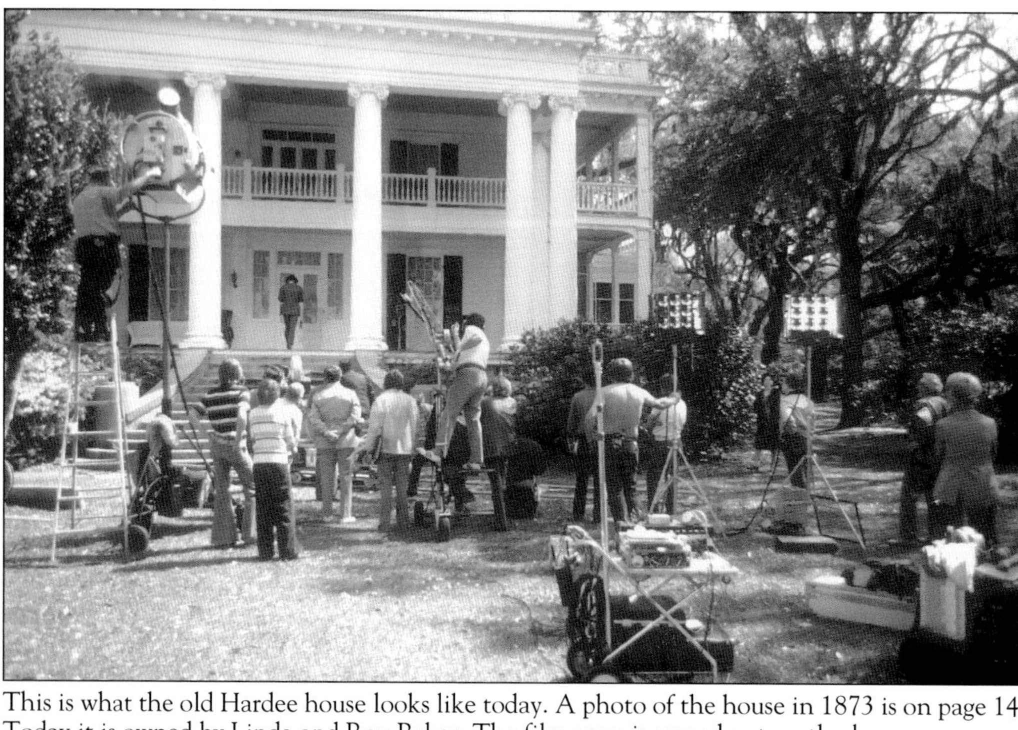

This is what the old Hardee house looks like today. A photo of the house in 1873 is on page 14. Today it is owned by Linda and Roy Baker. The film crew is spread out on the lawns.

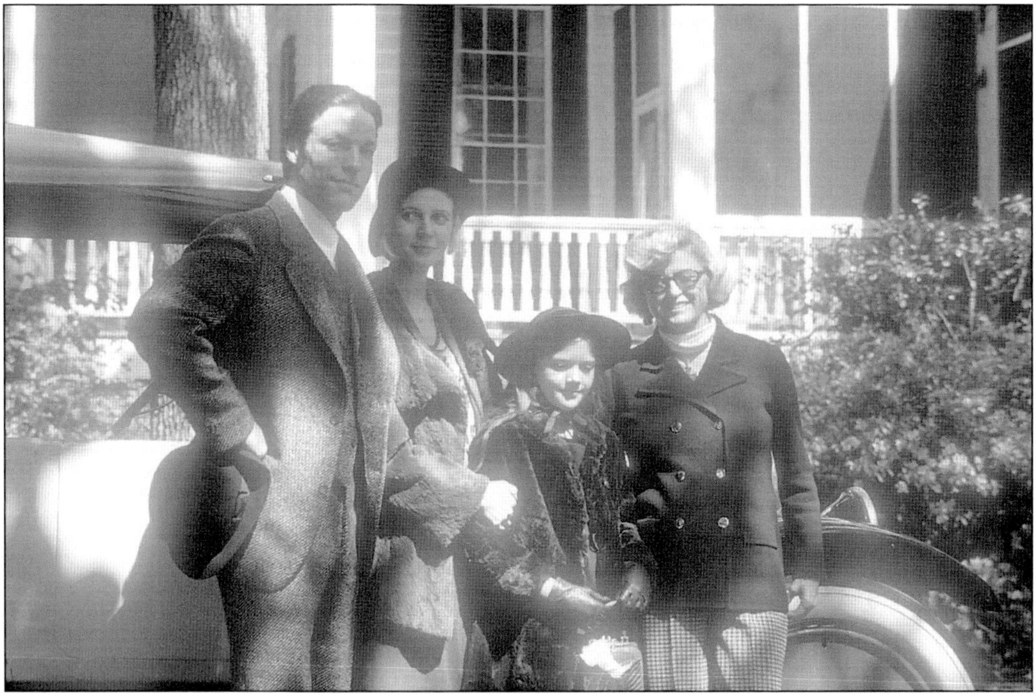

The stars lined up in a Hollywood constellation, from left to right, are Richard Chamberlain, Blythe Danner, and Leslie Williams, who is the daughter of Nick and Suzie Williams of White Bluff. Leslie Williams played the part of "Scottie" in *The Last of the Belles*. "Scottie" herself, Frances Scott Fitzgerald Lanahan Smith, the daughter of author F. Scott Fitzgerald and Zelda, is also pictured.

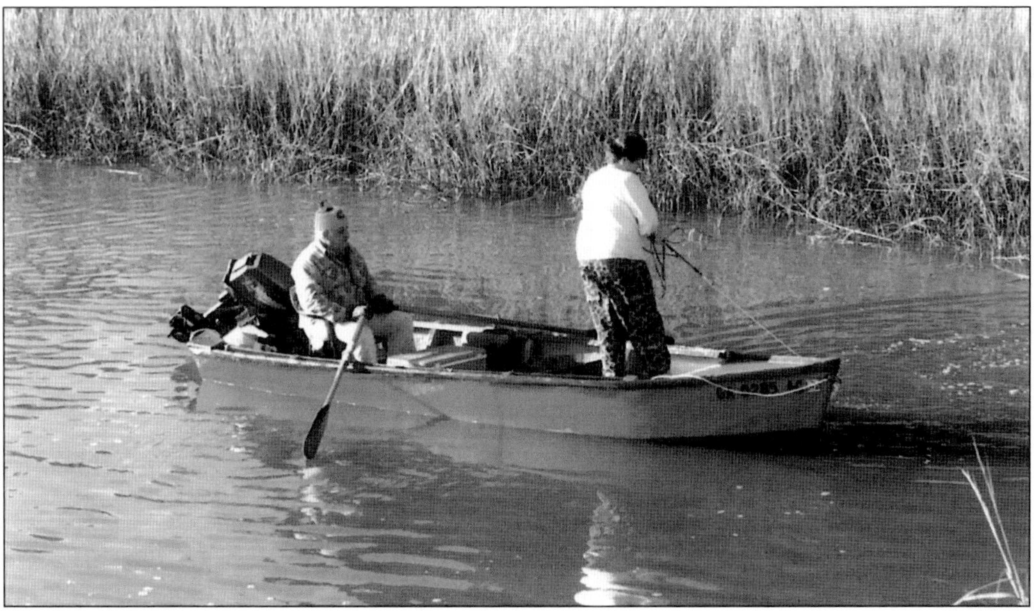

Blackie Barras rows the bateau in the creeks while his wife, Harriet, pulls in the cast net loaded with lively fall shrimp. Grits and fried shrimp have always been a southern favorite for supper. A few hushpuppies also go nicely with this classic southern dish.

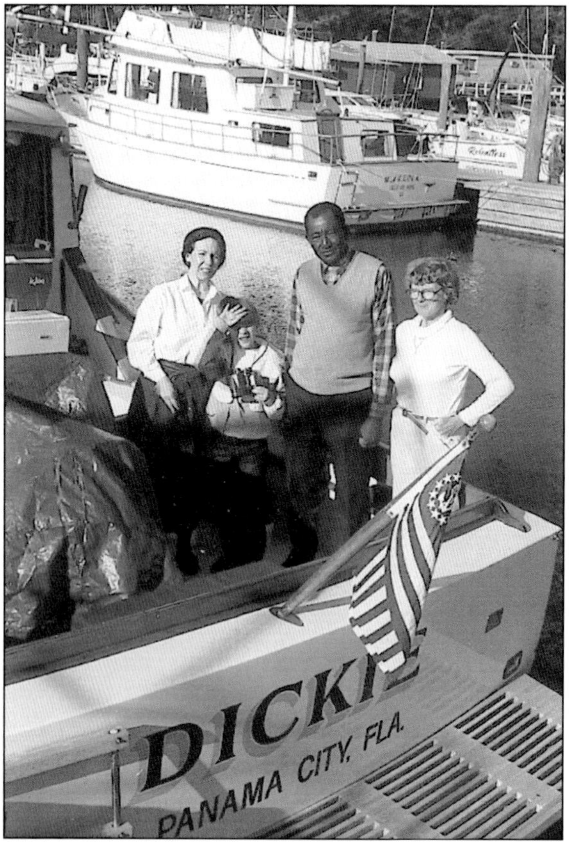

Mike Wright worked at Brady's Boat Works for years. He is pictured here on board the *Dickie*, a 40-foot Chrisovitch, owned by Wainwright and Eudora Roebling. Also on board are Pat Roebling, Charlie Roebling, and Eudora. Mike recalls, "Lots of little boys rode around in the river in bateaux. They were always low on gas. They'd say, 'Mike, can we drain the hose?' That hose'd hold four gallons after gassing up a big yacht. That way, they could ride all day—free." The *Warlock* visible in the background was owned by Hermann and Karen Coolidge.

Jacob Rauers cautiously inches his crab-line up to see if any crabs are eating his chicken neck bait while his brother, Chris, waits with the scoop-net. The dock is owned by their fun-loving grandmother, Carolyn Solana, who probably has the pot ready at a rolling boil and the newspaper spread over the kitchen table. This photo was taken by well-known Savannah photographer, Jack Leigh.

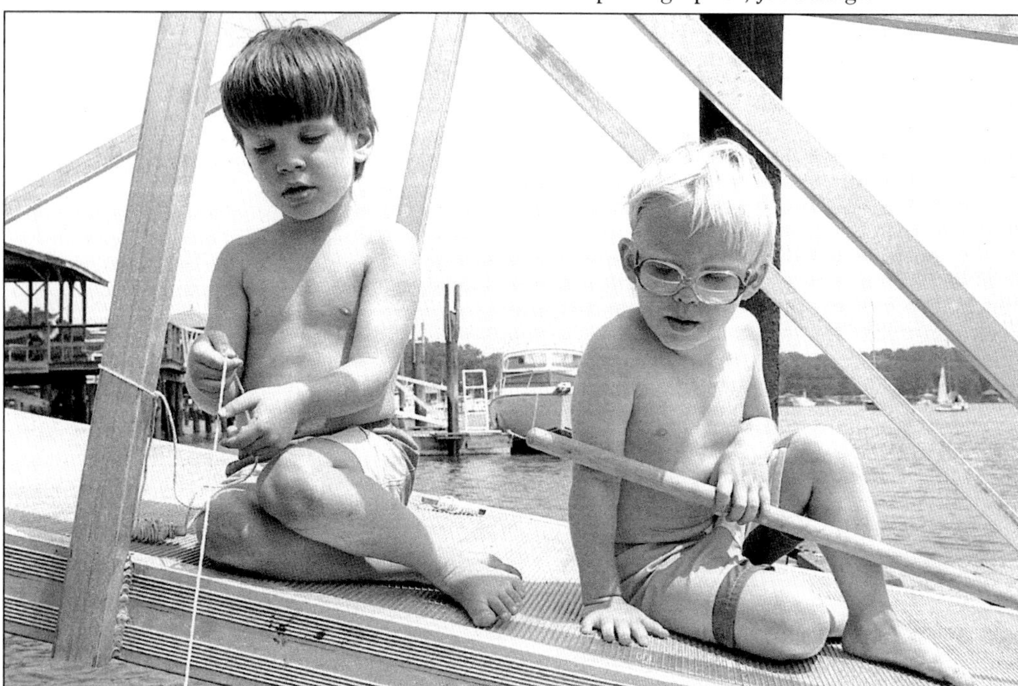

A section of the bluff near the marina was the focus of a heated battle in 1983 and 1984. Developers had plans to build condominiums, which panicked and outraged residents. Led by Janie Coslick, the community sprang into action. Their resistance was successful and the threatened historic homes were saved from the potential devastation. This is a photo of one of the lovely homes, which almost became a tragic pile of rubble. It is occupied today by Sam McCatchern and his son, Miller.

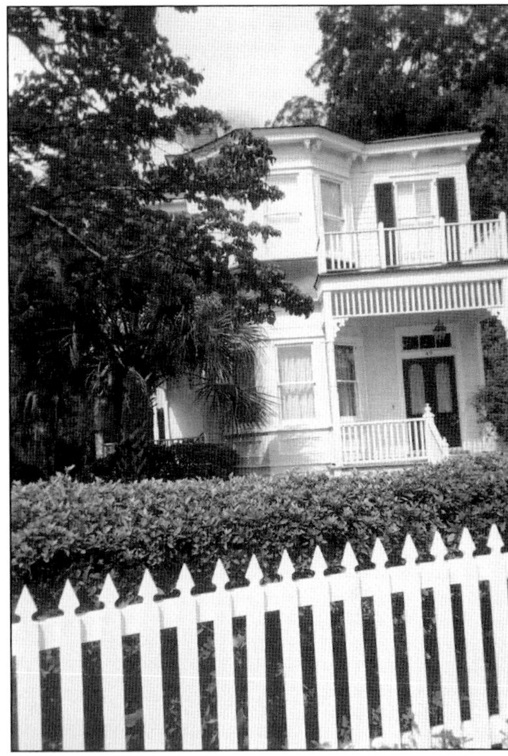

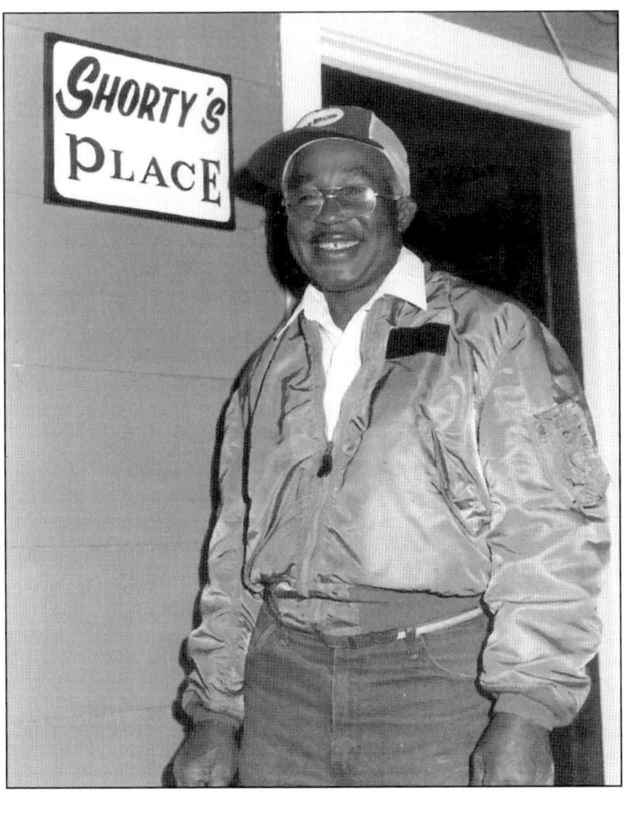

Many boaters remember Henry "Shorty" Grant, who painted and repaired boats at the marina for 27 years. Shorty always hummed while he worked—a sure sign of a contented soul. Two hundred guests attended his 66th birthday party on the dock where shrimp, venison, rice, and sausage were served. Shorty, now over 80 and retired from the marina, still works at local jobs, always humming. "It's work and hummin' and old friends that keep me going," he smiles.

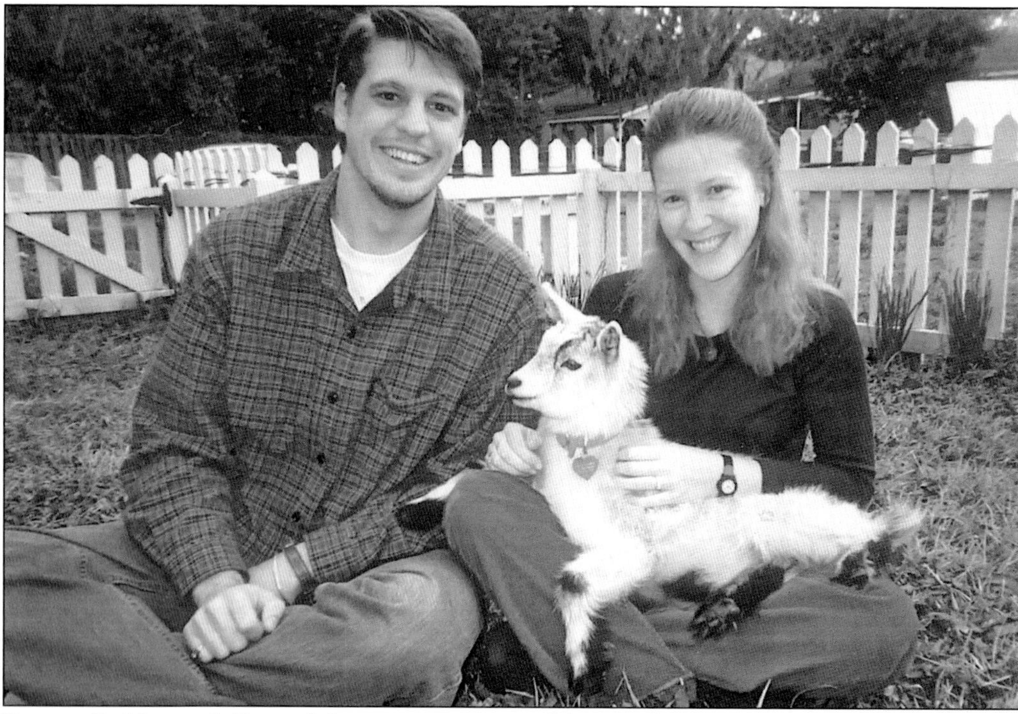

Dennis Befeler and Kasey Johnson enjoy a restful Saturday morning in their yard. Kasey is a graphic designer at Byrd Cookie Co. and Dennis is a professor and technical director of media and performing arts at Savannah College of Art and Design. "Minnie-Pearl" is an African Pigmy goat who resides with the author and takes daily walks on her leash to the glee of children.

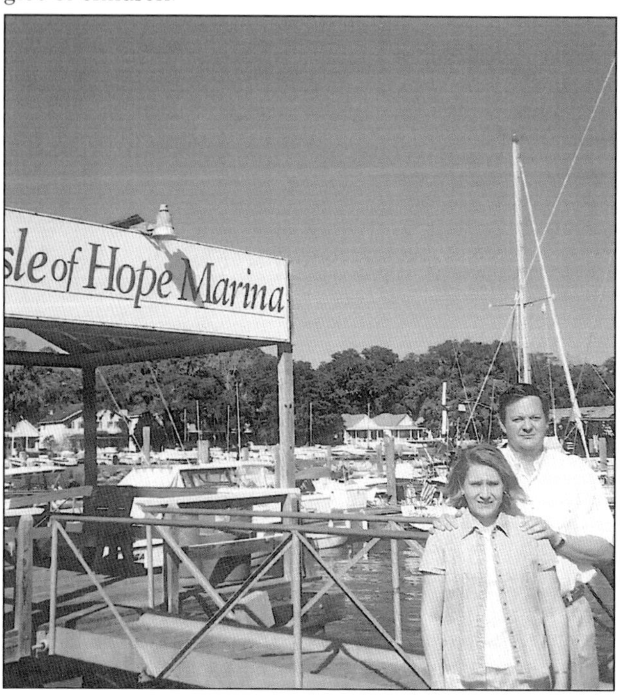

The Isle of Hope Marina services boats traveling up and down the inland waterway. Pictured are the owners, Charles and Suzanne Waller. The main runway decking is made of old hatch covers from a World War II Liberty Ship and the railway is one of the oldest in Savannah.

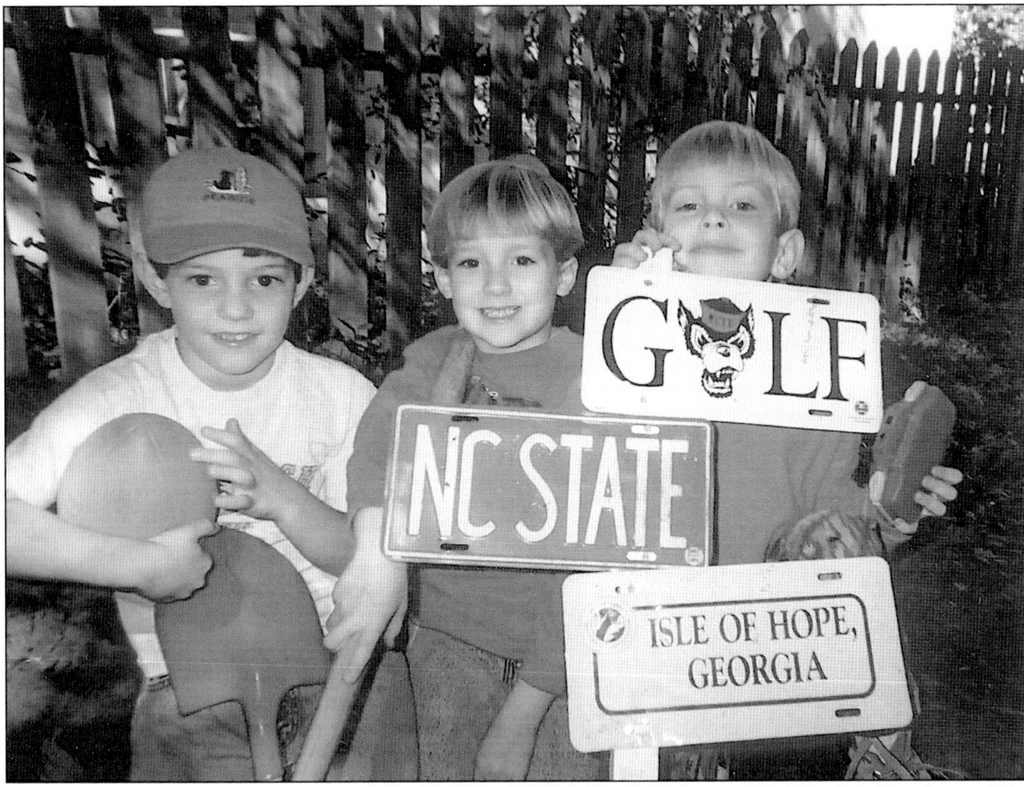

Pictured here, from left to right, are Clint Cail, Wright Wallace, and Miller McCatchern. The three youngsters dig foxholes and play happily in the backyard of the McCatchern home on Bluff Drive. The climbing trees, parks, rowboats, pools, and the river all make Isle of Hope an ideal place for children to grow up.

Playing in the Ebbie Paxton Memorial Park, which was given to the community by William Barbee, are, from left to right, Abigail (daughter of John and Tammy Ahlers of Hopecrest), Gigi and Jill (daughters of Blaine and Erin Williams of Jameswood), Mills (son of Carmen Johnson), and Natalie (daughter of Julian and Hali Cooper of Grimball Point Road).

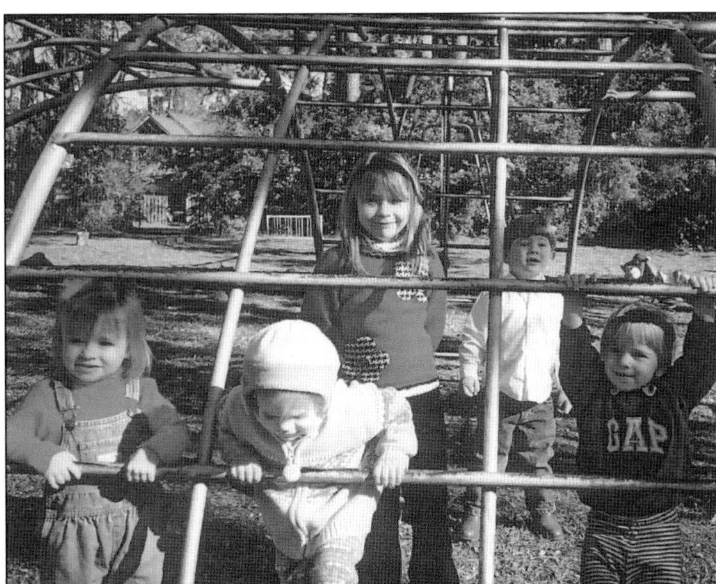

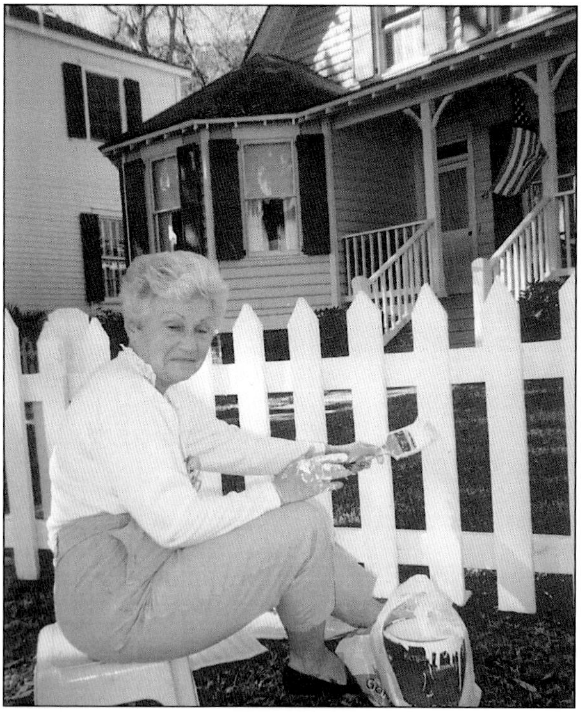

Betty Utsey paints pickets on a warm day in January. She and her husband, Jim, live in the house on the corner of Bluff Drive and Rosenbrook Avenue, which they designed with help from her two daughters, Janie Coslick and Trish Walton.

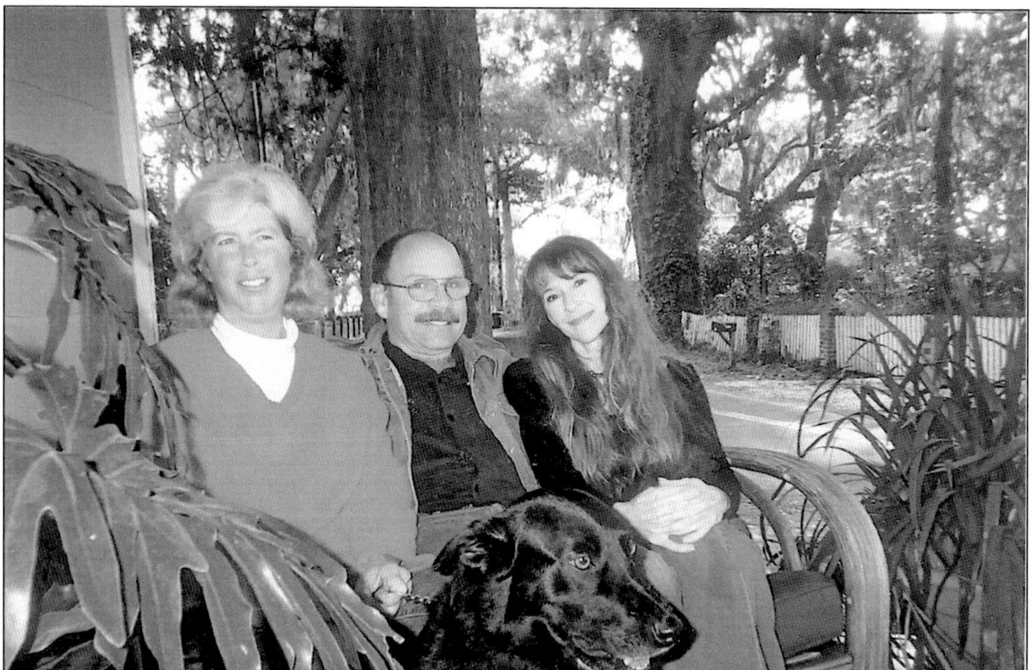

The following people are pictured from left to right: Caroline Glover teaches at the Isle of Hope School, Mike Gross works for Atlanta Gas Light Co., and Julie Wilde is an interior designer, vocalist, and pianist. Birdie is a professional squirrel chaser. Sitting on the porch with a glass of iced tea is a popular pastime during the warm spring days. After the "no-see-ums" and mosquitoes start to hatch, however, people without a screened porch stay indoors.

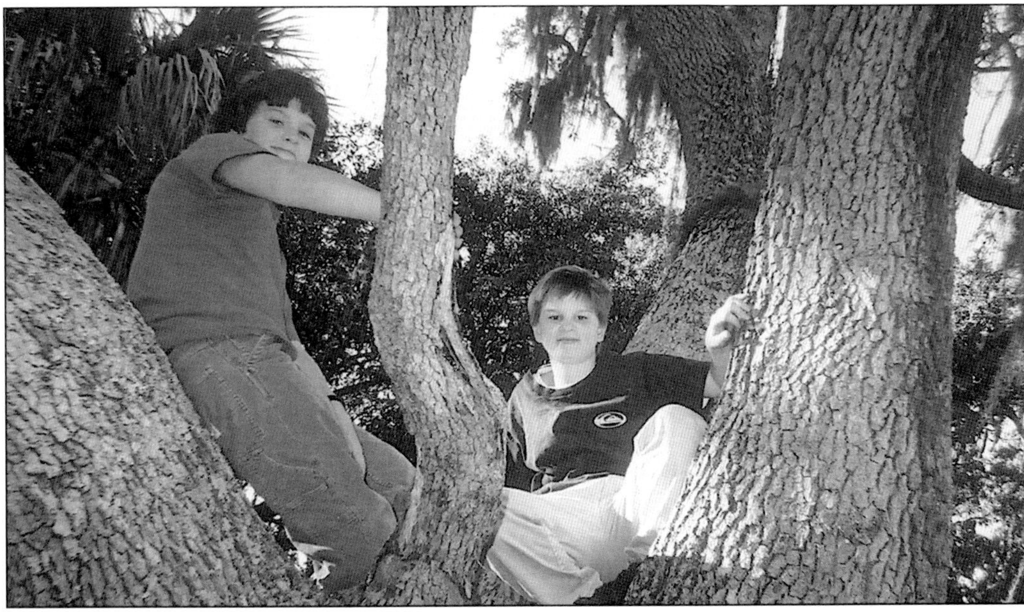

The giant oak trees all over the island make for great climbing. Max McKenna (left) of Richmond Drive and Spencer Ramage of Avenue of Pines look down the inland waterway for yachts heading south. Years before their time, children used to play here at the "Green Castle." The "Green Castle," once located on the bluff, was a tangled canopy of thick vines on which children climbed and played. Many spooky ghost stories were told inside this magical Sherwood Forest, which is no longer there.

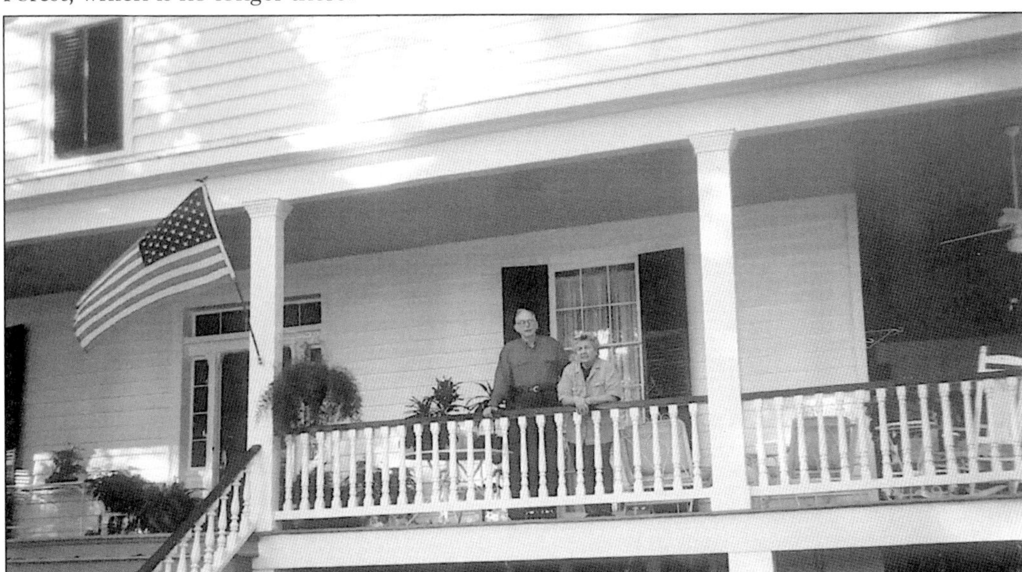

Ruthie and Noel Wright are the present owners of the Gallie-Wylly house. This lovely home is often photographed because it is similar to *Beauvoir* in Biloxi, Mississippi, which was once the home of Jefferson Davis. The Wrights hosted the Isle of Hope Artisans' League first annual art show in 2001 on the spacious porches and lawns. Several movies have been filmed here including *Gator* with Burt Reynolds and Lauren Hutton and a PBS film called *Bernice Bobs Her Hair*.

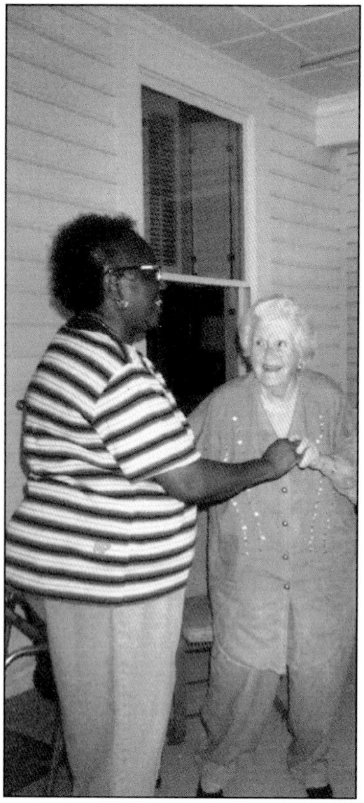

Mrs. John "Betty" Carswell smiles at Cora Belle Taylor, her friend and helper, as they dance to "Five Foot Two, Eyes of Blue." Anita Clay (not pictured), member of the popular music group The Crabettes, is playing her accordion in the garden. Mrs. Carswell's daughter, Betty, and her husband, Archie Morris, live on Island Drive.

The Rollings family makes Sunday rounds on bikes with Elmo, their polka-dotted pooch, in attendance. From left to right are Henry, Robert, Elmo, Jackson, and Erica. Their home is on the corner of Parkersburg Road and Bluff Drive.

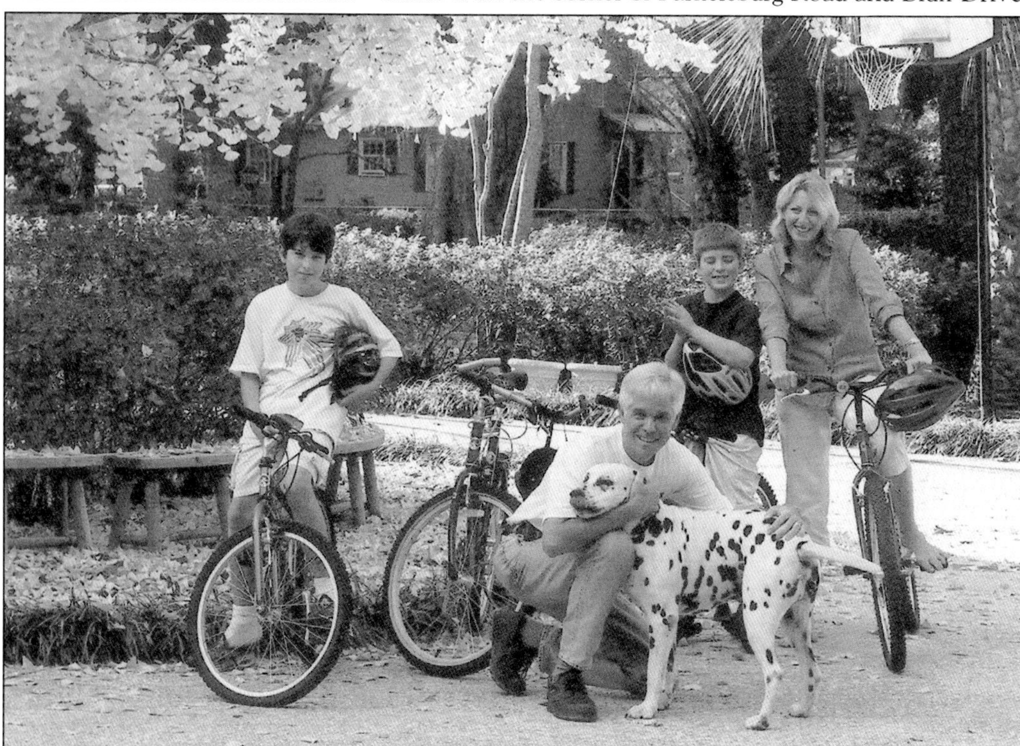

Chloe Mabry is focused on her buttery ear of fresh corn at an Isle of Hope Methodist Church function commemorating the 150th anniversary of the church. She is the daughter of Biza and Chad Mabry of Colonel Estill Drive, and the granddaughter of Fall and Bob Quattlebaum of the Landings.

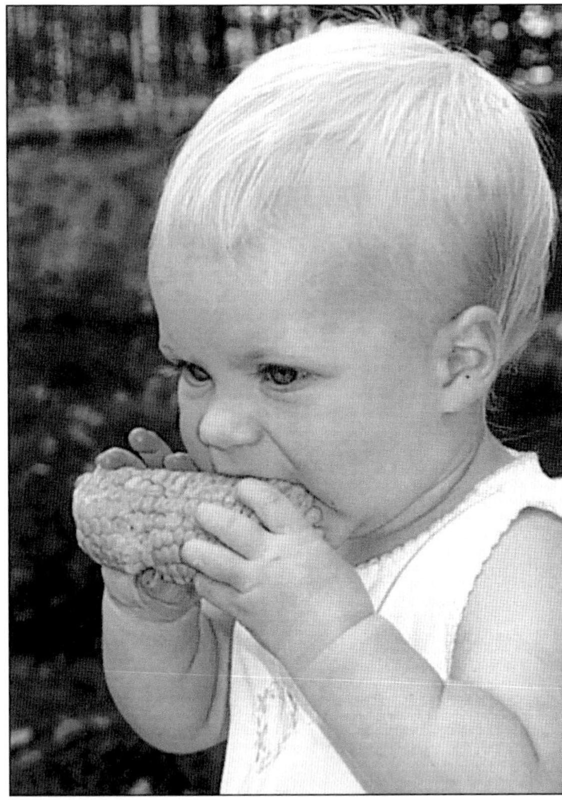

Fifty years ago, these ladies might have been playing canasta. Today they are enjoying a lively rubber of bridge. From left to right are Kathryn Waller, Beth Weeks, Polly Brooks, and Martha Summerlin.

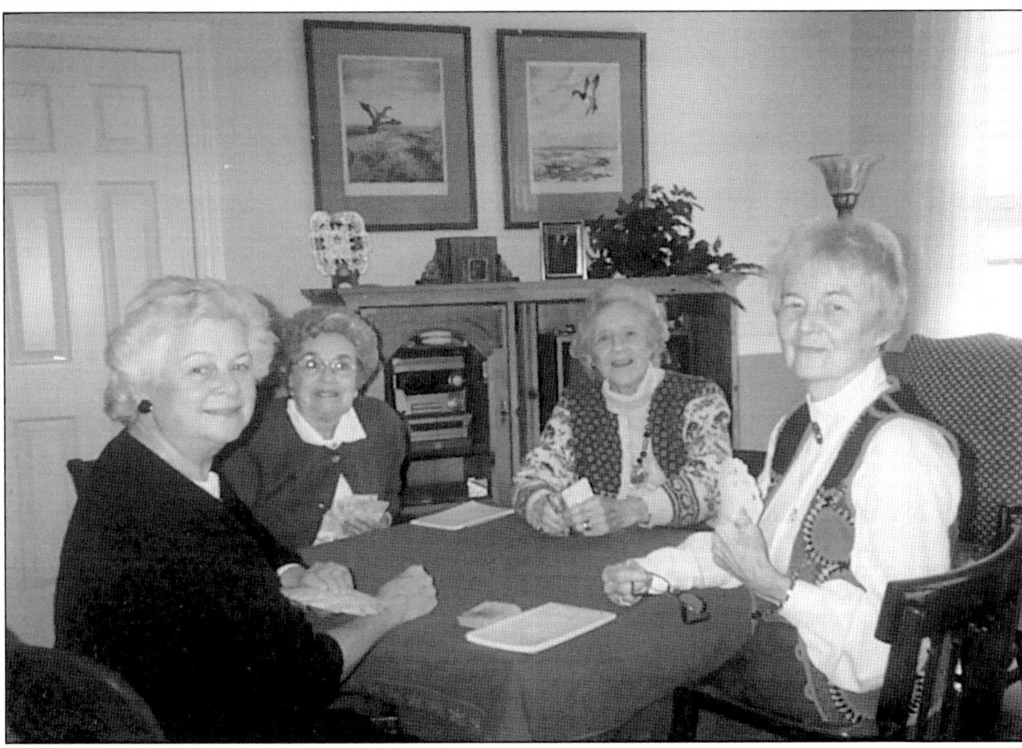

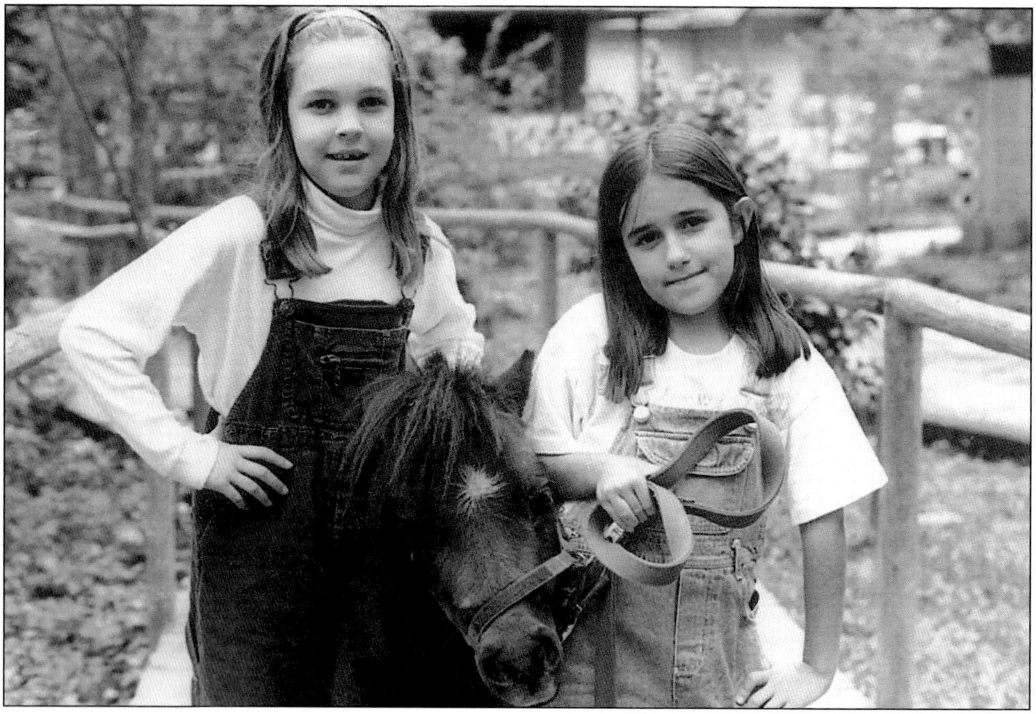

These two pals, Dancy Eve (left) and Anna Mayo, play with Roly, the miniature horse who had a small part in the movie *Midnight in the Garden of Good and Evil*. The carefree days of childhood still exist at Isle of Hope. Many moms "home-school" their children and teach them to grow vegetables and herbs in the garden.

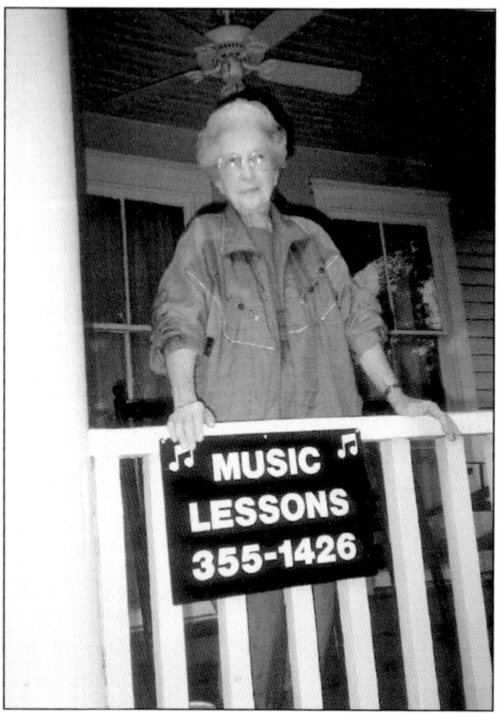

Adele Nielubowicz, the island's resident piano teacher, has taught many children and adults to play. Bikes leaning against the tree outside her home meant a lesson was in progress. She and her late husband, Chester, moved to Central Avenue in 1948.

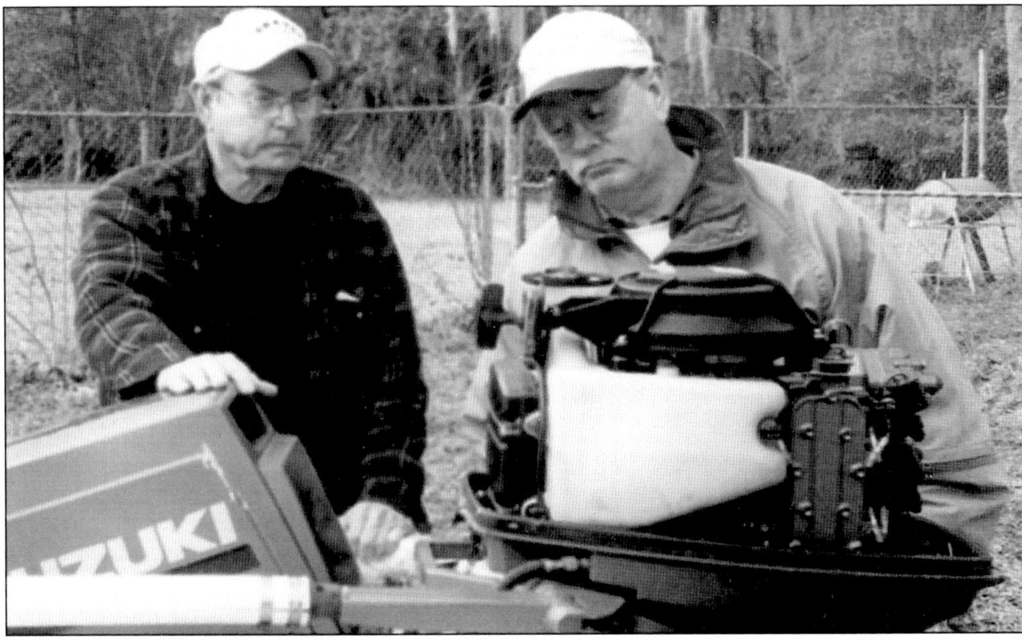

Brothers Carson and Harry Leagre Hucks have lived on the island for over 55 years. From a family of six children, they lived in the Wylly House on Rosenbrook Avenue for a few years and then on Henderson Avenue. Both attended Isle of Hope School, Washington Avenue Junior High, Savannah High, and Jenkins High. Hurricanes might blow other residents off the island, but these two are permanent fixtures.

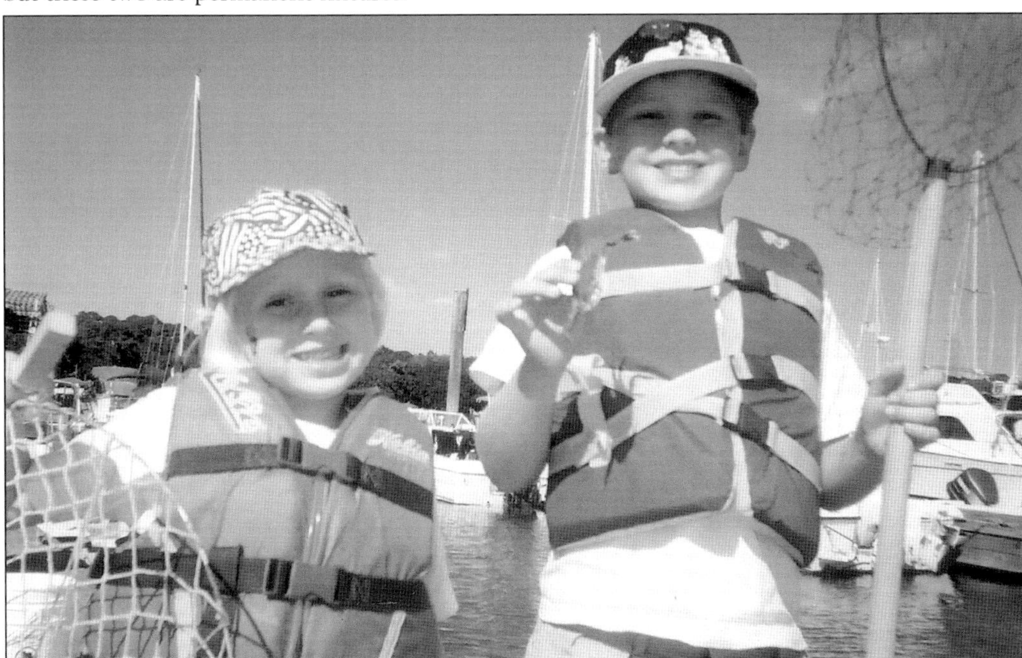

Sarah Mac and Hunter Bowman had a great time at the crab rodeo, which is held every year at the marina. Their parents are Catherine and Cam Bowman of Jameswood Avenue. Hunter threw the peewee crustacean, which he is holding, back into the river to do some more growing.

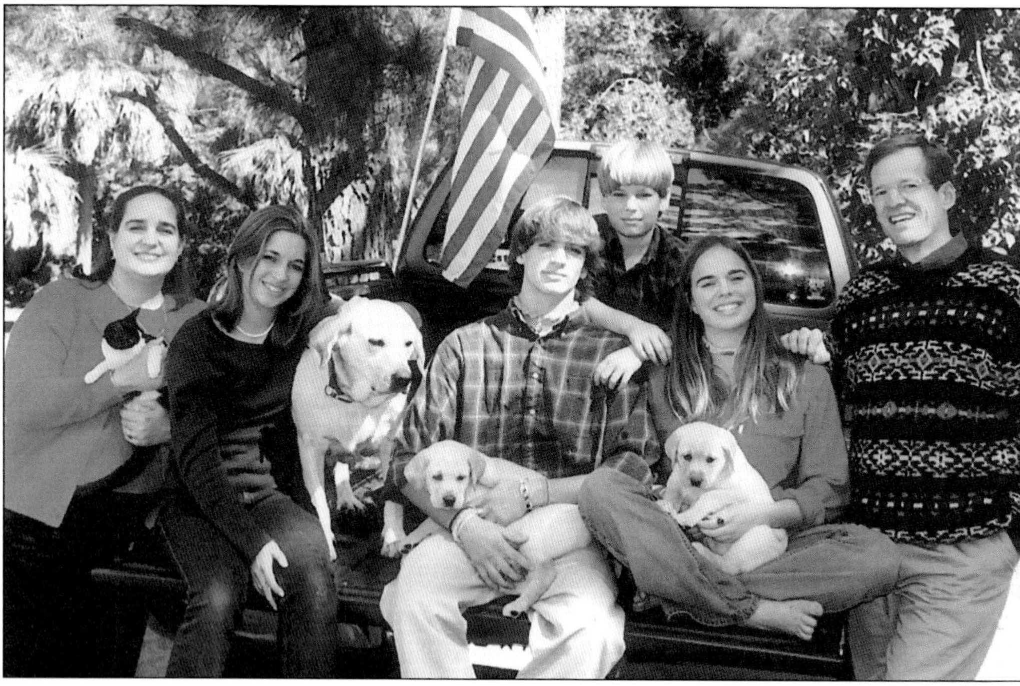

Congressman Jack Kingston and his family had this photo taken for their Christmas card. From left to right are Libby, Ann, Meshack (their Lab), John Jr., Jim, Elizabeth, and Jack.

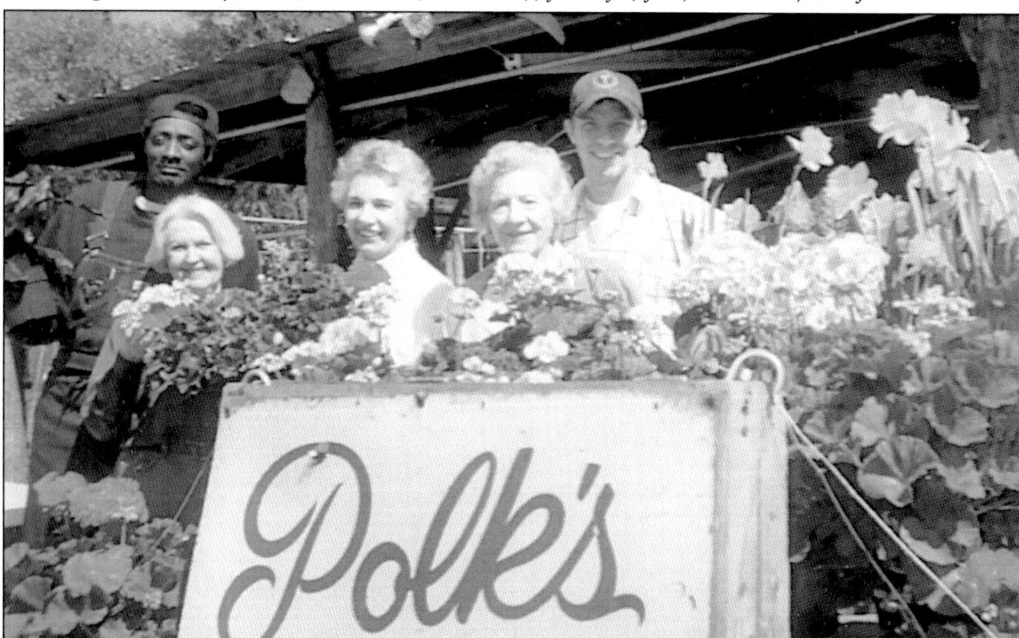

Boiled peanuts, ripe avocados, oranges, melons, and hanging baskets are a medley of temptation on the corner of Skidaway Road and Norwood Avenue. An old-time spirit prevails as friends bump into friends while choosing a melon or some stewing tomatoes. In this photo, from left to right, are Charles "Slim" Yarbourgh, Gayle Crawford, Virginia Lee, Polly Brooks, and Wesley Bashlor.

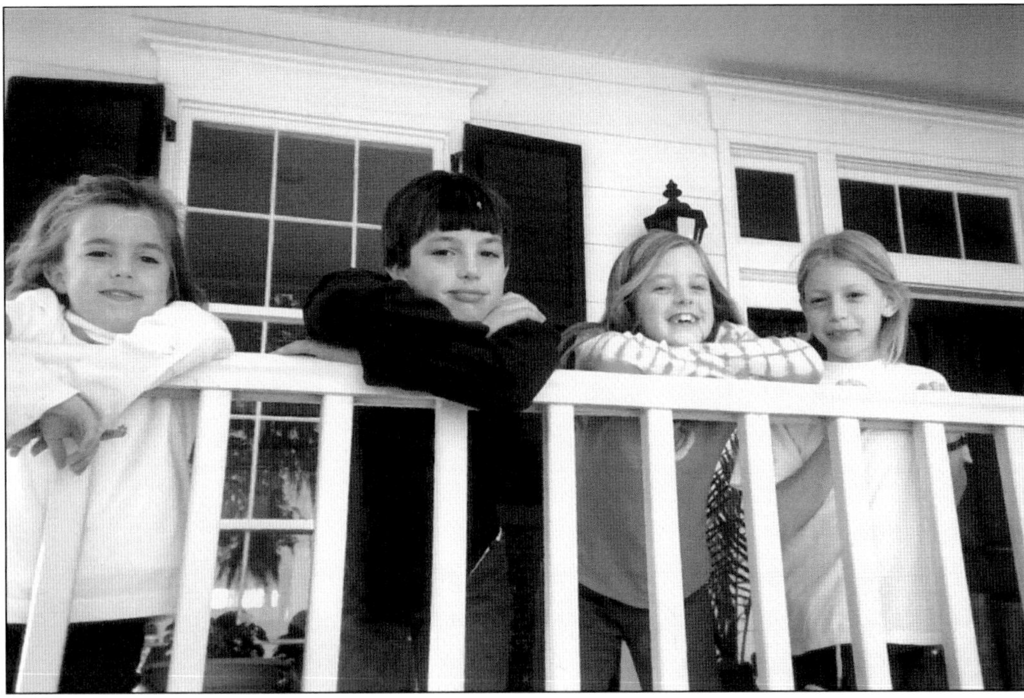

These children are probably anxious to get this silly picture-taking over with, so they can get to the playground. From left to right are Elizabeth, Sam, and Claiborne Stuber, and their neighbor, Emily Knopf.

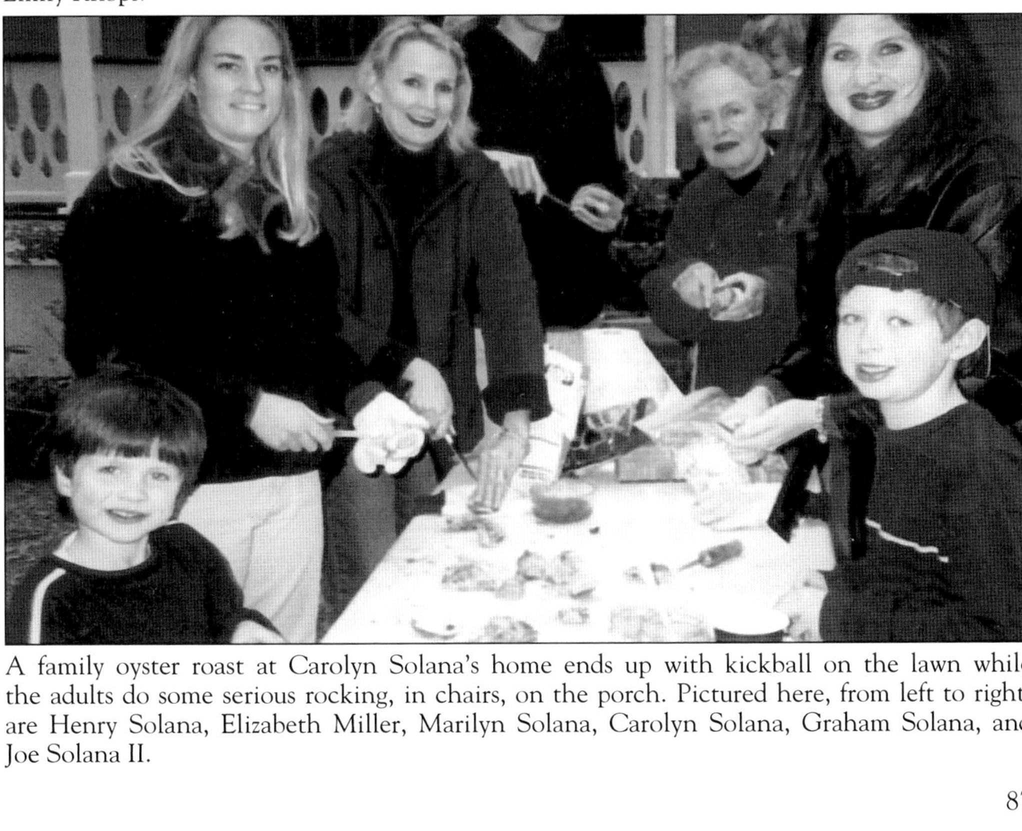

A family oyster roast at Carolyn Solana's home ends up with kickball on the lawn while the adults do some serious rocking, in chairs, on the porch. Pictured here, from left to right, are Henry Solana, Elizabeth Miller, Marilyn Solana, Carolyn Solana, Graham Solana, and Joe Solana II.

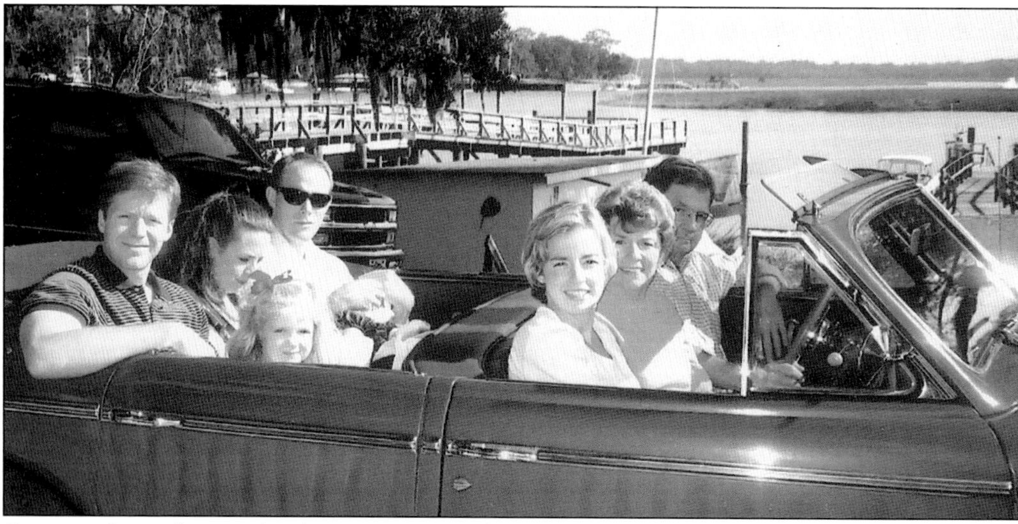

Cruising down the riverbank in a 1940 Buick Roadmaster convertible is the Minis clan. From left to right are David Slatinsky with Meg Graham in his lap, Amy Minis Graham, David Graham with Mac Graham in his lap, Florence Minis Slatinsky, and Margaret and Bobby Minis. The curve of the Skidaway River is in the background.

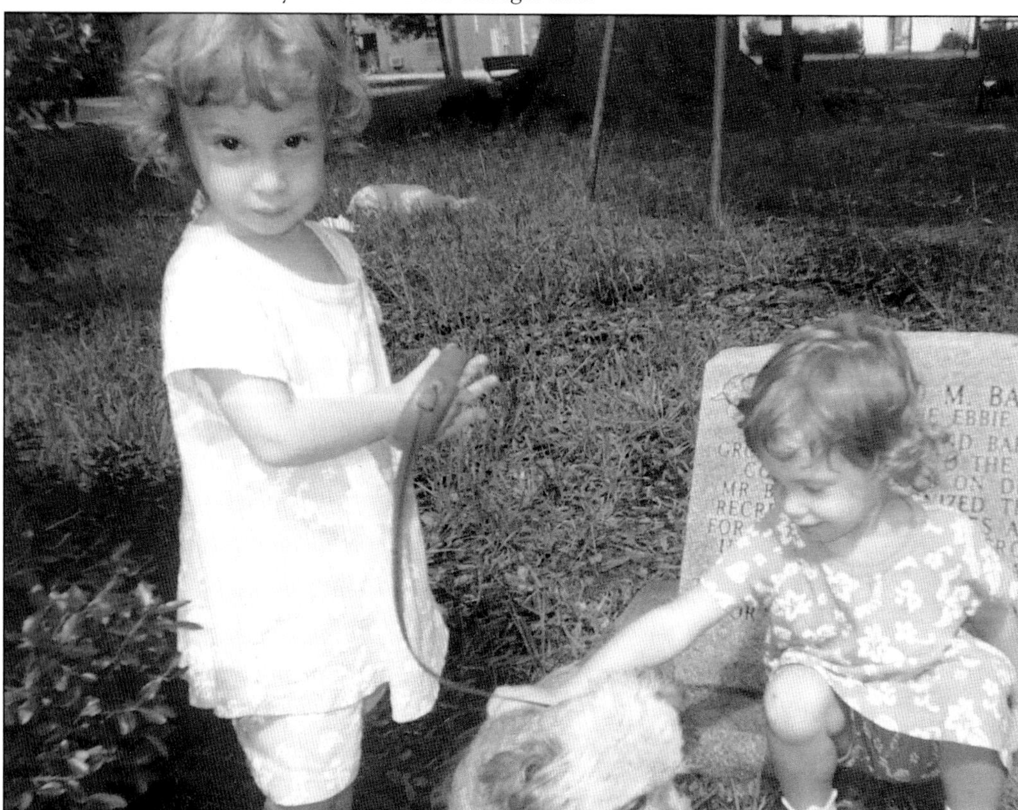

Twins Madelyn and Kate, the daughters of Cookie and David Hofele of Parkersburg Road, play with Tuffy in the Ebbie Paxton Memorial Park.

Amanda and Chris Everard from New Jersey recently bought a classic old cottage with an interesting past on Rosenbrook Avenue. Florence Martus is known worldwide as *The Waving Girl.* She waved at every ship coming into the Savannah River harbor for 40 years. Sailors knew to look for her lantern at night or her hanky during the day. After she retired, she rented this cottage with her brother, George. There is a statue of Florence Martus waving her hanky to ships with her dog at her side, on River Street on Savannah's riverfront.

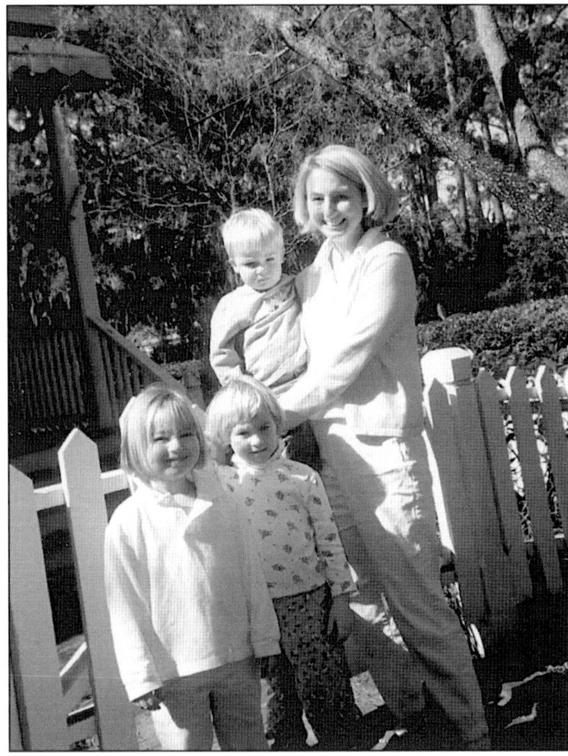

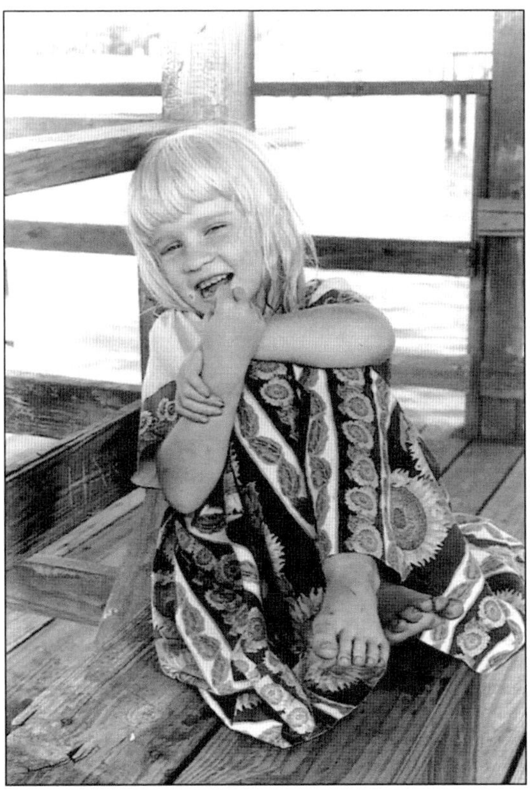

Claire Brodhead wraps up on the Wymberley Yacht Club dock after a swim. The club was, and is, a favorite spot for crabbing, casting for shrimp, and mud bogging. Claire and her brothers, Andrew and Ben, are the children of Janie and Peter Brodhead of Flynn Drive. The Brodheads own Brighter Day Natural Foods on Park Avenue, in the city.

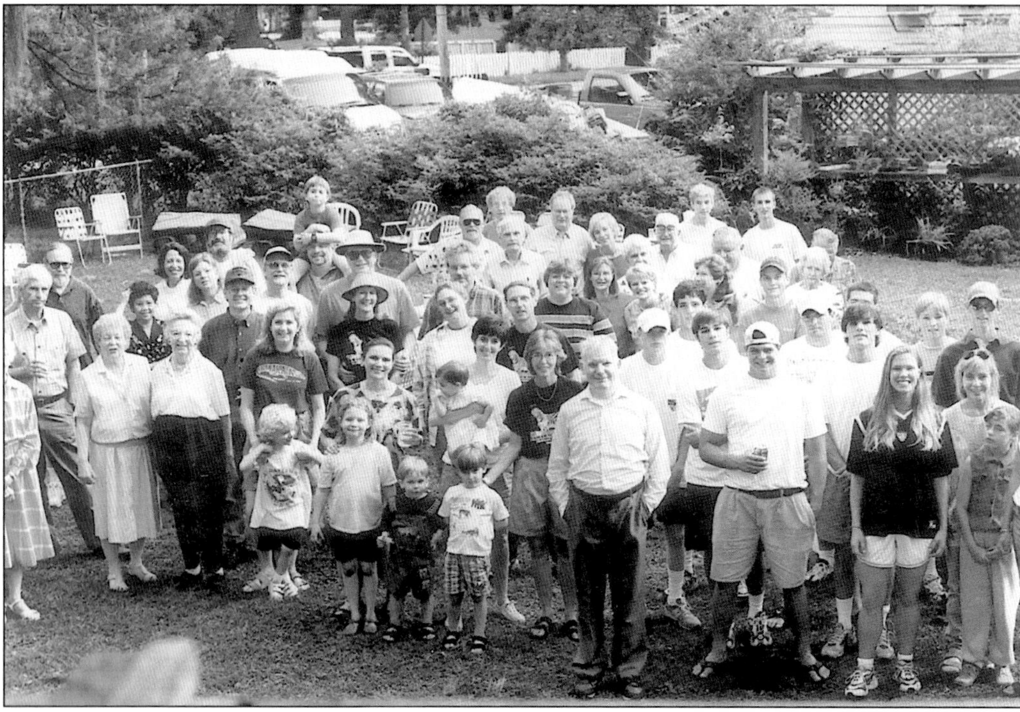

For 25 years, Tamarack Holiday, held on May 14, was an Isle of Hope tradition. Laden with shrimp casseroles, crab cakes, okra gumbo, red rice, watermelon, and boiled peanuts, families gathered in the garden of Nancy and Jim Tamarack to catch up on the past year. This photo was taken in 1988 and has many familiar faces.

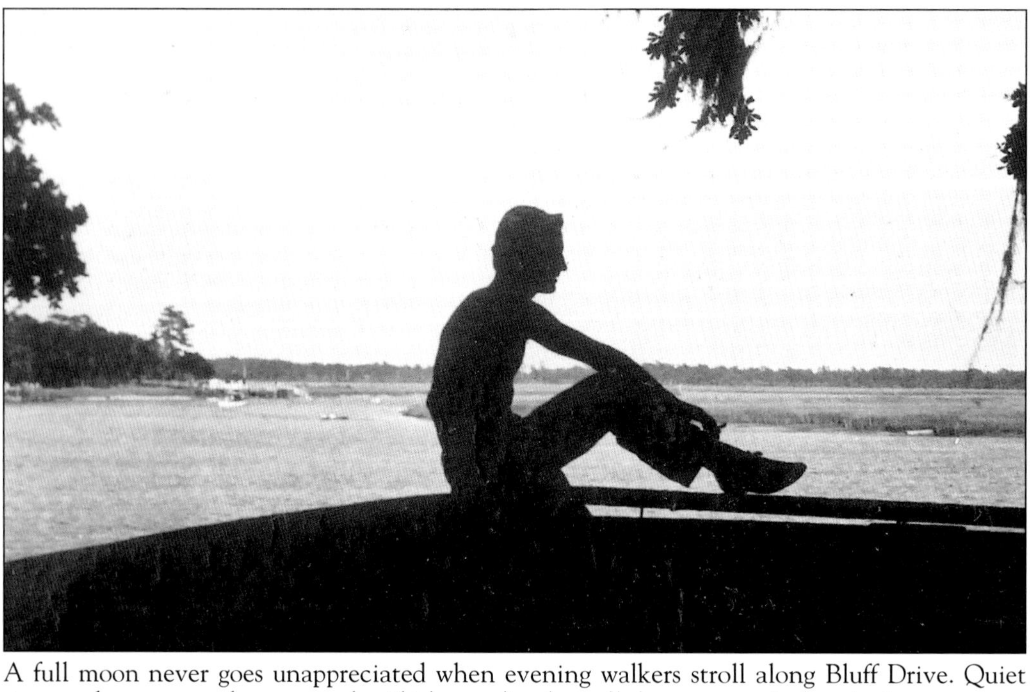

A full moon never goes unappreciated when evening walkers stroll along Bluff Drive. Quiet time as the sun goes down over the Skidaway dissolves all the stresses of a hectic day.

Two

Churches

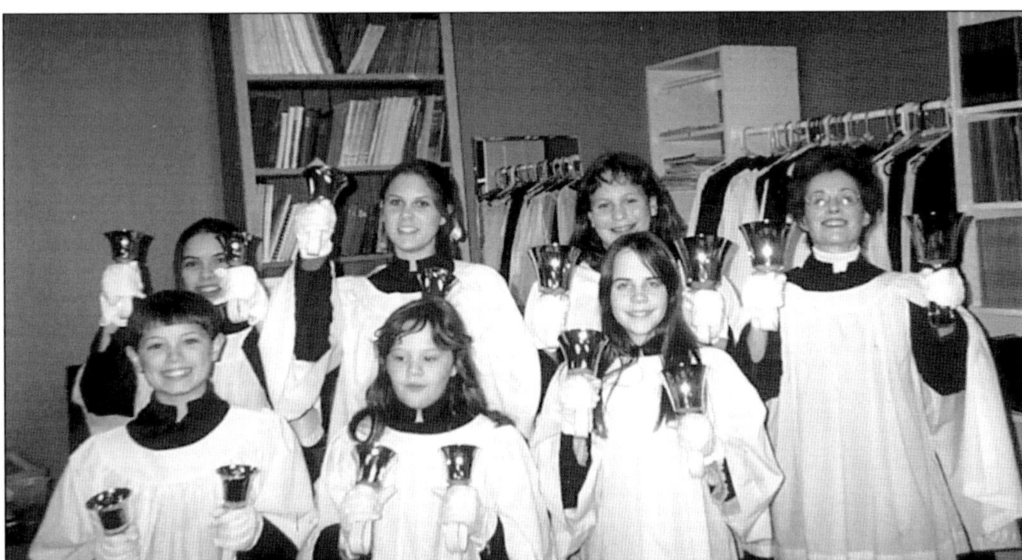

For years the Methodist Church was the main place of worship on the island. People of many faiths attended services there. As a welcome symbol, a large key hung outside the door for many years. Today there are Baptist, Episcopal, Catholic, and Methodist churches on the Isle of Hope. Practicing bell-ringing at St. Thomas Church are, from left to right, (front row) Mac Woo, Tori Quante, Anna Quante, and Pamela McCaslin (organist-choirmaster); (back row) Devin Woo, Allison Caldwell, and Chandler Case.

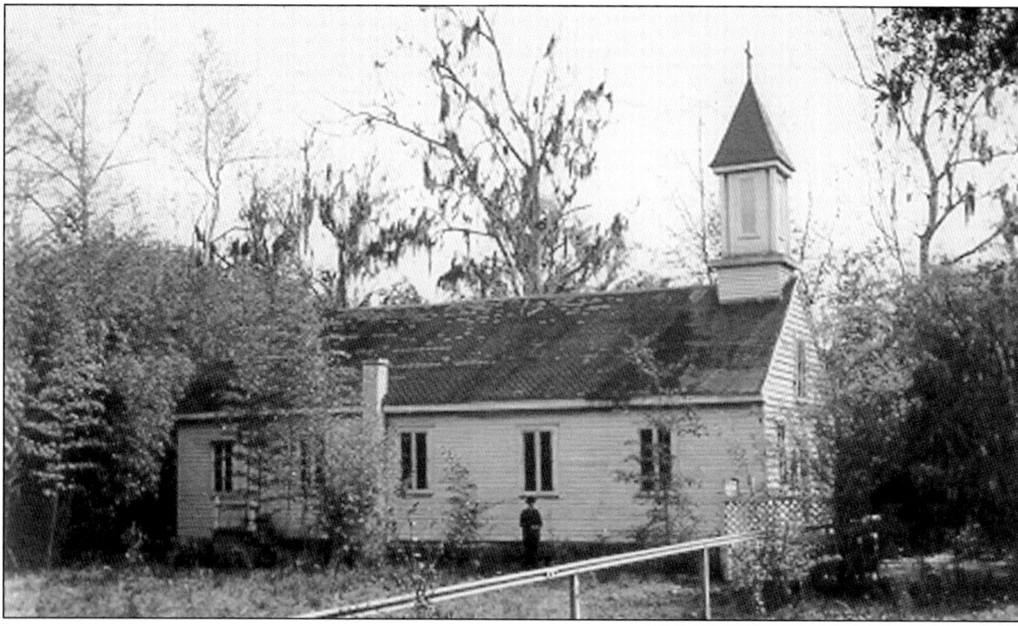

Our Lady of Good Hope is often photographed today. In 1874, Father John Wissel, OSB, purchased the land on Isle of Hope in trust for the Congregation of Benedictine Fathers within the diocese of Savannah. The first home in the South for a Benedictine community was built. For years it was a mission of Sacred Heart Church. In 1876, Father Gabriel Bergier acquired an adjacent lot deeded from Dr. Stephen Dupon's estate. Our Lady of Good Hope was built. Father Bergier died of yellow fever in 1876. The remaining Benedictines moved to Oklahoma to minister to the Native Americans. Today mass is said by a priest from the parish of St. James each first Sunday of the month. The chapel seats approximately 100 people.

Dear little chapel! How often have these hands scrubbed its floors, decorated its little altar and dusted the benches. I recall the goodhearted Dr. Dupon's gift to our struggling little band.......for the Christian education of colored people....Others came to aid in the good work Several were colored, thus making an unique community....

Dark clouds were gathering, however, and in spring of 1876....yellow fever had reached our beautiful Forest City....with what heroic courage our priests and sisters faced the scourge. Alas! Many of the dear faces of my early youth went down to the cold grave with but few to see or shut their eyes in the sleep of death.

Among the little workers out at the Isle of Hope.....Father Gabriel Bergier, OSB, visited all classes and colors...even when his own health ...demanded his close, faithful watchfulness....The writer...felt the fever eating into his very bones. How fierce the burning...On the same bed...lay one who within twenty-four hours was a corpse. Next evening there was another. Who was to bury the dead, but a mere boy? What could one or two do to check our fear, our suffering?...

A few weeks later and our beloved superior was carried off...Our little band broken up, but the two named escaped to continue, out in the wilds of Indian Territory...

May peace and joy be the share of the worshippers in the little chapel of our Lady of Good Hope. Asking a prayer from all and hoping I may again visit the sacred place, I am, sincerely in Corde Jesu.

Rt. Rev. M. Bernard Murphy, OSB

Written from Oklahoma in 1908, this condensed version of a poignant letter by a Savannah boy who spent his novitiate at Our Lady Of Good Hope, graphically tells of the grim experience of the yellow fever epidemic.

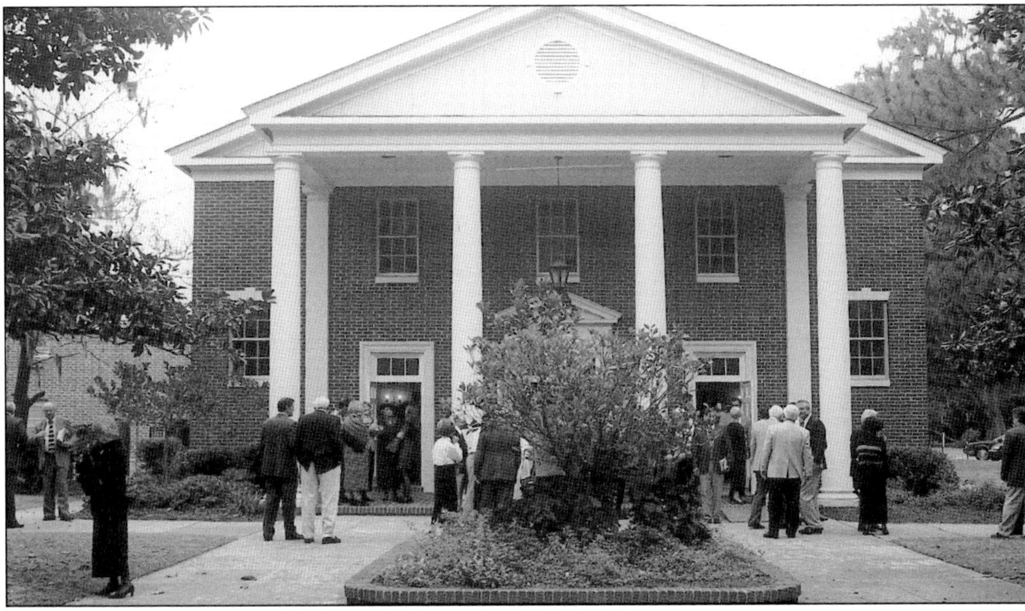

The Isle of Hope Baptist Church dates back to the early 1950s. Dr. Searcy Garrison, pastor of Bull Street Baptist Church in Savannah, worked with local families to start a mission at Isle of Hope. The first service was held in the Community House on June 7, 1952. Lawrence Hardy, a seminary student, served as pastor to 26 people. In 1953, the mission became a constituted church and the sanctuary on Rose Avenue was completed and dedicated in 1966. In the '70s a gym was built. The Hugh Jackson Youth Room has an after-school program. In 1991, the Child Development Center opened to ages six weeks to four years.

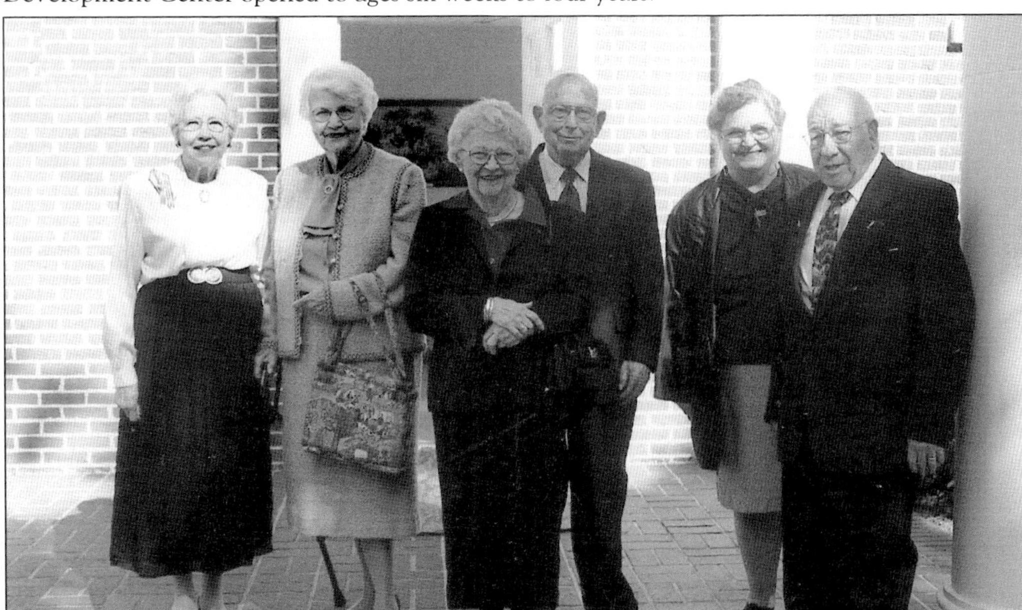

Charter members of the Isle of Hope Baptist Church line up for the camera. From left to right are Leila Norton, Betsy Jackson, Dot Orton, Paul Orton, Sophia Barnes, and Bob Barnes. Logan Dixon is not pictured.

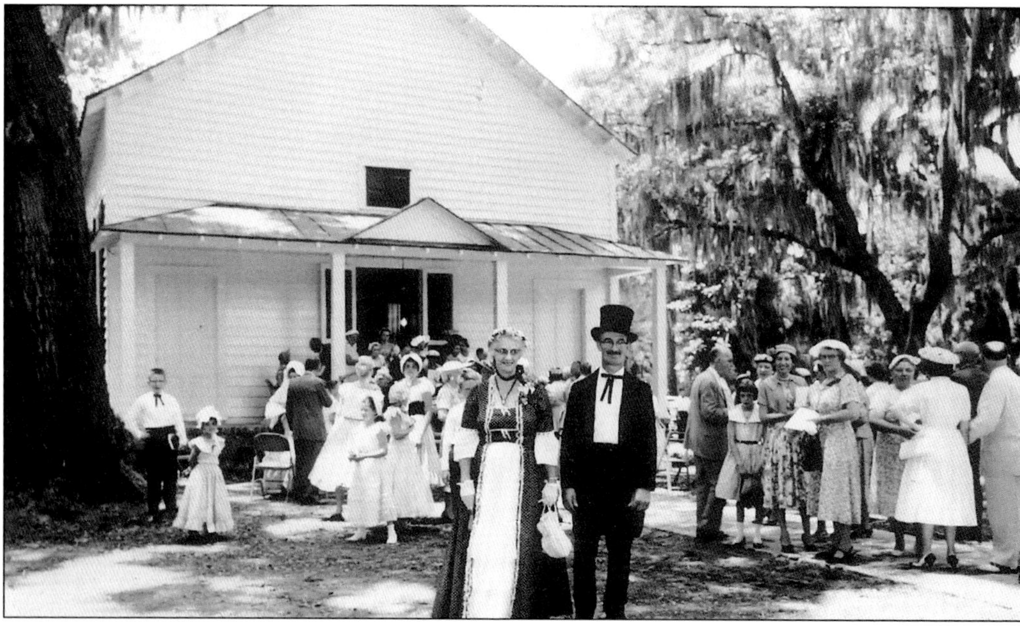

The Isle of Hope Methodist Church was organized in 1851 near Skidaway and Bethesda Roads. Dr. Stephen Dupon gave the land on Parkersburg Road in 1859 and the church was moved to the island. During the War Between the States, pews served as sick beds for soldiers at Camp Claghorn on the bluff and the Chatham Artillery. Many carved their names into the pews while recovering. The bell was melted to make ammunition for Union troops and was later replaced by George Wylly. The church was used as a camp by Sherman's men during the occupation of Savannah. This photo shows the 100th year re-enactment.

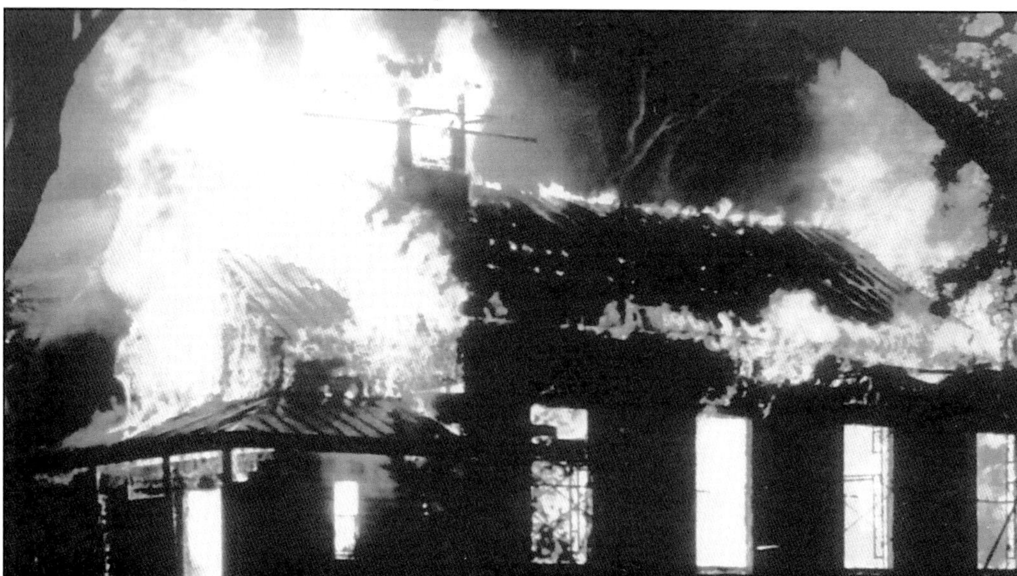

Despite the heroic efforts of the Isle of Hope and Southside firefighters, a dreadful inferno consumed the building in 1984. Fortunately, the original pews, chancel rail, and furniture had been removed for renovation and were therefore spared. The rebuilt church resembles the old one and was paid for entirely by contributions.

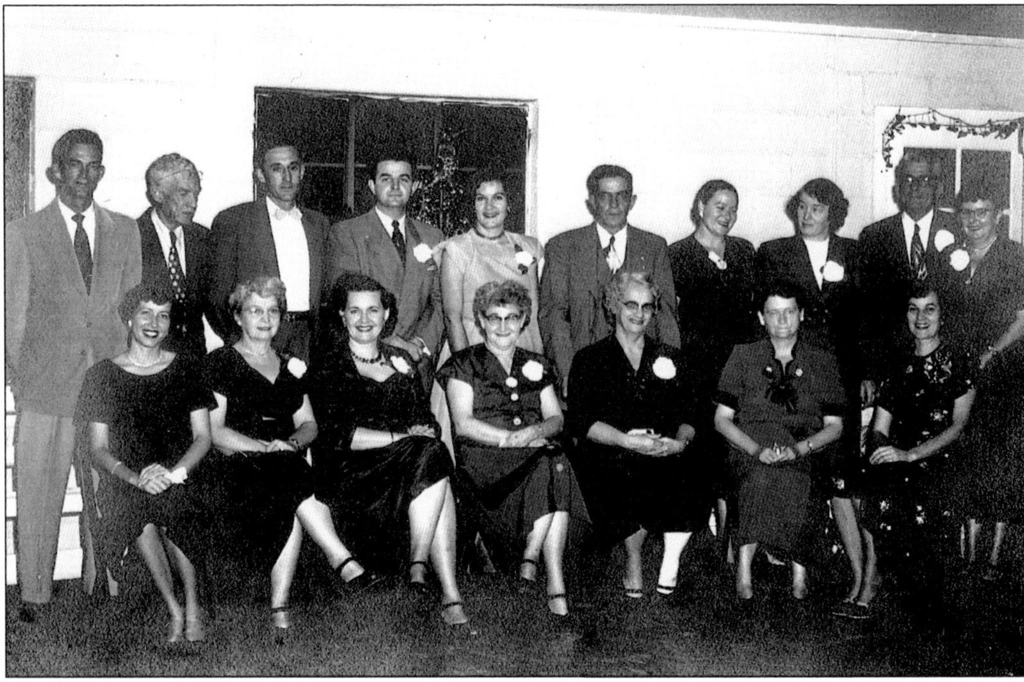

Here are the members of the Lula Smith Circle of the Methodist Church in 1953. Pictured from left to right are (front row) Leila Norton, Mary Taylor, Betty Wilson, Thelma Mell, Julia Mintz, Jean Caphton, and Mildred Salnikoff; (back row) Howard Norton, F.W.B. Taylor, Gerald Wilson, Rev. C. Edward Reeves, Sara Roberts, Harry Mintz, Connie Hagan, Gertrude Reynolds, Jim McGregor, and Sarah Hontz.

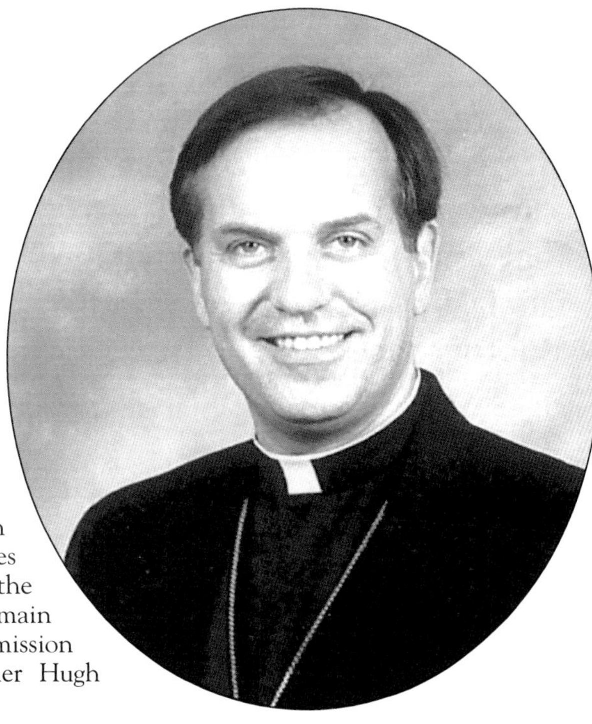

St. Thomas Church is on the northwest corner of Cornus Drive and St. Thomas Avenue. Local Episcopalians kept a mission in operation starting before 1859. Services were held in the Methodist Episcopal "union" Church until the chapel was built on land given by Maria Henderson. With the dedication of members like Charles Hardee, Anna Roberts, and others, the mission became a parish in 1954. The main church was built in 1964 and supports mission work at home and worldwide. Father Hugh Bromiley is the rector.

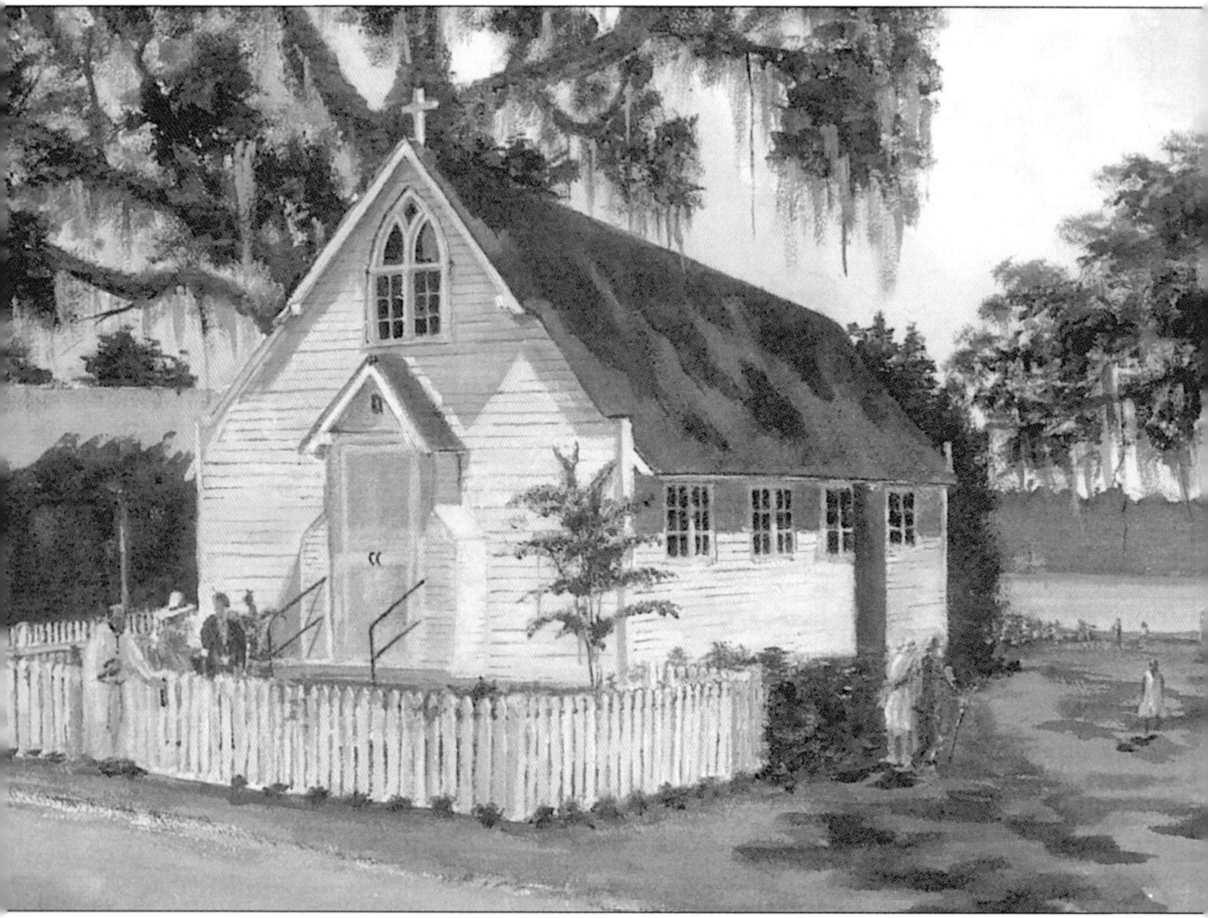

The St. Thomas Chapel was dedicated on St. Thomas Day, Dec. 21, 1923, by the Right Reverend Frederick Focke Reese, Bishop of Georgia. In 1922, this land was given by Maria Henderson, whose family acquired a tract of land from Christ Church in Savannah. The building is made of heart pine, and the windows were poured in sheets resulting in classic ripples and imperfections. The original heat source was a pot-bellied stove that kept the priest's chair toasty warm. Visitors to the chapel are reminded of the favorite old hymn "Church in the Wildwood." This is a charming painting by local artist Chip Goldsmith.

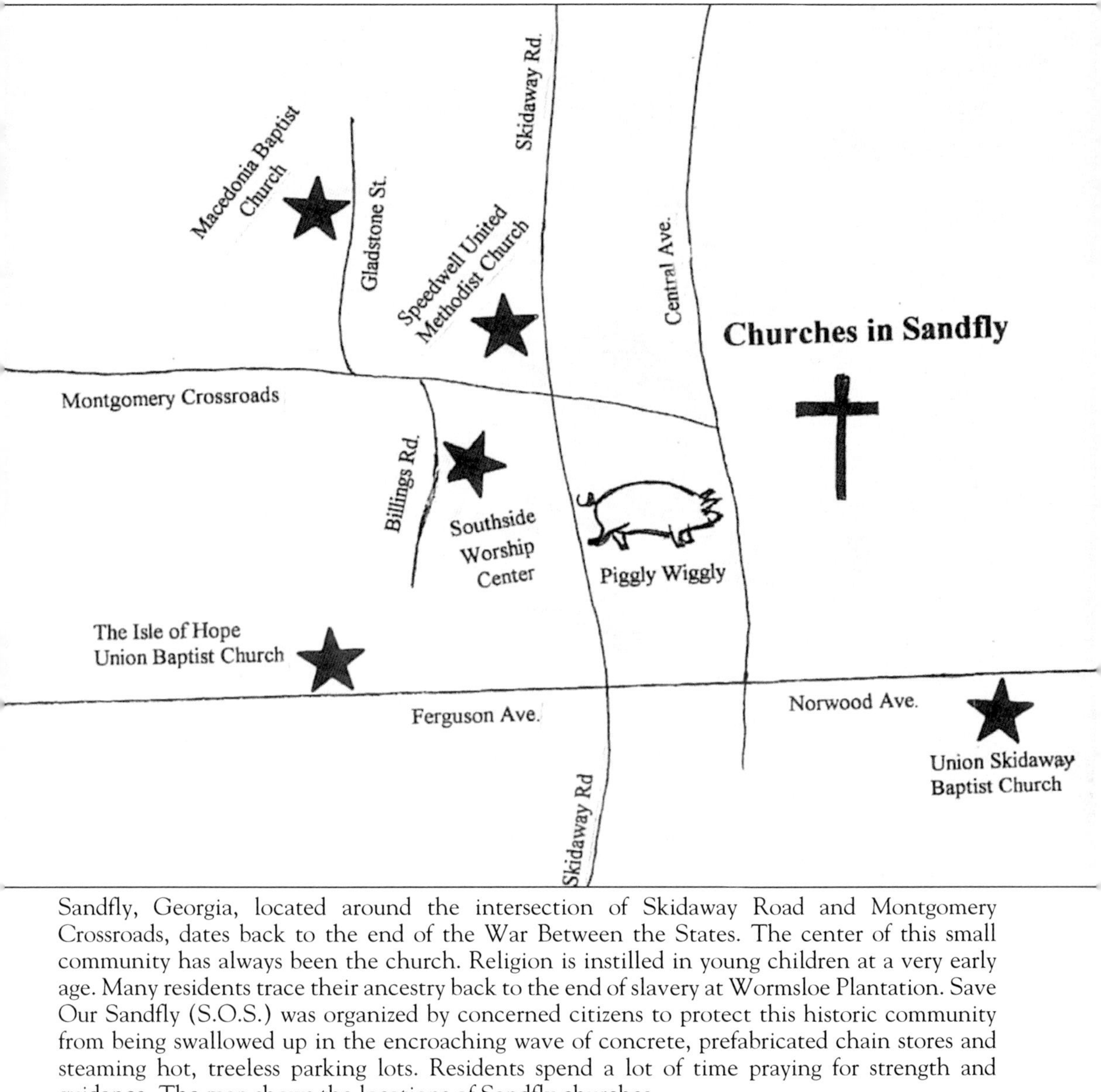

Sandfly, Georgia, located around the intersection of Skidaway Road and Montgomery Crossroads, dates back to the end of the War Between the States. The center of this small community has always been the church. Religion is instilled in young children at a very early age. Many residents trace their ancestry back to the end of slavery at Wormsloe Plantation. Save Our Sandfly (S.O.S.) was organized by concerned citizens to protect this historic community from being swallowed up in the encroaching wave of concrete, prefabricated chain stores and steaming hot, treeless parking lots. Residents spend a lot of time praying for strength and guidance. The map shows the locations of Sandfly churches.

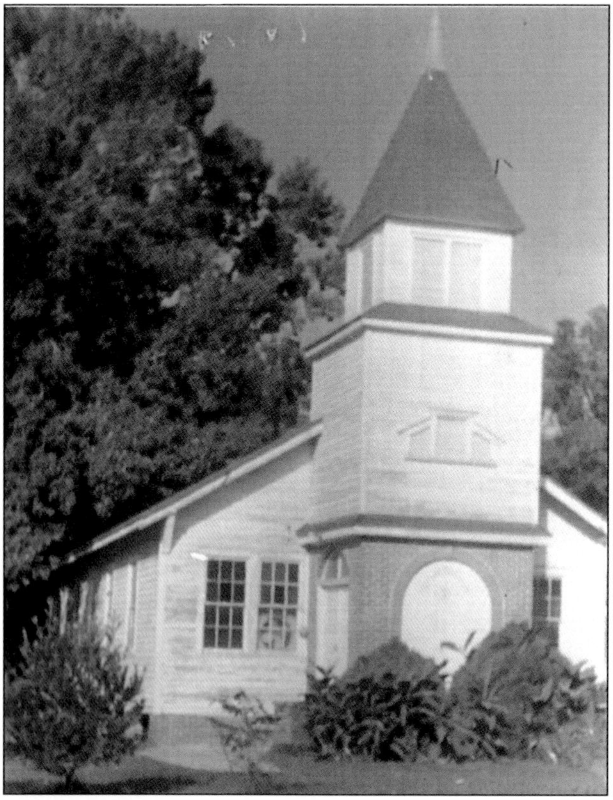

Speedwell Methodist Church was founded in 1884 by Sandfly residents and The Women's Home Missionary Society of the North General Conference. In the early 1800s, missionaries Viola Baldwin and Emma Lewis came to Sandfly to teach about Christ. Sunday School was held under a spreading oak tree until Irene Hayes offered her log cabin. Brother Thomas Kemp gave land on Skidaway Road for a church that burned in 1932. Services were held in Hines Chapel and led by 44 various pastors.

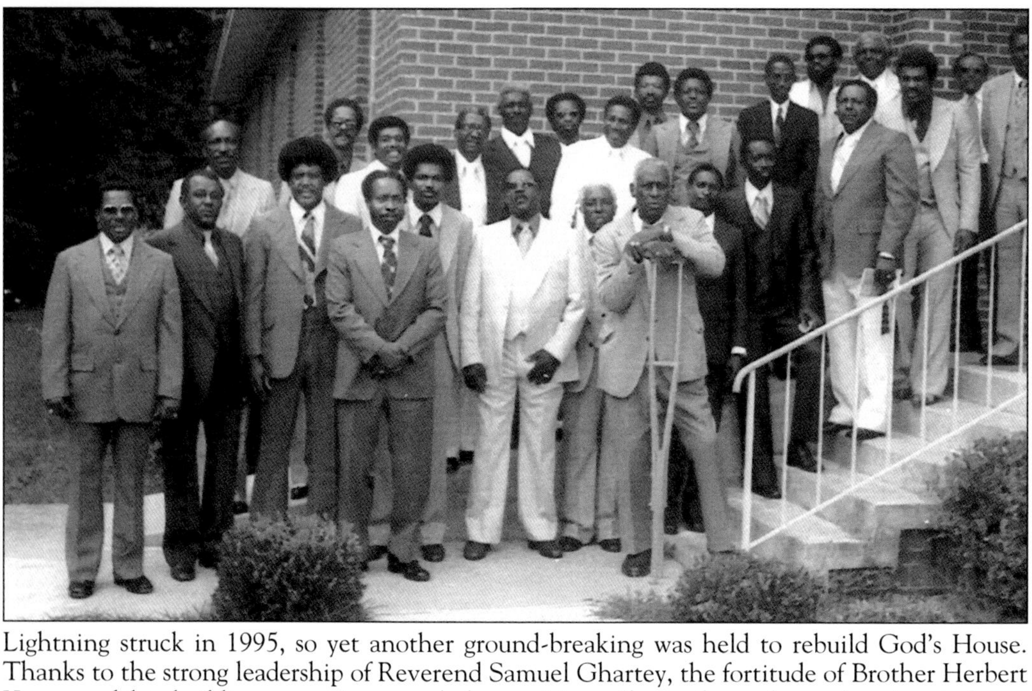

Lightning struck in 1995, so yet another ground-breaking was held to rebuild God's House. Thanks to the strong leadership of Reverend Samuel Ghartey, the fortitude of Brother Herbert Kemp and his building committee, and the untiring efforts of members, the church has a congregation of 325 today.

The Union Skidaway Baptist Church had an unpretentious beginning. A small number of Baptists met on December 13, 1872, to consider forming a church. They erected a small building of worship and called it The Union Baptist Church of Skidaway Island. As there were so few members at this time, they invited various brother ministers to preach until they could hire a pastor. Reverend P.J. Framble was the first to minister at the church. The church was rebuilt in 1963.

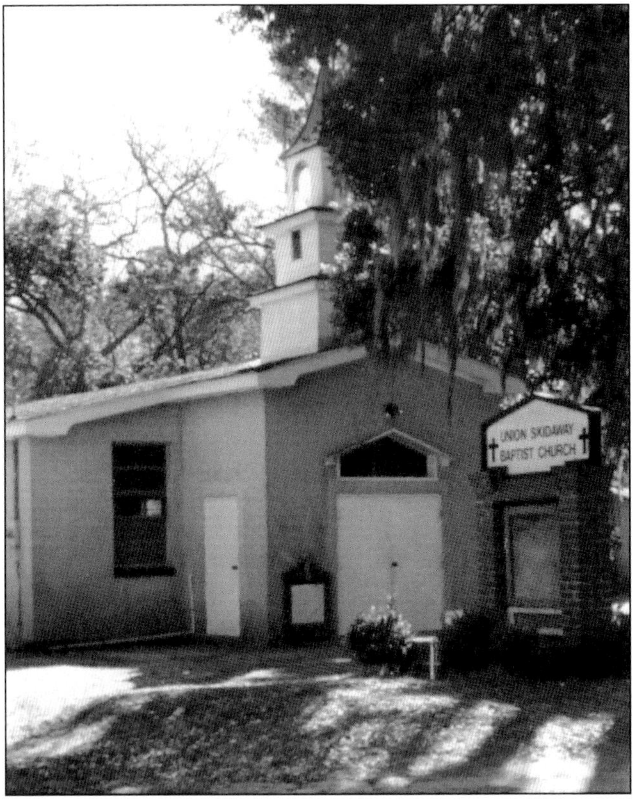

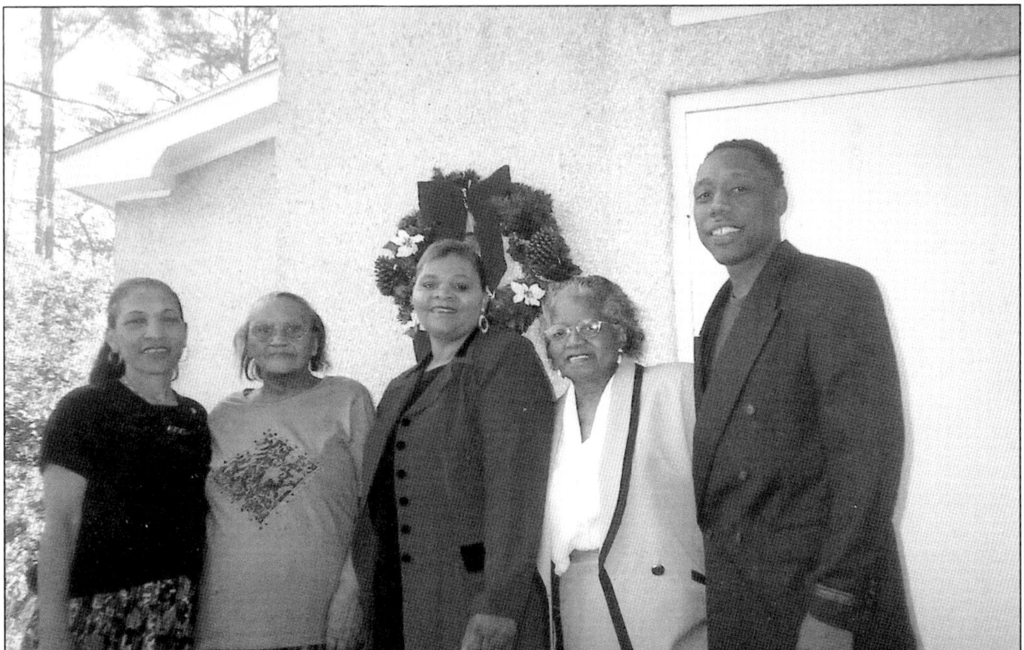

Posing in front of their church on Norwood Avenue are, from left to right, Loressa Williams, Alethia Cruse, Dolores Jackson, Lillian Battiste (pianist), and the Rev. Alan O'Neal Sr.

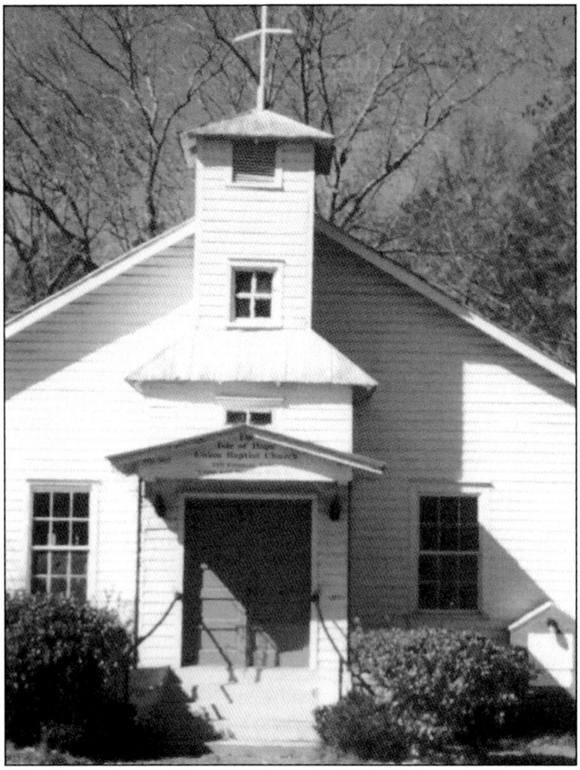

Isle of Hope Union Missionary Baptist Church was organized in 1872 by Reverend Lucius Houston and Quives Frazier. The land, given by Barney Lee, was opposite the new Isle of Hope School. In 1941, the wooden building was moved to its present location on Ferguson Avenue. Jacob Golden, with the help of deacons and enthusiastic members, reassembled it. A kitchen and meeting room were later added.

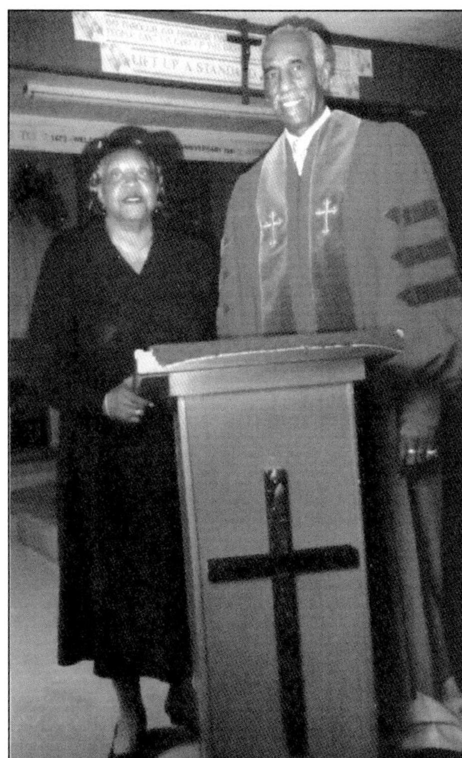

Twenty one years later, led by Deacon Isaac Golden, the church was remodeled and dedicated. The small congregation of 50 members and a vibrant choir are led by the charismatic Rev. Joseph Jackson and First Lady, Sister Veronica Jackson. Upon entering, one feels a sense of calmness and belonging inside the small, lovingly-tended sanctuary.

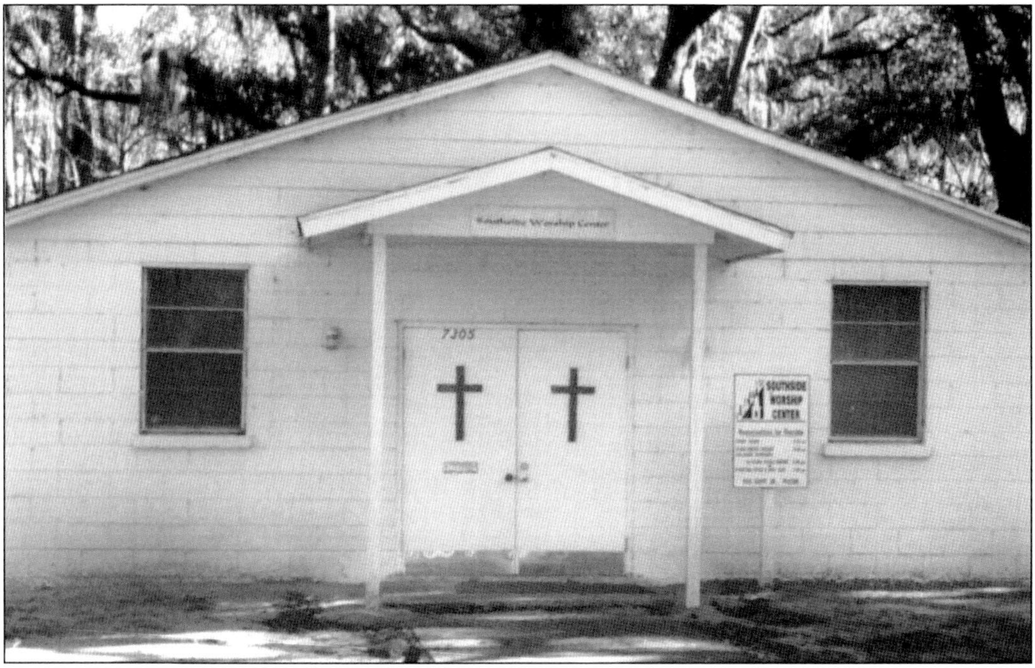

Southside Worship Center, this tiny house of worship pictured above, was originally called The Sandfly Holiness Center. It is located at Billings Road and Montgomery Crossroads and was founded in 1927. Some of the past clergymen include Rev. Joseph Lewis, Pastor Ernest Williams, Pastor Griffin, Pastor Carrie Bell Griffin, and Pastor Smalls.

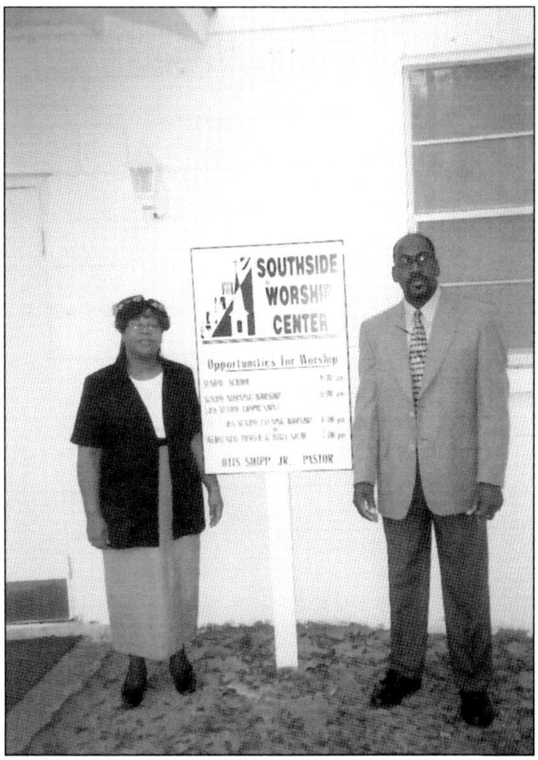

Standing in front of the small frame church are Janice Marie Shipp with her husband, Pastor Otis Shipp Jr. Attending this church are fourteen members and two followers. Their philosophy is, "Where God is worshipped in spirit and in truth."

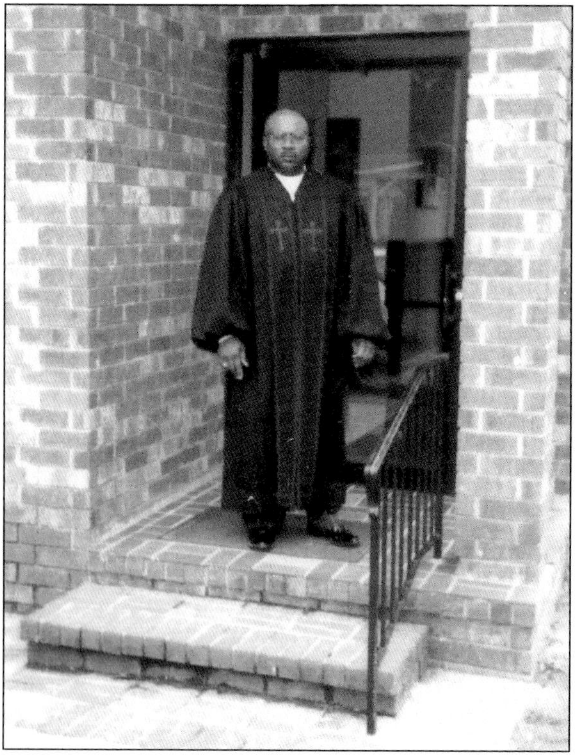

The Macedonia Baptist Church entrance is pictured on the left. In 1877, a few Christian brethern organized Prayer House led by Father Amos Morrell. The church then moved to Dutch Town and subsequently Sandfly. Sister Nellie Saunders opened her home for worship and donated the land in 1917. Former pastors were Revs. Isaac Anderson, Frank Daniels, W.H. Washington, E.K. Fair, T.B. Arline, Peter Framble, Freddie Bonds, Alton Anderson, Nathaniel Hamilton, and Richard Hall. Presently, Reverend Jerome Stokes (pictured), assisted by Associate Pastor Vernon Galloway, minister to the flock.

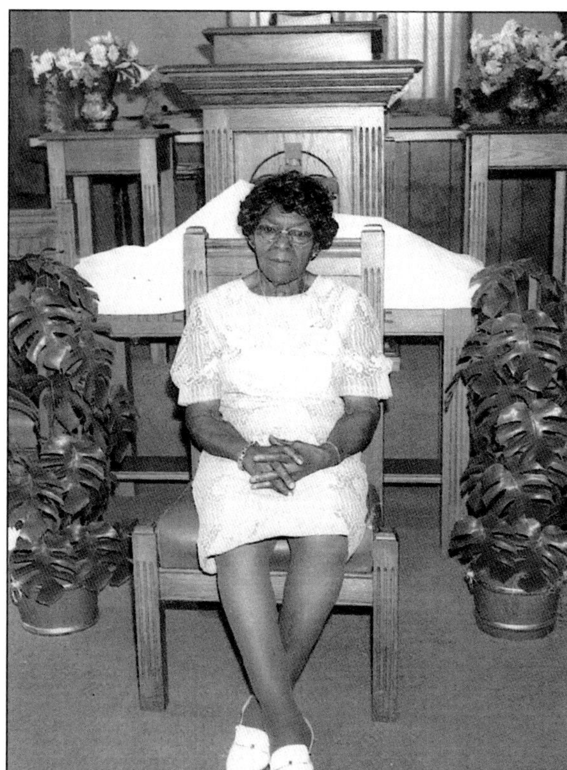

The church was remodeled in 1993 and has grown to a membership of 200. Mother Ethel Mack (1893-1979) was a vital member, contributing much of her time to the choir and held various offices of responsibility. She was one of the founders of Zion Baptist Association and president for 27 years.

Three

WORMSLOE HISTORIC SITE

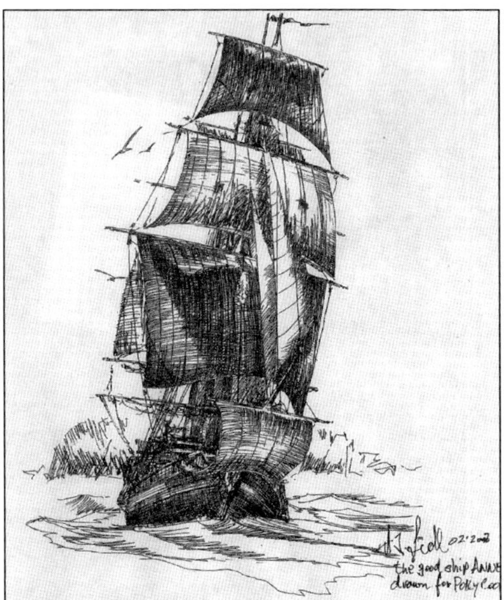

Noble Jones sailed from England aboard the frigate *Anne* in 1732 with Gen. James Oglethorpe and 114 other colonists. With him were his wife Sarah, three-year-old Mary, and ten-year-old Noble Wimberly. The mission was to establish the 13th British colony in America. His second son, Inigo, was born in 1734. A daughter, Sarah, died in infancy. Jones leased 500 acres on the Isle of Hope from the Trustees of Georgia and called it Wormslow (spelled "Wormsloe" since the 1840s). In 1756, King George II granted him ownership. The pen-and-ink drawing of the *Anne* is by Albert Seidl, eminent Savannah maritime artist.

God hath chosen a mate for me.
I'll honor him in loving the.
There did I find, the did I choose;
The do I bind, but death must lose.
As I expect, so let me find
A faithful heart and constant mind.
God hath kept my heart for the,
Grant that our love may faithful be.
Such pleasure I find, choice I find
That naught but death shall change my mind.
Wit wilth and beauty all do well,
But constant love do these excill.
The eye finds, the hart chooseth,
The hands bind, but death looseth.
P. S.
Miss, keep this in remembrance of me
when you look at it, think of them that
wrote it who perhaps may be many a
mile off.

Noble Jones held his beloved wife, Sarah Hack, in high esteem, as evidenced by this touching poem that he apparently wrote to her in the early 1720s. They were married at Lincoln's Inn Chapel in London on July 30, 1723. The poem is typed exactly as it was written in his original letter. (Courtesy of Georgia Historical Society.)

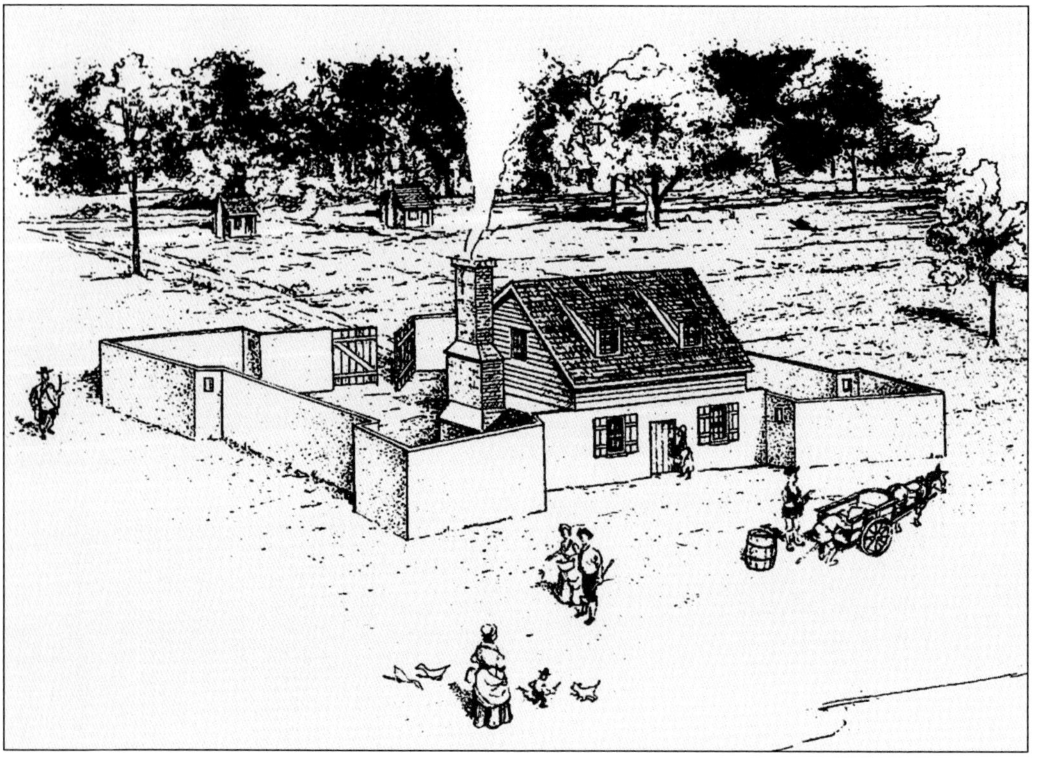

From the onset, Oglethorpe had feared an attack by the Spaniards in Florida, who resented the settlers on land they claimed as theirs. He instructed Jones to build a "watchhouse" to guard the Skidaway Narrows, the inland waterway from the south. Jones' Fort was completed around 1744. Members of the military garrison slept in huts near his house. A vista of three miles was cut through the woods to Whitefield's orphan house, Bethesda. (Courtesy of Wormsloe Historic Site.)

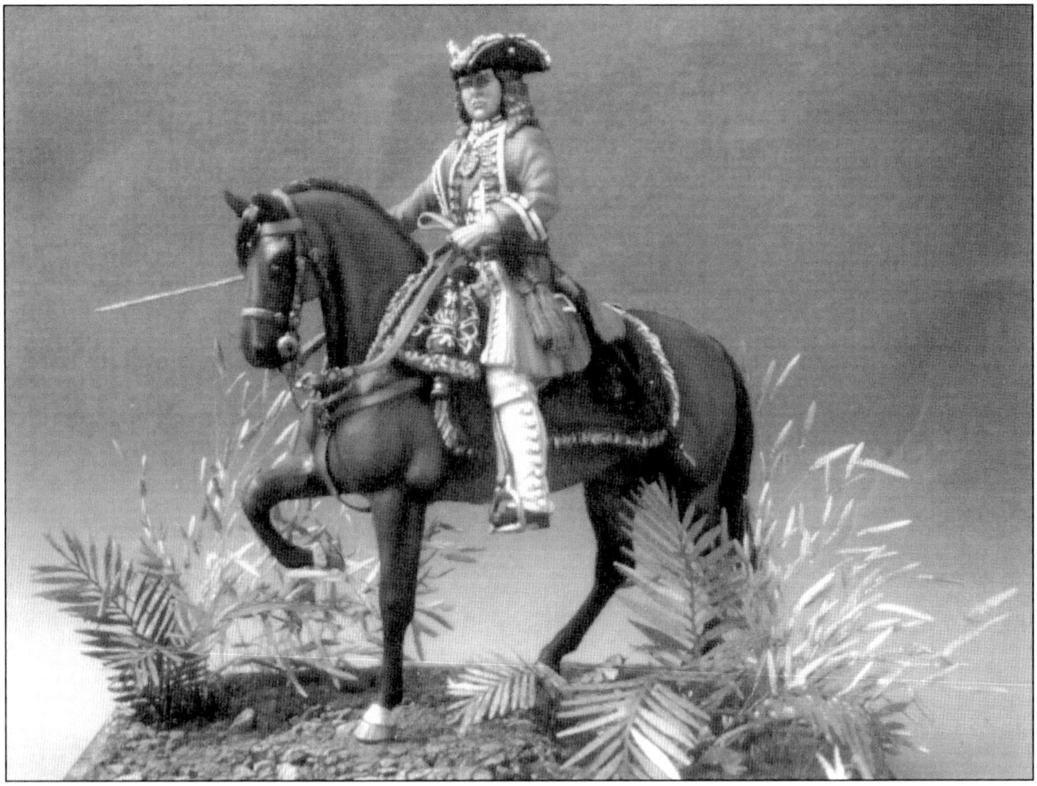

In 1736, Oglethorpe was made commander-in-chief of His Majesty's troops in Georgia and the Carolinas. He regularly rode on horseback to visit the outpost he had built farther south at Frederica. The photo is of a lead model fashioned by Preston Russell, a local published historian and retired pathologist.

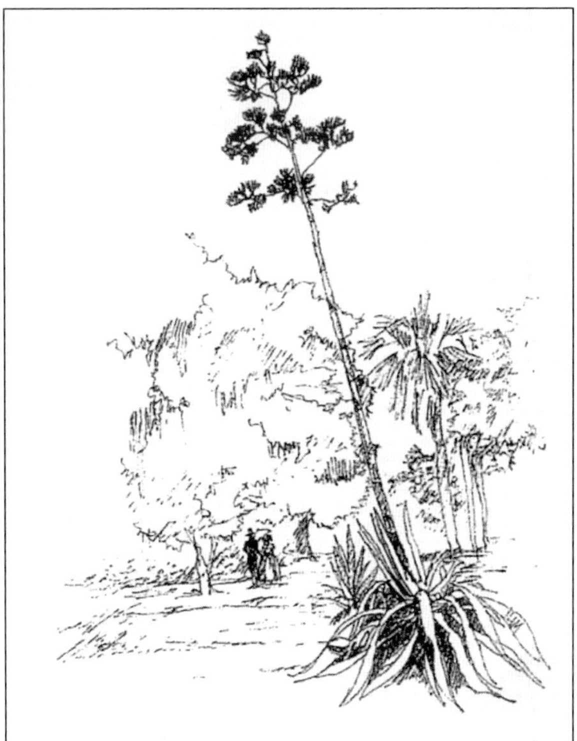

By 1740, Henry Parker and James Fallowfield had settled on Isle of Hope and each had leased land from the Trustees. Due to misfortunes, Fallowfield abandoned his land, which was granted to Jones. He called it *Wimberly*. Townsfolk came in horse-drawn carriages in July of 1765, to admire a rare Agave plant of the Amaryllis genus, known as Century Plant, grown by the Honorable Noble Jones. It was 27 feet tall and was probably imported from South America. The drawing is by Jean Lim, a Savannah artist and woodworker.

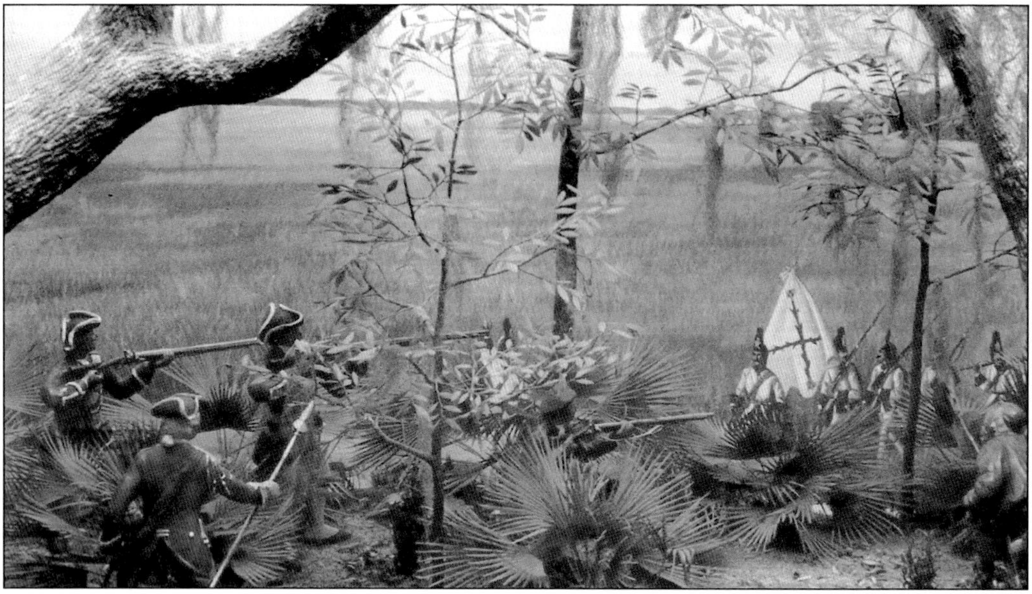

In 1742, General Oglethorpe defeated the Spaniards at the Battle of Bloody Marsh on St. Simons Island. After successfully defending Fort Frederica, Oglethorpe's men ambushed the Spaniards, making the marsh run red with Spanish blood. The Marine Guard continued to be stationed at Wormsloe, even though the Spanish threat had been quelled. Noble Jones was given the title of captain. (Courtesy of the Fort Frederica Foundation.)

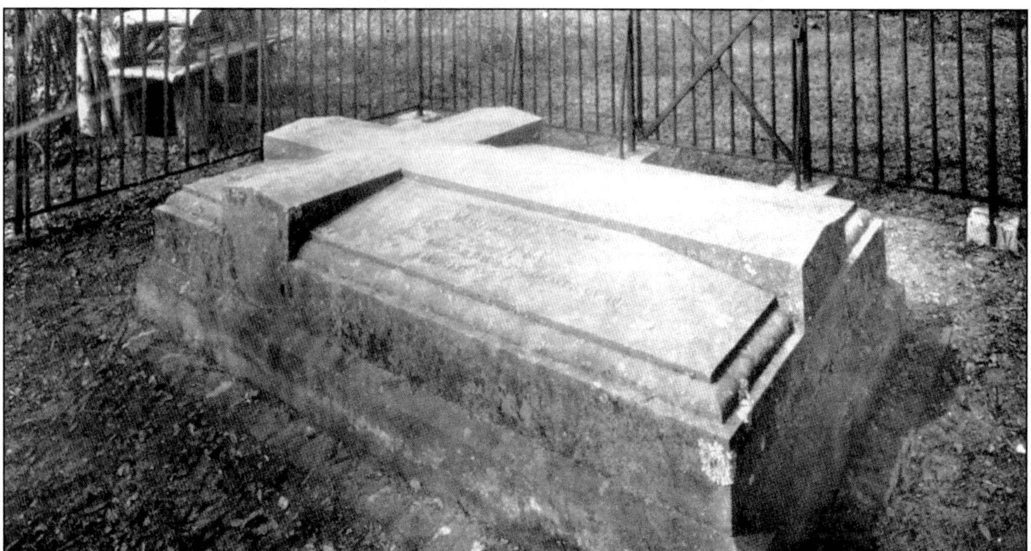

Noble Jones was a physician, carpenter, surveyor, rum agent, constable, and military man with a keen interest in agriculture. The Trustees desired silk production, so Jones planted mulberry trees and attempted sericulture. To see what might grow in the new world, in 1772 Ben Franklin, agent to the colony, sent Upland rice from Cochin China, which grew on dry ground. He also sent seeds of the Chinese Tallow tree. Noble Jones died in 1775. His first gravesite was at Wormsloe; he was then moved to Colonial Park Cemetery, and was then moved to his final resting place, Bonaventure Cemetery. This photograph shows the Wormsloe burial ground with the family monument that was erected in the 1870s.

Trained in medicine by his father, Noble Wimberly Jones (1723–1805) was the first president of the Georgia Medical Association in 1804. He had strong allegiance to the patriots and was influential in directing several Revolutionary War efforts. Jones was elected as Georgia's representative to three Continental Congress sessions. Because he was a Son of Liberty, his political views differed radically from those of his father, but the two were very close and their mutual admiration held steadfast. The elder Noble Jones died in 1775, just before royal authority collapsed in Georgia. Noble Wimberly chose to stay with his father instead of attending the First Continental Congress. (Courtesy of John Duncan Antique Books and Maps.)

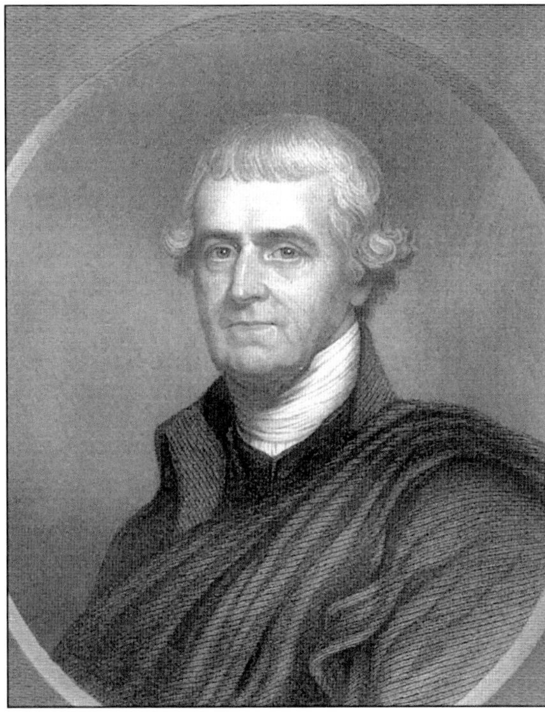

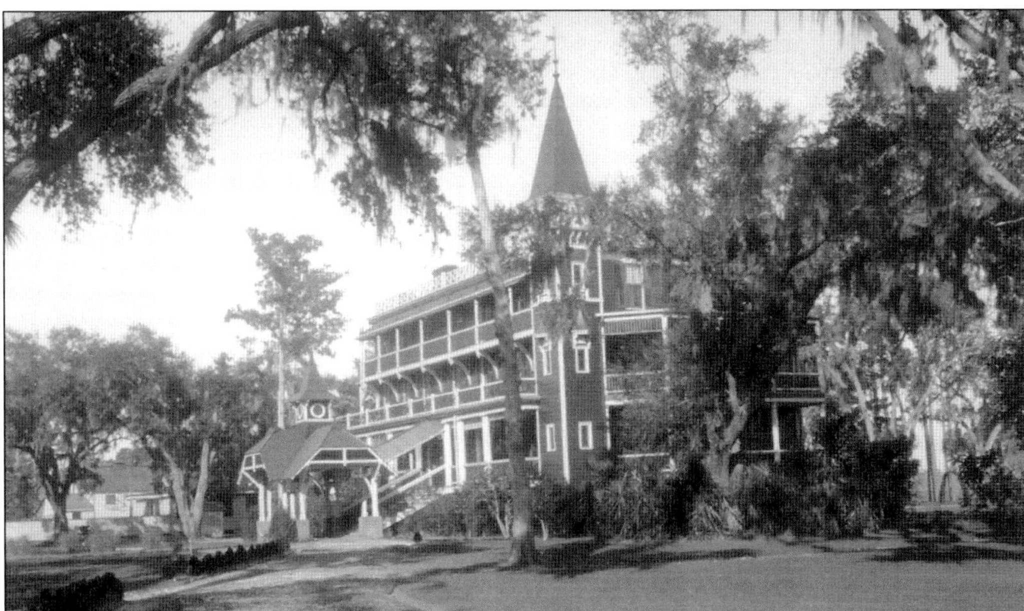

Dr. George Jones (1766–1838) was the third owner of Wormsloe. He served as the mayor of Savannah from 1812 to 1813, was elected representative to the state assembly, and served as a judge in Georgia's Eastern Circuit. He was also a physician and a planter with extensive acreage in Chatham County and elsewhere. Dr. Jones built the original house at Wormsloe, which was later greatly expanded. Like his father, he was also the president of the Georgia Medical Association. This is a later photo taken after the house was purchased by W.J. De Renne of the fifth generation. (Courtesy of Eudora De Renne Roebling.)

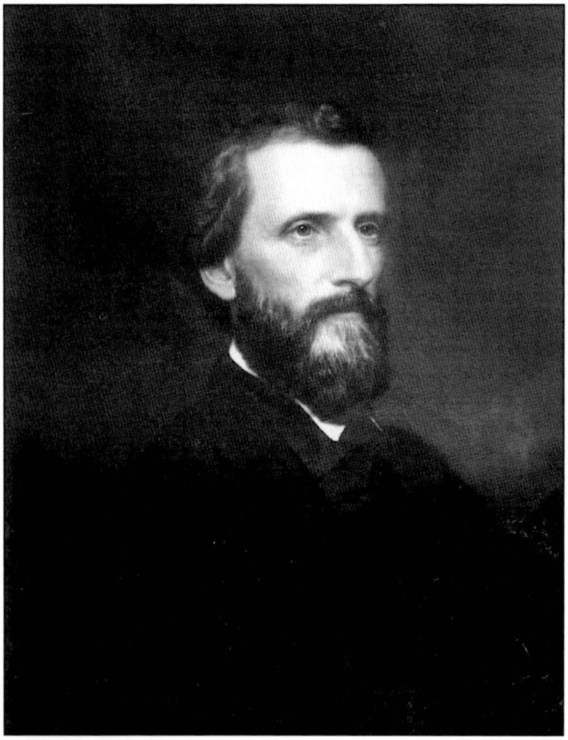

When Gen. William Sherman invaded Savannah during the Civil War, George Wymberley Jones (pictured) and his family were living in the house at Wormsloe. To escape the federal invasion, the family fled to Augusta and the deserted house was damaged by federal soldiers. Jones and his father owned a valuable collection of Georgia books and documents that were lost or destroyed during the invasion. In 1865, George W. Jones added De Renne to his name because Van Deren had been his grandmother's maiden name. He also changed Wimberly to "Wymberley" and Wormslow to "Wormsloe." (Courtesy of Eudora De Renne Roebling.)

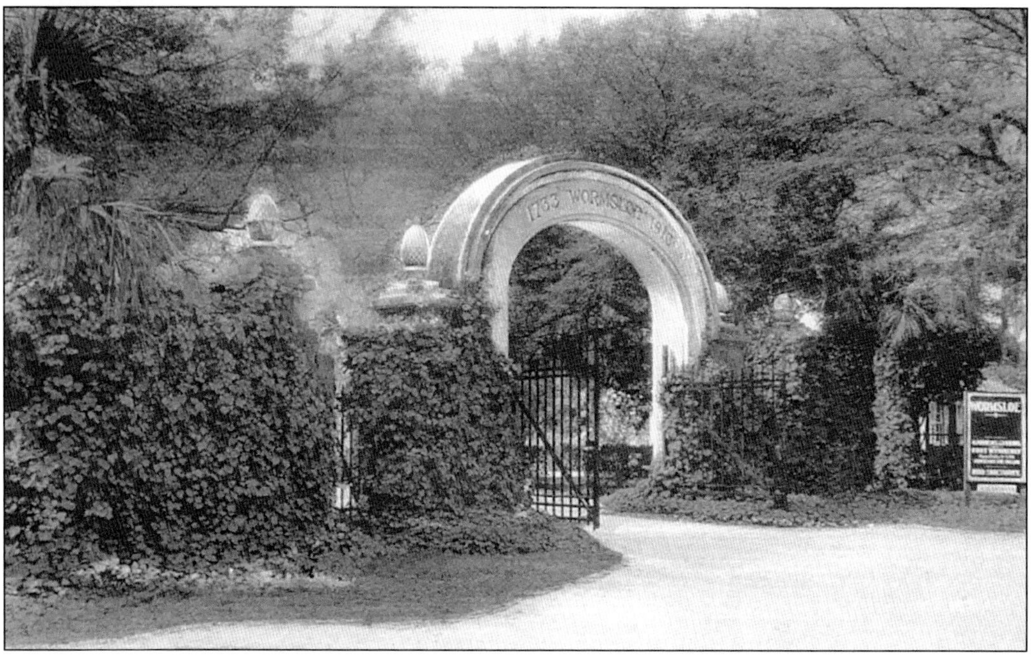

The impressive masonry archway at the entrance to the main driveway was erected in 1913 by Wymberley Jones De Renne (1853–1916), of the fifth generation, to commemorate the 21st birthday of his son, Wymberley Wormsloe. The dates engraved on the arch are 1733, the year of the founding of the colony of Georgia, and 1913, the year of the construction of the archway. (Courtesy of John Duncan Antique Books and Maps.)

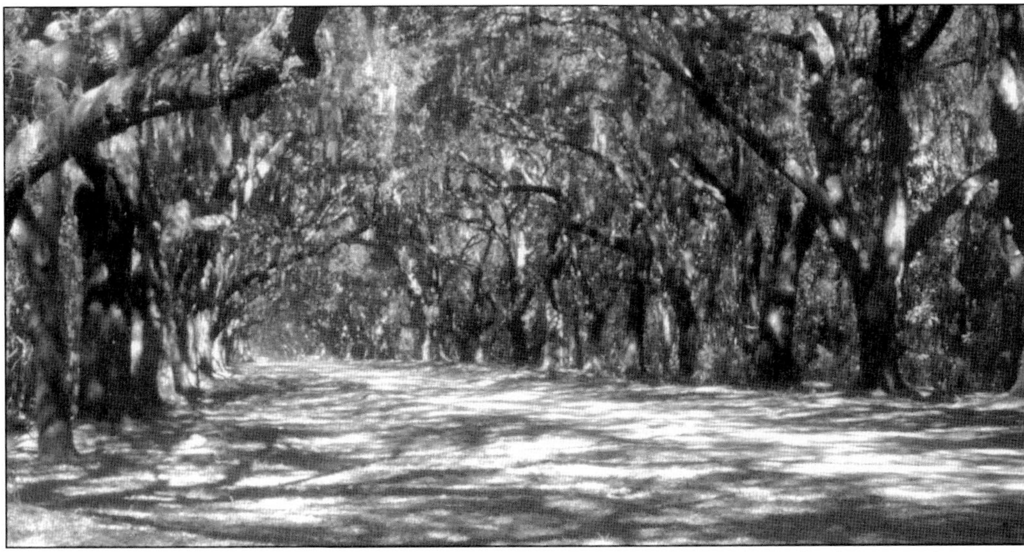

The driveway is 1.5 miles long and flanked by 400 stately live oaks, which were planted by De Renne as a continued celebration of the birth of Wymberley Wormsloe. The grand home is not available for tours because descendants of Noble Jones still occupy the house, but the museum offers visitors a short film about the early colonists and excavated artifacts. There are also nature walks to the tabby ruins of Jones' Fort, his original gravesite, and a colonial life area. The walking trails in the forest have exhibits along the way displaying wildlife prints, which are the work of early naturalist Mark Catesby. (Courtesy of Eudora De Renne Roebling.)

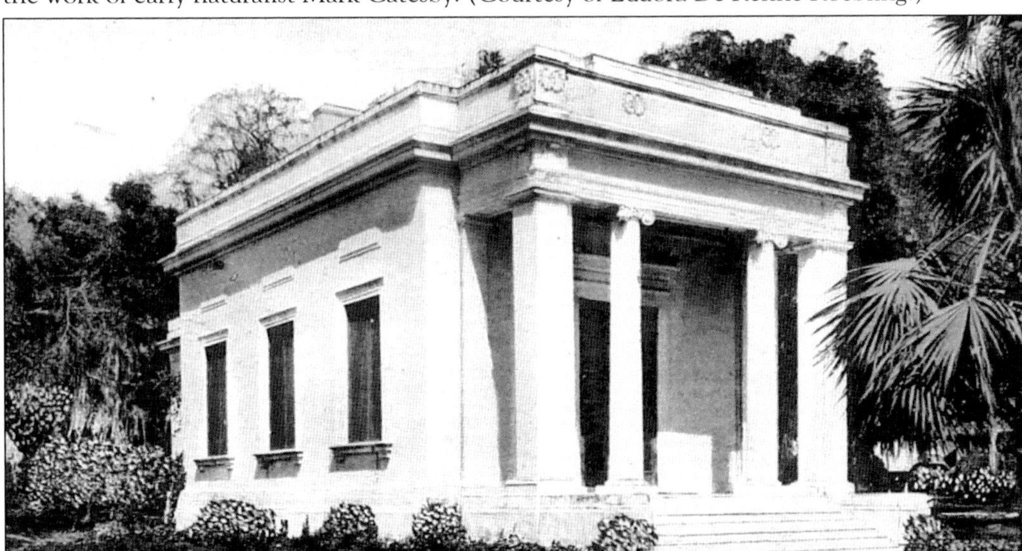

Knowing of W.J. De Renne's passion for Georgia historical documents, Charles Jones Jr., and other friends of De Renne helped him rebuild the family collection. In 1907, De Renne built a fireproof library. The library once housed the permanent Confederate Constitution, Sherman's telegrams to General Grant telling of Savannah's surrender, letters from Ben Franklin to Noble Wimberly Jones, and transcripts of the original acts of the Georgia Trustees. The library is guarded by a cannon used against the British in 1812. (Courtesy of John Duncan Antique Books and Maps.)

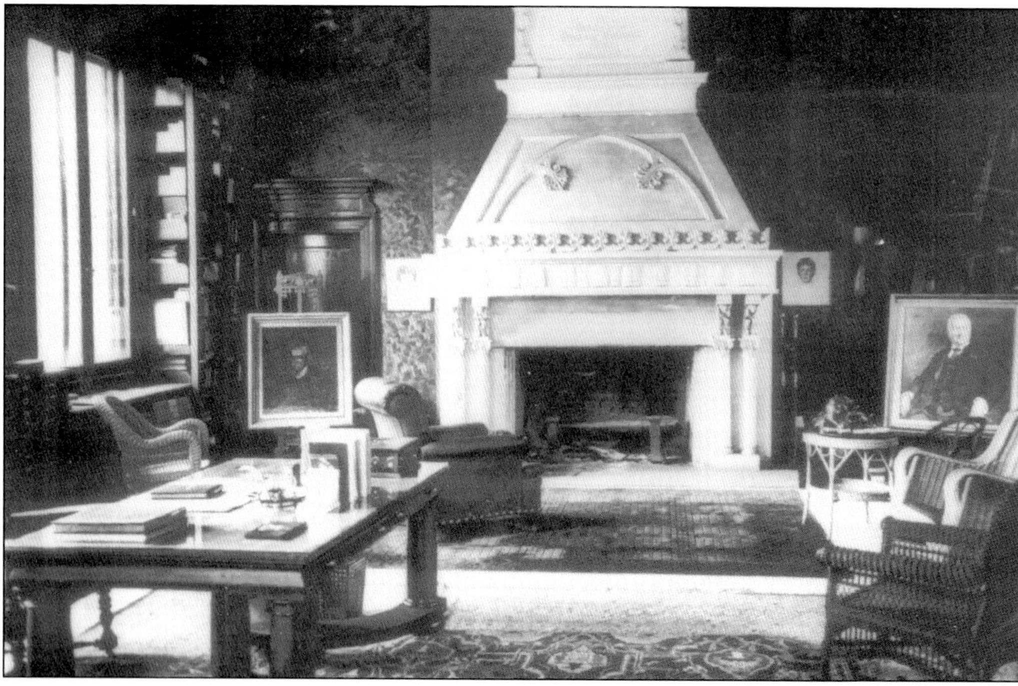

In the library's interior, shown here in a photograph of the 1920s, a painting by Gari Melchers of Wymberley Jones De Renne was displayed to the right of the fireplace. Noble Wimberly Jones is to the left. The library had, by this time, attracted numerous scholars and students of Georgia history. (Courtesy of Wormsloe Historic Site.)

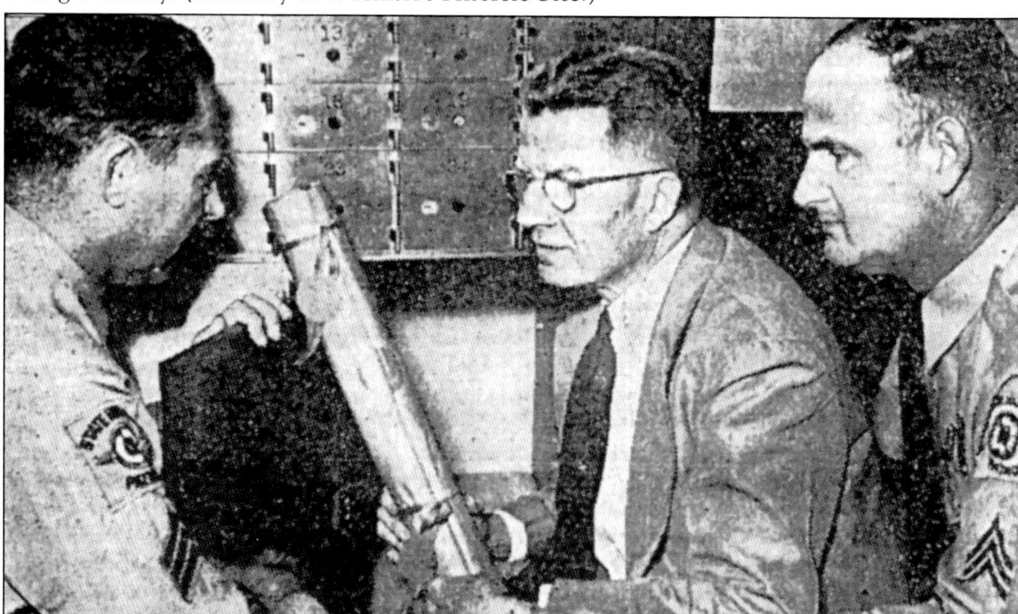

This is a photo of the state patrol escorting Wymberley Wormsloe De Renne, with the Confederate Constitution in hand, to Norfolk, Virginia. In 1951, De Renne took this document to the final reunion of Confederate veterans. It is now part of the De Renne Library Collection at the University of Georgia Library. (Courtesy of Eudora De Renne Roebling.)

Elfrida De Renne (1884–1970) was Wymberly Wormsloe's sister and was married to Dr. Craig Barrow. She hosted many famous writers, painters, musicians, and sculptors. Her love of fine arts was profound. In her home on McDonough Street, she held meetings with Mrs. Malcolm Bell, Jane McIntire (Hewitt), Mrs. Francis McIntire, Mrs. Paschal Strong Sr., and Harriet Lawrence (Huston). They named themselves the "Prosodists" and founded the Poetry Society of Georgia in 1923. Mrs. Barrow wrote *Anchored Yesterdays*, which was co-authored with Laura Palmer Bell. The book is a highly acclaimed history of Savannah's first century. (Courtesy of Wormsloe Historic Site.)

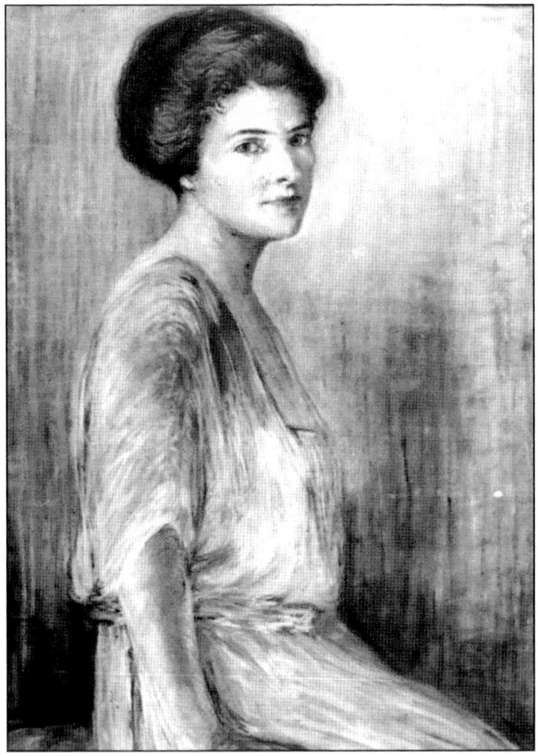

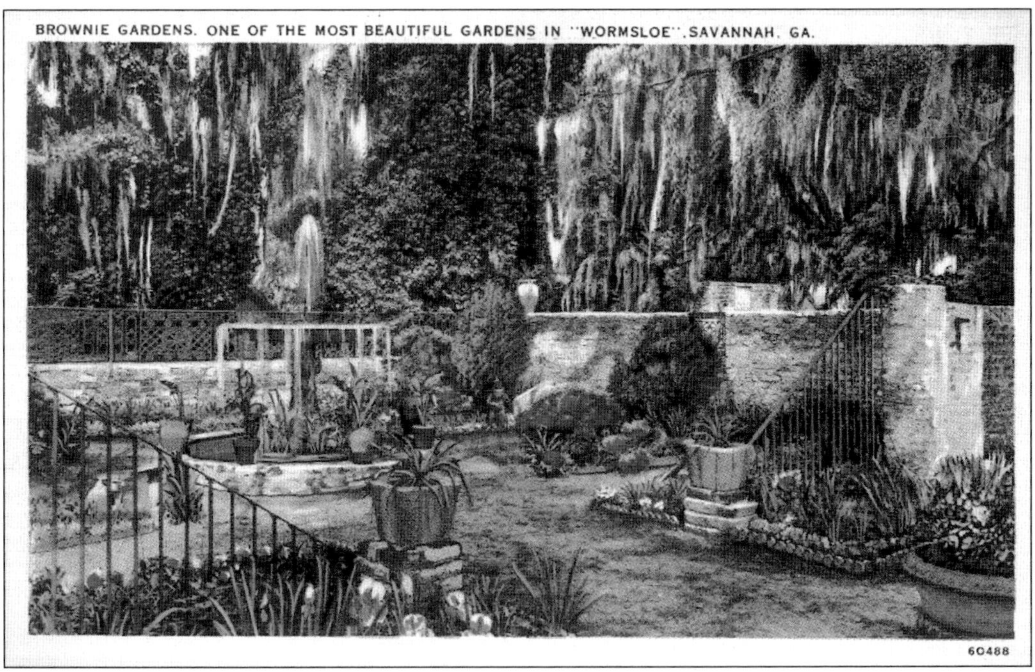

The gardens were designed with old materials—bricks from slave huts, stones, and rocks were used for the flagged walks and handsome ironwork. With local plants, rare plants, and expert landscaping, Wormsloe Gardens, opened during the 1920s and 1930s, and was one of the most delightful places around Savannah.

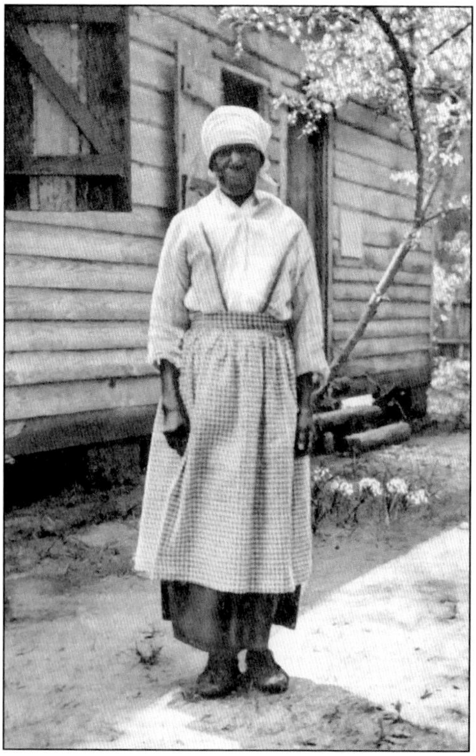

From the earliest days of Wormsloe Plantation, slaves lived and worked there. Some tended cattle and others worked in the cotton fields. It is believed that "Aunt Liza," who is pictured here, was born at Wormsloe. G.W.J. De Renne donated a building on West Broad Street for the education of black children. Later, his widow donated a building on East Broad Street to the city for the same purpose.

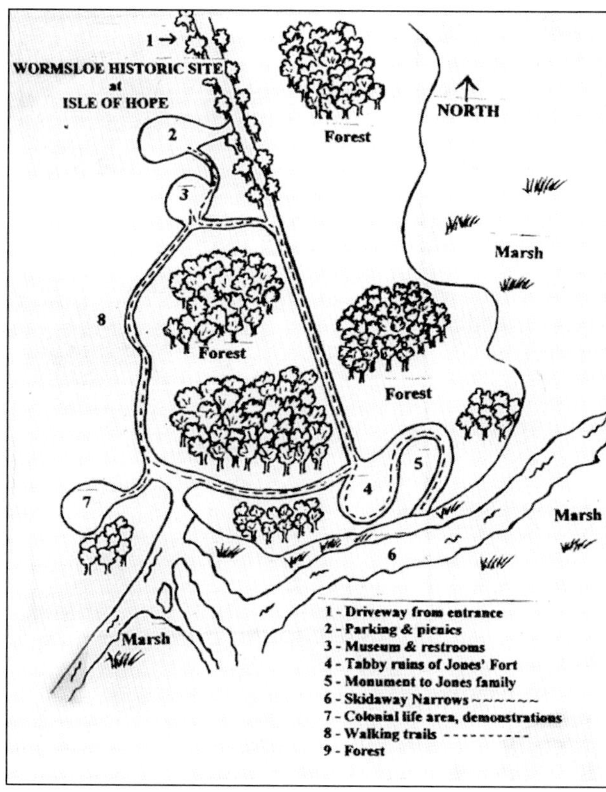

In 1972, the family conveyed 750 acres to the Nature Conservancy, which transferred the property to the State of Georgia. The 1828 house and 48 acres surrounding it are owned and occupied today by the eighth generation of the original founder. Each year, more than 66,000 visitors drive under this archway to visit Wormsloe Historic Site. Hours are 9 a.m. to 5 p.m., Tuesday through Saturday, and 2 p.m. to 5:30 p.m. on Sundays. It is closed Mondays, Christmas, and Thanksgiving. For more information call (912) 353-3023.

Four

Bethesda

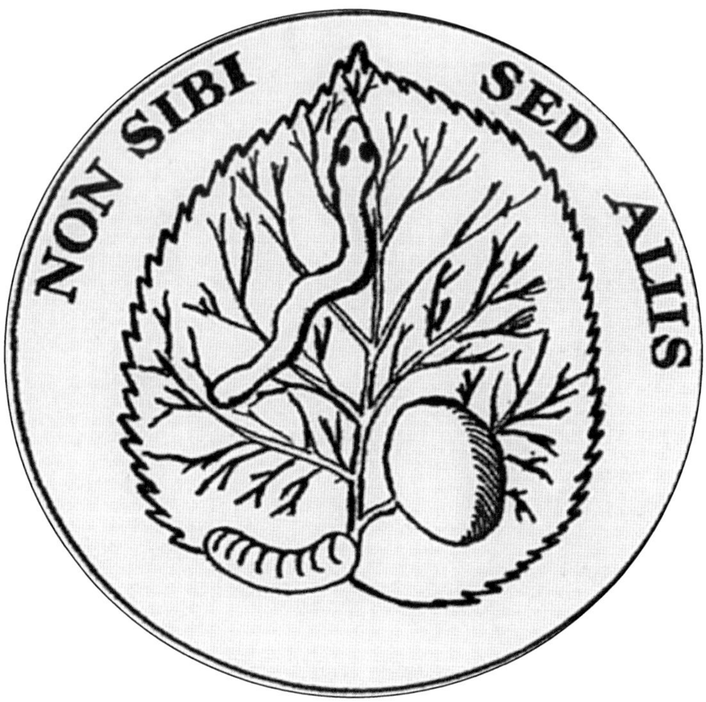

Bethesda is a fine institution that expresses the spirit of the original colony of Georgia. Their motto, at the time of its founding, was "Non Sibi Sed Aliis," which translates to mean "Not For Ourselves But For Others." The crest shows the mulberry leaf with a silkworm. It was hoped that the early colony would produce silk for export.

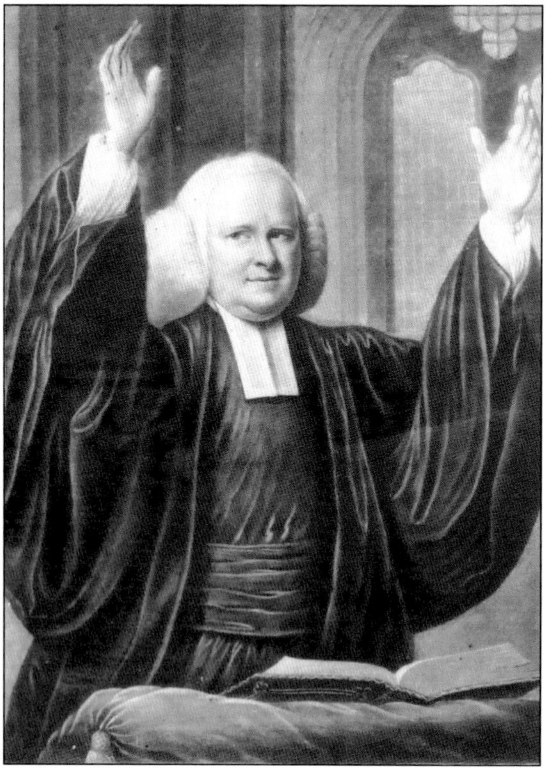

Bethesda Home For Boys is America's oldest existing orphanage. Anglican minister George Whitefield and his friend James Habersham came from England in 1738 and saw the sorry state of children orphaned by malaria, yellow fever, and heatstroke. The flamboyant orator broadcast his desire to build an orphanage, crying out, "Ye must be born again!" His sincerity pierced hearts and opened pocketbooks and the Georgia Trustees granted him 500 acres. Habersham chose the site on the Vernon River. (Courtesy of the Bethesda Museum.)

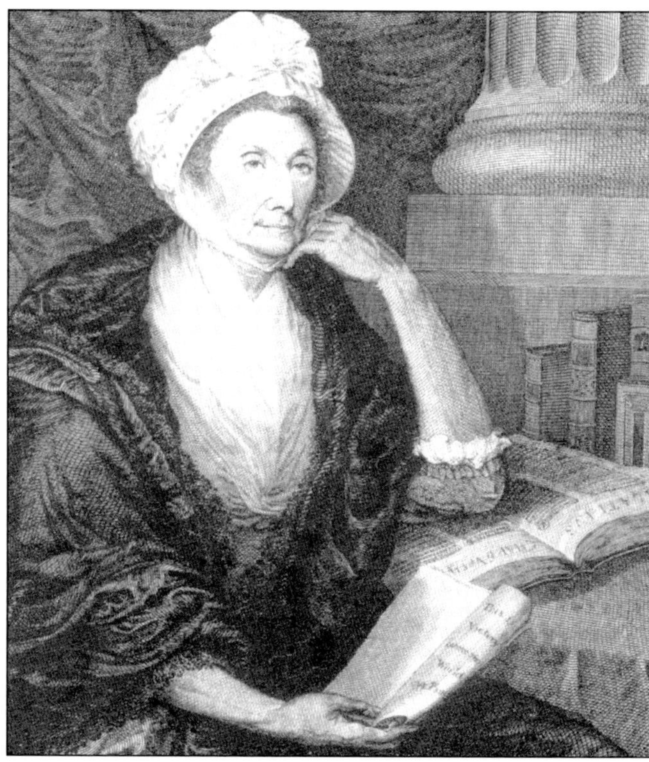

Selena Hastings, the Countess of Huntingdon, was the most prominent noblewoman in evangelical circles in England in the 18th century. A friend of John and Charles Wesley, she was a builder of chapels, the founder of Trefecca College in Wales, and the founder of the Countess of Huntingdon's Connexion. She generously backed George Whitefield's orphan home. Her full-length portrait, painted by John Russell, hangs in the museum at Bethesda. In 1750, Peter Tondee, Richard Milledge, and Benjamin Scheftel founded the Union Society, a group of men from Christian and Jewish religions working in understanding for the common civic good. (Courtesy of the Bethesda Museum.)

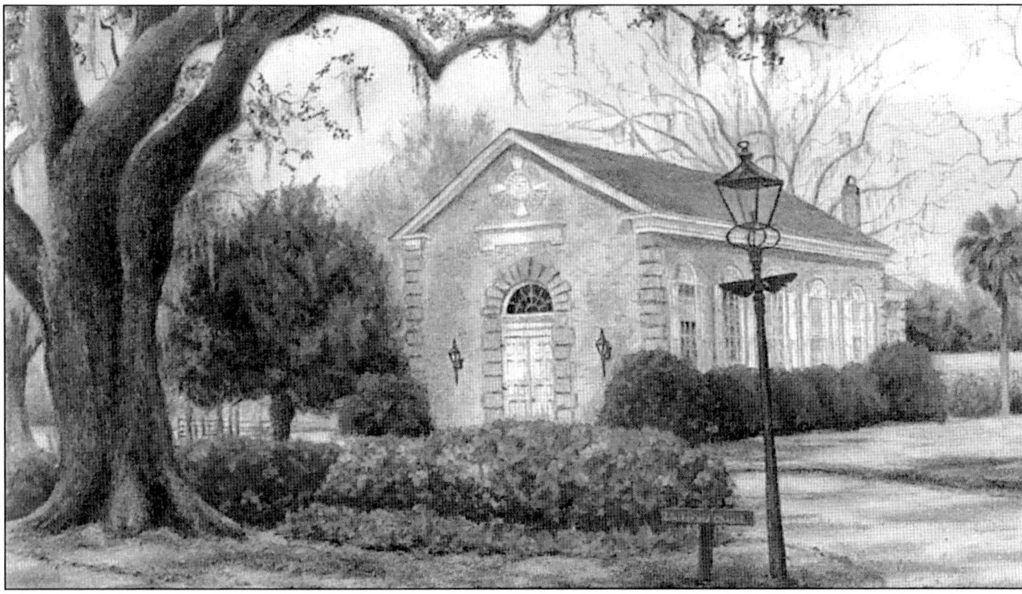

The Georgia Society of Colonial Dames raised funds to build the Whitefield Chapel. Over the entrance is inscribed, "To the Glory of God and in Memory of George Whitefield, founder, 1740." The pews were given to the chapel by the Georgia Society of Colonial Wars; the alter was donated by Mrs. B.F. Bullard, and Mrs. Clarence Anderson donated the stained glass alter window. The alter window shows Christ blessing a child under the burning bush, which is the emblem of Bethesda.

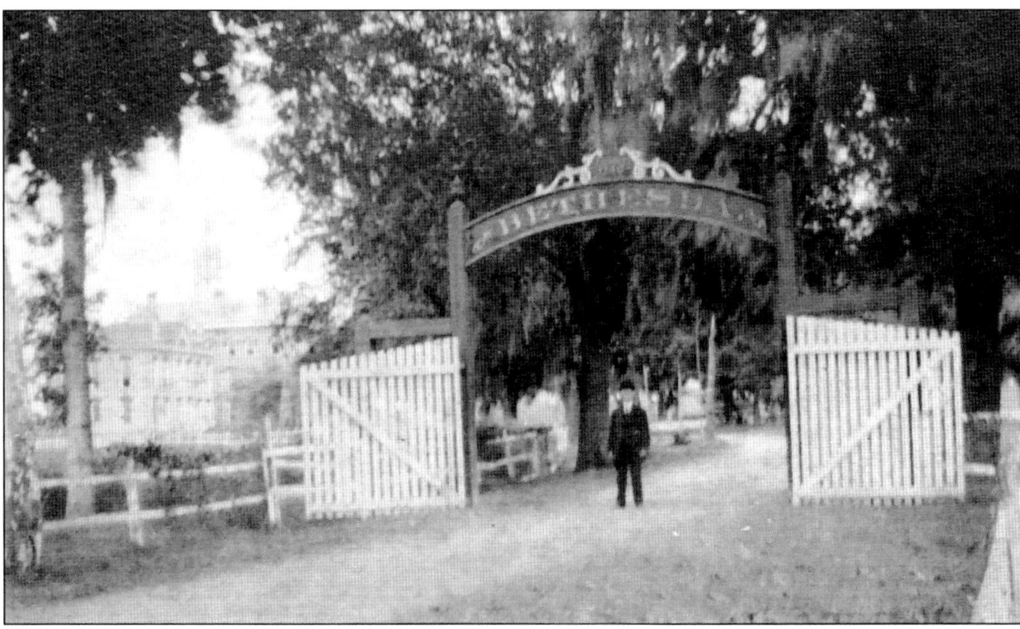

This early photo was found in Betty (Wylly) and Jim Collins's attic on Coosaw Island, South Carolina and is entitled "Leaving My Happy Home." The word "Bethesda" comes from Aramaic, the language that some believe was spoken by Jesus. It was originally spelled "Bethisda," of which the translation is "house of mercy." Many Bethesda boys have become outstanding citizens and fathers in Savannah and elsewhere.

They were known to all as the run-away boys
Every time they were caught, they were put in jail
And nobody was allowed to go their bail.
I remember washing turnips down by the big gate,
And two frisky mules named Red and Kate.
Mum Rosa, Mum Bertha and Cary Cox,
And how Mr. Hearn would teach us to box.
I remember Mrs. Nellie would call A.V.C.
Our matron, Mrs. Martin, could really drink tea.
The Gardner brothers, Jacob and Roy,
Miss Lillian Chaplin was called a tomboy.
I remember ol' Winkster saying, "Boy, stop that car!"
His chinkepins [sic] were really the best, by far.
But we didn't stop that car, it was surely a sin.
After that we got no more of Winkster's chinkepins.
I remember the well was in the backyard,
And Phil Carter was sweet on Mary Girard.
He started a fire, boy, how he did blow,
Then put it out, just to be a hero.
I remember Wylly Keck had only one leg.
As a baseball catcher, boy, how he could peg!
One-arm Tucker could make the ball hum.
First baseman John Larsen was called "Jug-o-Rum."
I remember our haircuts we got from Bob Tate.
Ol' "Gator's" real name was Carroll Wingate.
There was Charlie, Gordon, and Wellington Knott.
When Wellington threw shells, I was put on the spot.
I remember Ben Wright; he was always on time,
Said, "Look in my vest pocket and bring me dat dime."He
gave Alfred Mulling the name of "Ol' Ting,"
Walter Johnson was known to all as "Pee Wee King."
I remember Mum Lou would run up and down,
Saying, "Git out de way, boy, lemme fling myself around."
She had an old horse by the name of Nellie,
And when Mum laughed, she'd shake like jelly.
I remember the silo, the dilapidated barn,
And Mum Rosa telling me, "Dat Sekie's martus corn."
The day after Christmas, we'd break up our toys,
But there's an old saying that "boys will be boys."
And last, but not least, I'm glad to say,
That Bethesda's in the good ol' U.S.A.
There, I hope it's safe from enemy bombs,
However, I pray it will befall no harm.
I hope I've brought memories to all former boys
Who shared with me the happiness and joys.
I wish we could all again meet one another,
For to me, each one of you seems like a brother.
I'm sorry things happened that I can't remember.
As the years rolled by from January to December.
There is one thing sure, I have no regret,
For my stay at Bethesda, I'll never forget!
—John Albert Martin

This poem, written by John Albert Martin, who lived at Bethesda from 1907 to 1917, paints a realistic, verbal image of daily life in the orphan home.

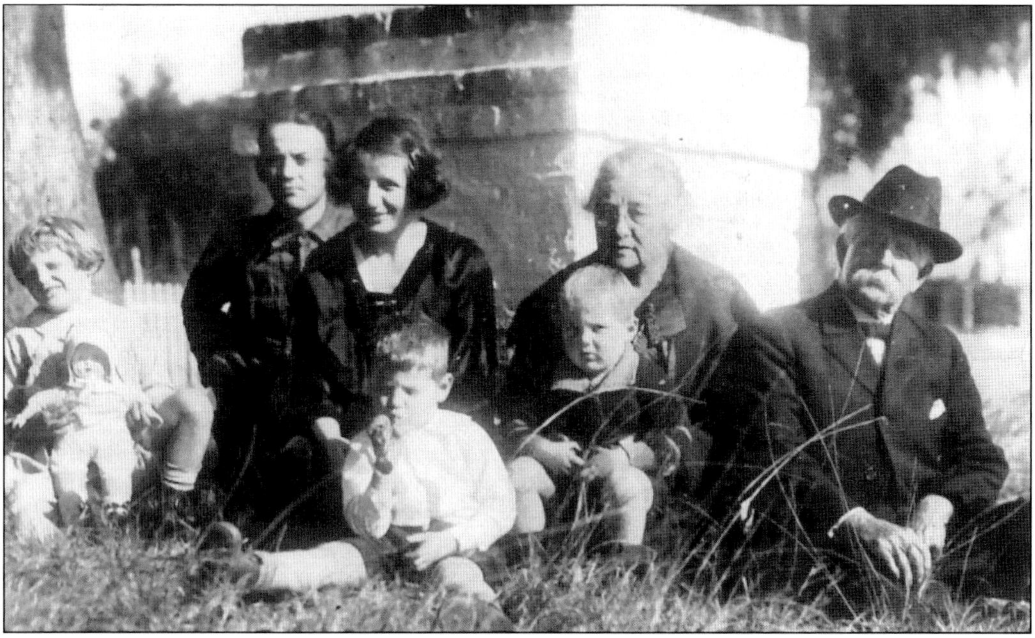

Papa AVC, as his family affectionately called him, sits by the beacon firebox on Bluff Drive on Christmas day, 1922. A marker in his memory in the center of the Bethesda campus reads: "A.V. Chaplin, 1876–1914, beloved superintendent of Bethesda for 38 years. This tablet is placed here by the Society and the old boys who knew and loved him for his kindness and justice." Pictured, from left to right, are (back row) Ken Bragg, Lillian Chaplin (Bragg), Helen Flora Wallis (Chaplin), and Albert Vernon Chaplin; (front row) Lillian Chaplin Bragg (Davis), and Sonny and Vernon Chaplin.

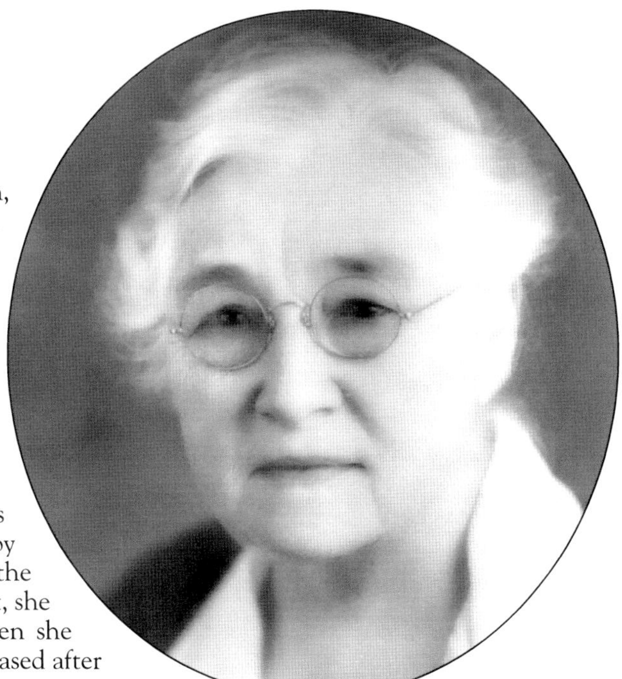

Helen Flora Wallis grew up in Bluffton, South Carolina and came to Bethesda as a seamstress and teacher. She was called "Mama Nell" by the boys. She married A.V. Chaplin and they had four children of their own. Social time was in the assembly hall where plays, dances, and musical performances were held. For one special event, Mama Nell made a surprise dress for the boys. This magical dress featured hundreds of live fireflies, each held in place by a single strand of thread, all over the wide skirt and bodice. With lights out, she glittered like the starry heavens when she came on stage! The fireflies were released after the show.

Bethesda

'Twas a cold and dreary evening.
Everyone was hurrying on,
seeking shelter, rest and safety,
for the day had come and gone.

Yet, amid the stir and bustle,
while the sleet and snow fell fast,
came a faint and childish whisper
as the throng was hurrying past.

"Well, my little lad?" I questioned,
as I halted on the street,
and thus beheld a boy in rags -
no shoes or stockings on his feet.

"Don't you think a little fellow
like you ought to be at home?
Go back to your home and mother -
'tis too late for you to roam."

"I ain't got no home, kind mister,
and no mother either, sir.
Mother - she went home to heaven,
'cause the angels came for her.

And my daddy, he is dead, sir.
One day he took sick and died.
His eyes - they got big and red, sir,
after my mother left his side.

This is Rex, my little doggie,
and there's just us two, you see."
"Yes, my little lad, and won't you
come and go along with me?"

"Have you any room for Rex, sir?
I can't part with him, you know,
'cause we've been so long together,
and I love my doggie so!"

"All right, then, just come with me now,
and you'll soon be nice and warm.
We'll go where such little fellows
as you are safe from what might harm."

Presently we reached Bethesda,
where we found an open door,
and kind hands there to receive him;
food and clothing there - and more.

Then a future was before him.
He was not a cast-away.
He was made to know life's lessons,
and life's service, day by day.

He was won from homeless pity.
He was saved to all that's good.
and grew to a godly manhood,
just because Bethesda stood.

This touching poem appeared in the *Savannah Morning News* in 1923. It was written by Louise Hughes of Statesboro.

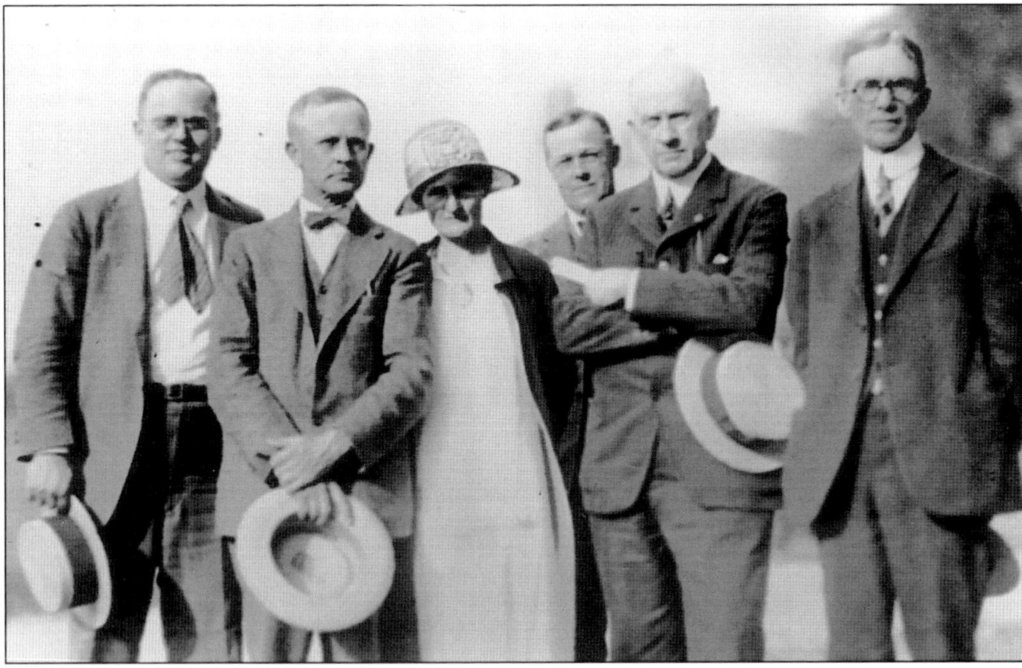

The dedication of the Whitefield Chapel was in 1925. In this photo, from left to right, are Clifford Lebey, Ole and Henrietta Burroughs, George Elton, Savannah Mayor Robert Hull, and Union Society President George Mercer (father of songwriter and lyricist, Johnny Mercer). George Vaden, a Savannah native, spent seven years at Bethesda. In his latter years, he liked to be driven around the grounds of Bethesda to savor fond memories. His wife, Catherine "Snookie" Vaden, drove him there almost daily. He lived well into his 90s. (Courtesy of the Bethesda Museum.)

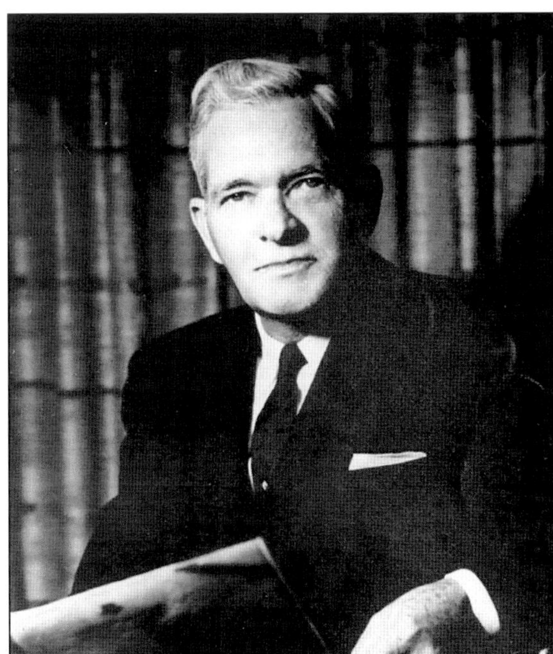

Barney Diamond of Savannah, an alumnus of Bethesda, worked diligently to organize the memorable 200th anniversary reunion that was held in 1940. He generously remembered his alma mater in his will and gave Bethesda 150 acres of land adjoining the grounds. (Courtesy of the Bethesda Museum.)

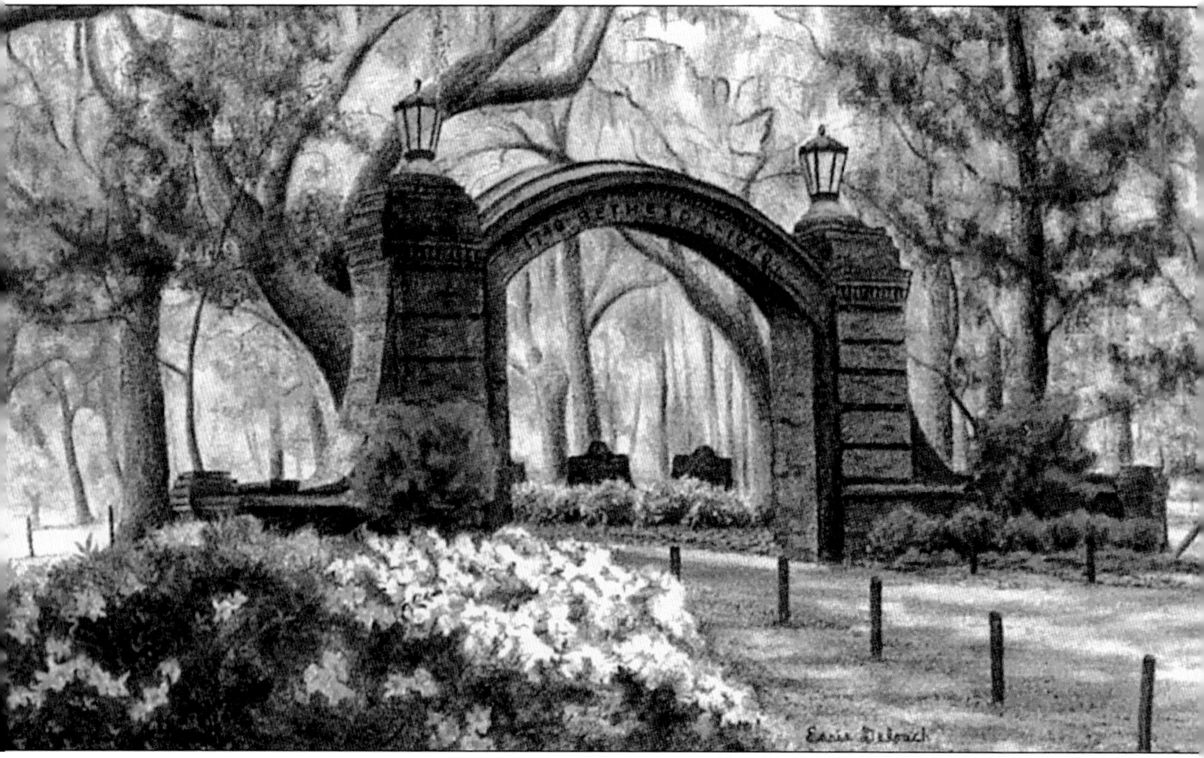

Today, visitors admire the graceful archway, which was rebuilt in time for the 200th anniversary of the home in 1940. The boys carried the bricks from the old swimming pool to the building site. Electric lights from an old building on the Savannah River were added 30 years later. This is a charming painting by Essie DeLoach, a Savannah artist.

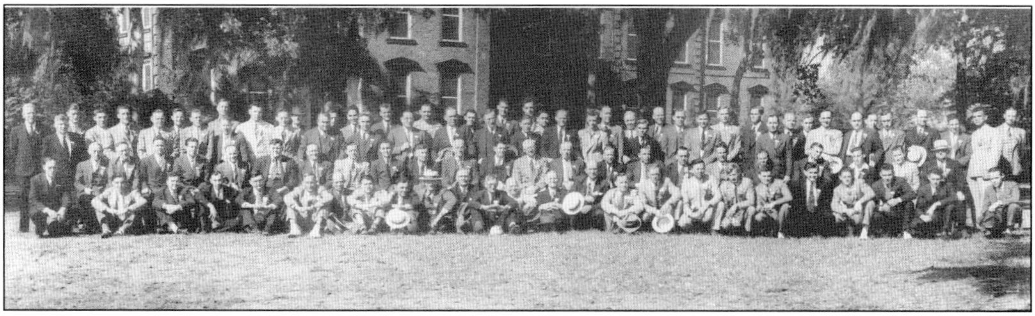

In this April 23, 1940 photograph taken at the Bethesda Home for Boys 200th Anniversary reunion are, from left to right, as follows: (front row) Worrell, Crevis, Hinely, Tuten, Strickland, Lewis, Jones, Martin, Lovett, Rabler, Williams, Stevens, Gilmore, Papot, Sloan, Christiansen, Tate, North, Strobert, Strobert, Crevis, Hinely, Bandy, Coleman, and Jessup; (middle row) Seyle, Ash, Vaden, Clements, Tucker, Dickerson, Elliott, Elliott, Elliott, Baker, Roberts, Torrance, Atkins, O'Bern, Elkins. Elkins, Hart, Hart, Moore, Reddick, Schuman, Simmons, and Berry; (back row) Snead, Ward, Conner, Clements, Clements, MaKay, McKay, Groover, Williams, Weeks, Richardson, Lewis, Baum, Carter, Perkins, Winchester, Carter, Simpson, Richardson, Strickland, Draughon, LaRoche, Defield, Roberts, Weeks, Flowers, Evans, Tidwell, Waters, Buchanan, Muse, Pope, Wolfe, Brinkley, Taggart, Schafer, Diamond, Martin, McKay, Hodges, George, Sweat, Maulden, Green, Larsen, Godfrey, Vause, and Hatcher. (Courtesy of the Bethesda Museum.)

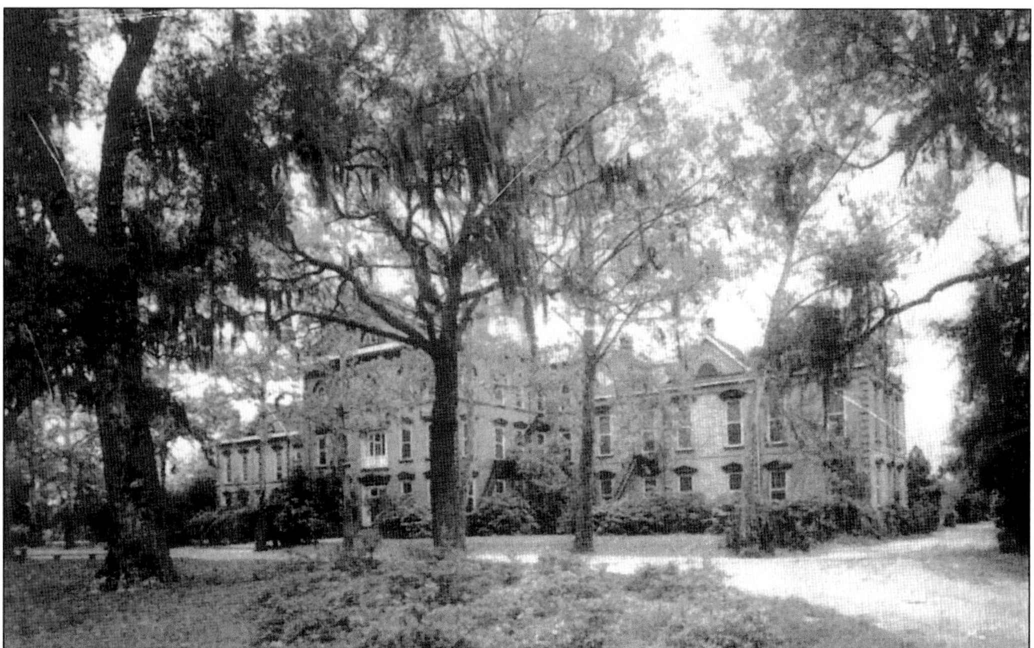

This photo shows the "Big House" as it looked in 1953 before the Central Hall was removed. Only the two end buildings stand today. (Courtesy of the Bethesda Museum.)

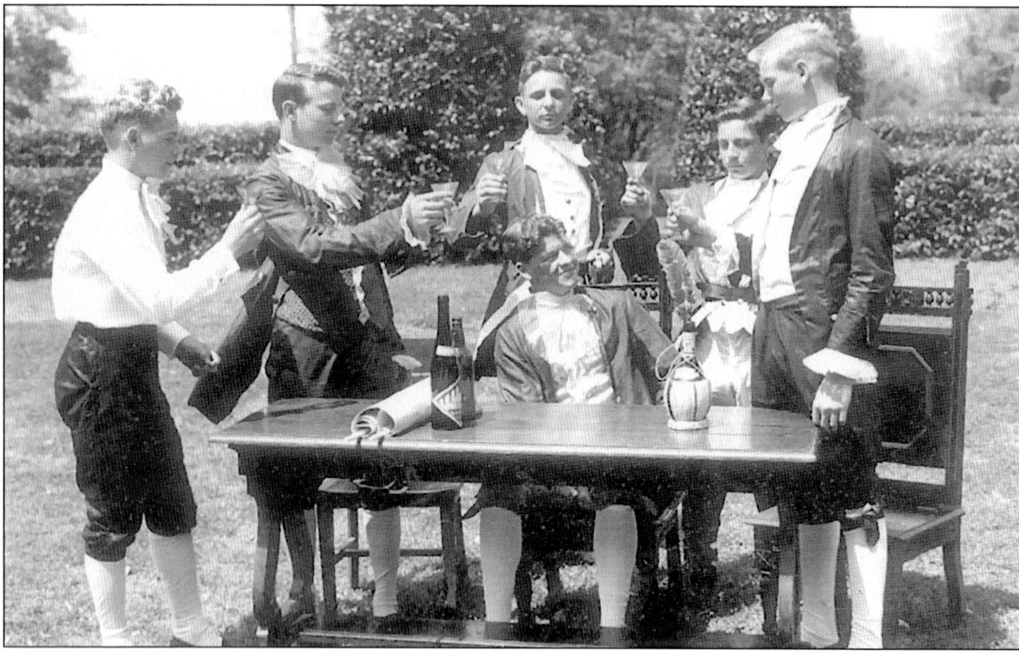

Ole Burroughs, who was the superintendent at Bethesda from 1915 to 1945, took pleasure in putting on re-enactments in the amphitheater down by the marsh. In authentic-looking uniforms, the young actors in this photo portray the signing of the Declaration of Independence. (Courtesy of the Bethesda Museum.)

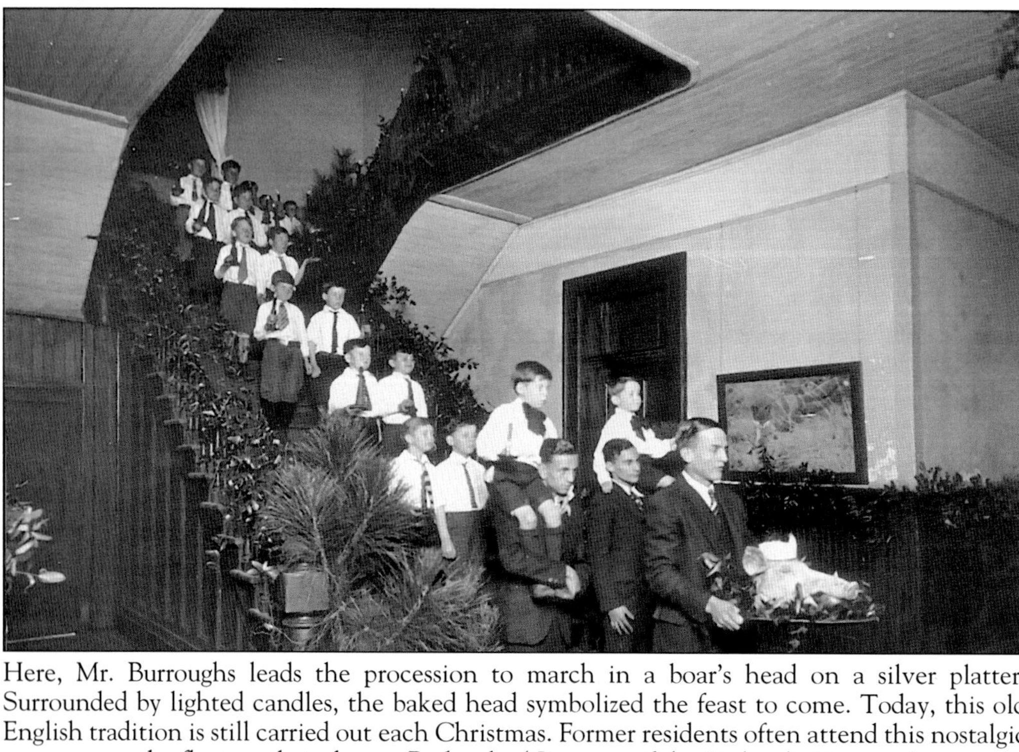

Here, Mr. Burroughs leads the procession to march in a boar's head on a silver platter. Surrounded by lighted candles, the baked head symbolized the feast to come. Today, this old English tradition is still carried out each Christmas. Former residents often attend this nostalgic ceremony and reflect on their days at Bethesda. (Courtesy of the Bethesda Museum.)

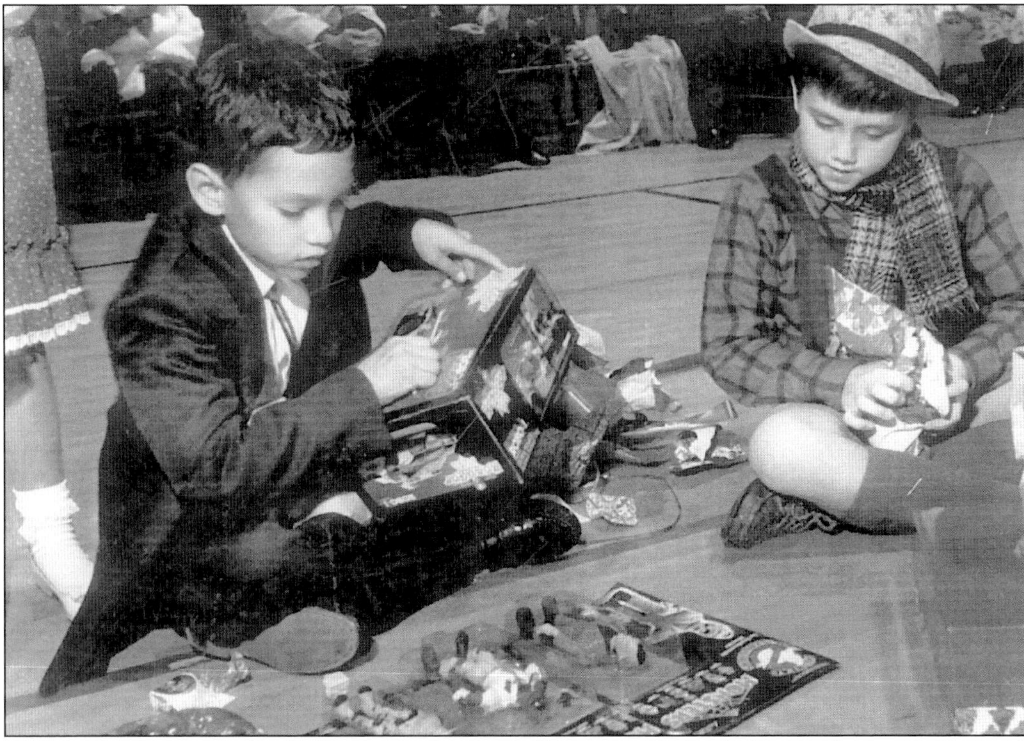

Alex Miller (left) and Scott Price open their gifts on Christmas morning, 1987. The Bethesda Women's Board understands that it is especially difficult to be away from family during the holidays. (Courtesy of the Bethesda Museum.)

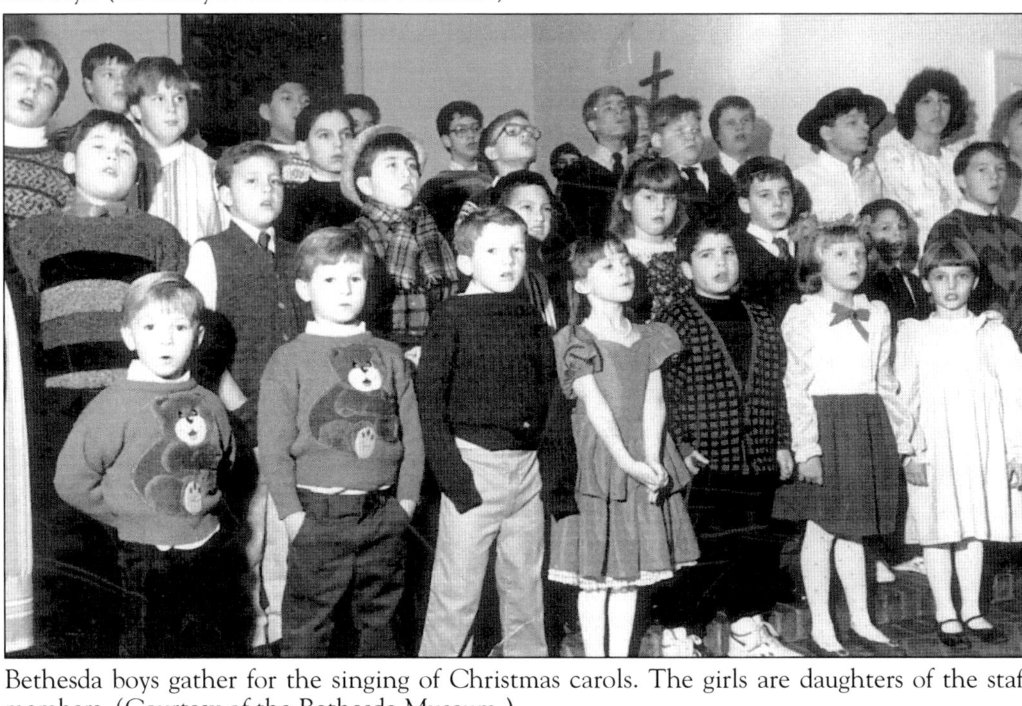

Bethesda boys gather for the singing of Christmas carols. The girls are daughters of the staff members. (Courtesy of the Bethesda Museum.)

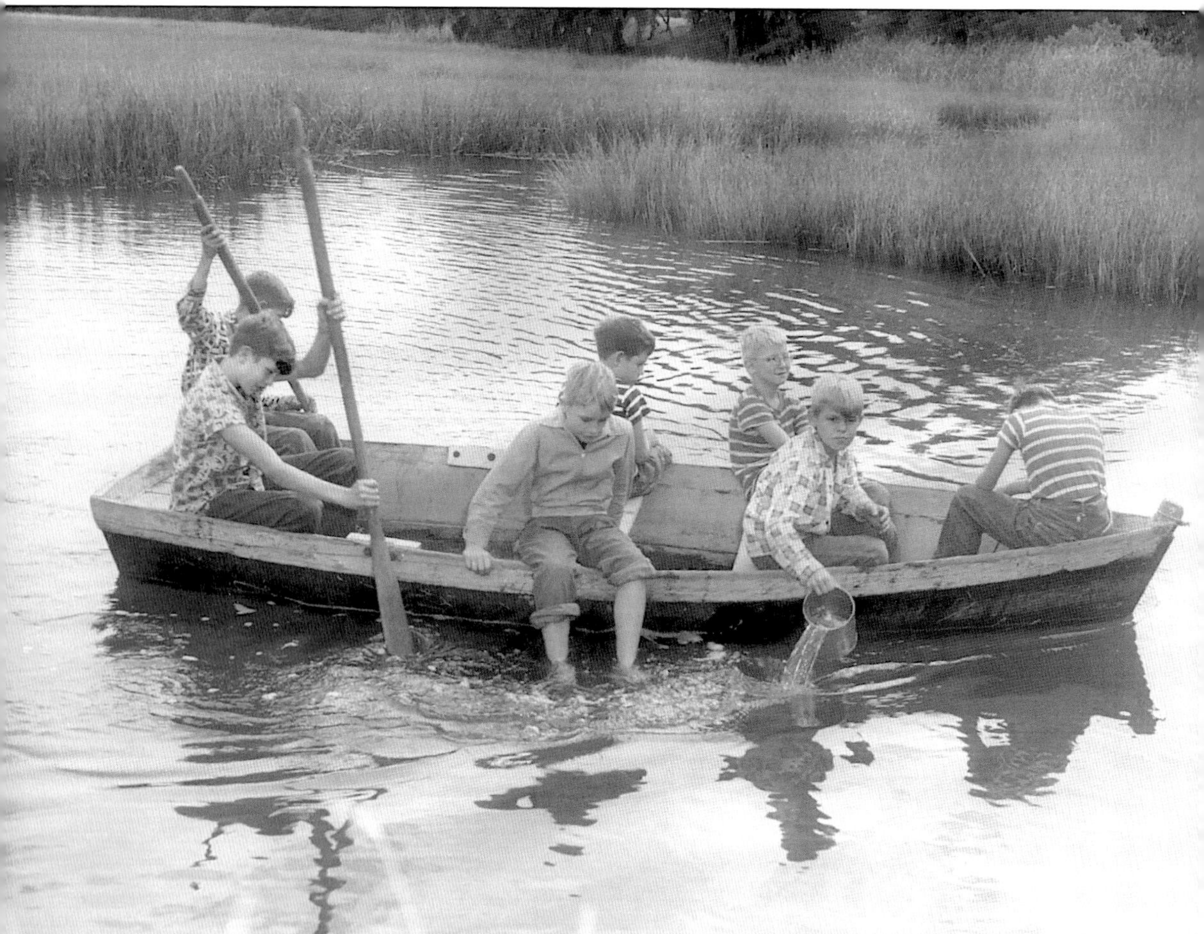

Seven Huck Finns in a leaky bateau paddle around in the Moon River. The camera has captured a special moment in childhood tranquillity. This river was originally called Back River. The city changed the name after Johnny Mercer wrote the popular song, *Moon River*. Somehow, "Back River, wider than a mile...." didn't sound quite as romantic!

Five

Dutch Island

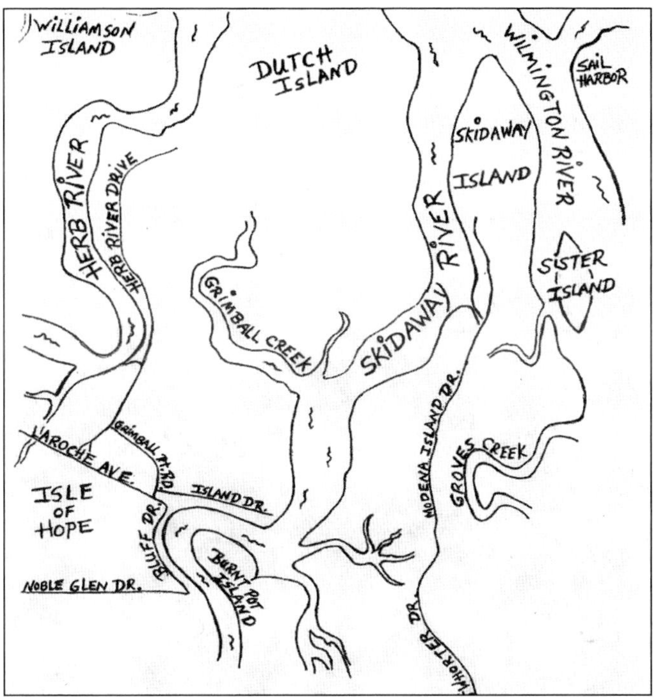

In early 1700s, this island was called Providence and was renamed Liberty Island after the Revolutionary War. Many German families lived here and it became known as Deutsch Island—shortened to Dutch Island. The first campers were the Yamacraw Indians. Chief Tomochichi roasted oysters here and at Thunderbolt, which was one mile away by water. Deer, bear, wild turkeys, curlews, and alligators thrived. In 1759, King George II granted the southern half of Providence to Michael Radick and Henry Danzler, a relative of Dr. Julian Kelly. In 1762, King George III granted the north end (Gnann Hammock) to John Young, who was a local cabinetmaker. At some point, Young's portion was sold to Frederick Herb. The Youngs and the Frederick Herbs occupied that end of the island.

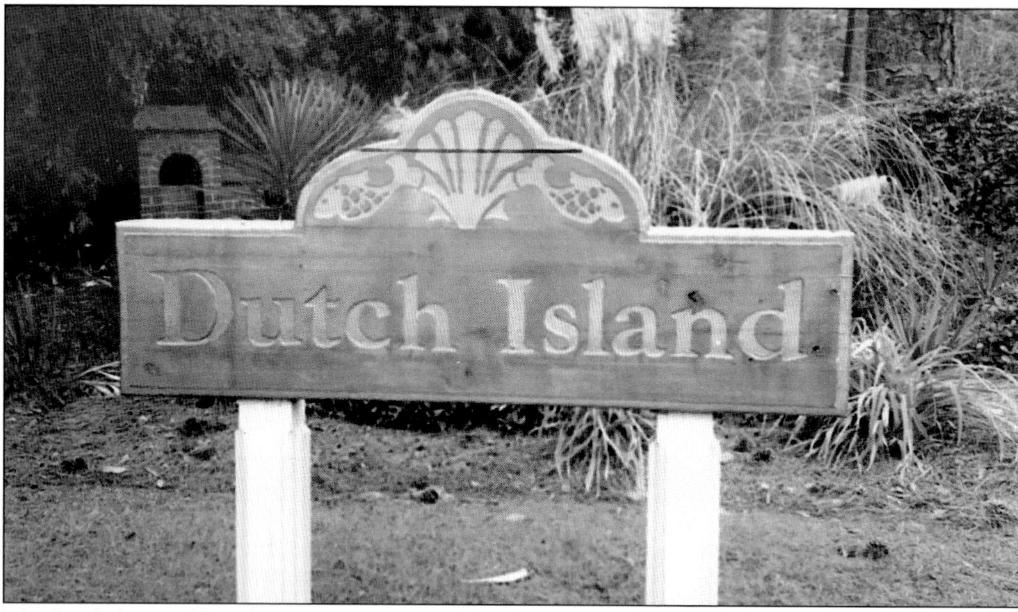

The land changed hands several times over the years. Fires, storms, and neglect deteriorated the buildings and fields grew wild. Then, in 1928, the Wessels family bought the island and tended to it for almost six decades. Today, it is a delightful community of ecological excellence, with stunning trees, ponds, wildlife, and marshes, three deepwater rivers—the Herb, Wilmington, and Skidaway Rivers, and a population of 2,637. Frank W. "Sonny" Seiler and Robert Cooper have researched the Batson project and provided much of the following information.

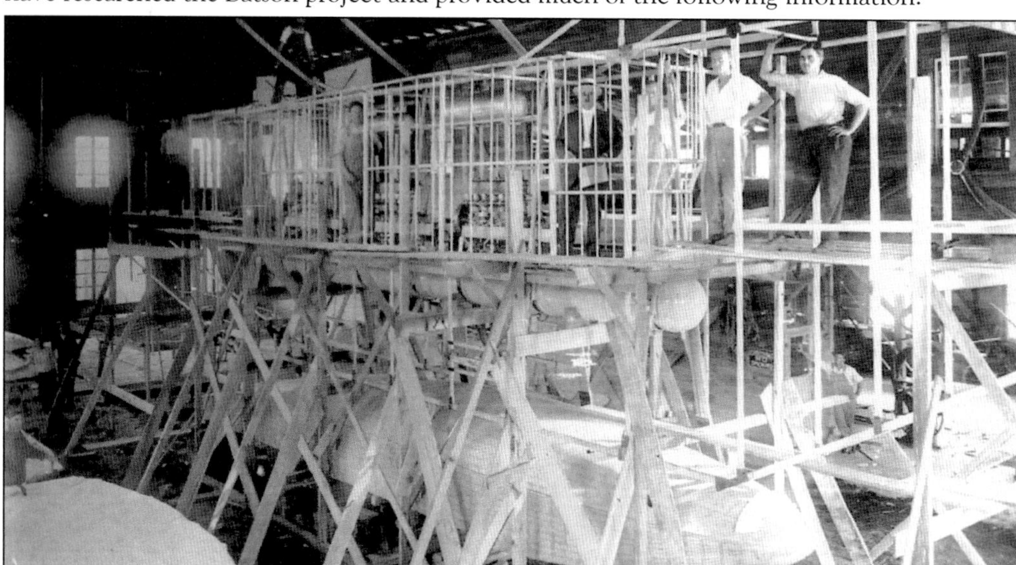

In 1913, Capt. Matthew Batson came to Dutch Island from Anna, Illinois and bought land from the Laroches. He and his co-workers knew his aero-yacht, though only on the drawing board, would flit through the skies at 40–65 mph. It would fly non-stop to Ireland via the Azores. The initial voyage would be to New York City and on to Newfoundland for the big take-off. Dutch Island was the ideal secluded place for his experiments. Batson is seen inside the scaffolding in his straw hat.

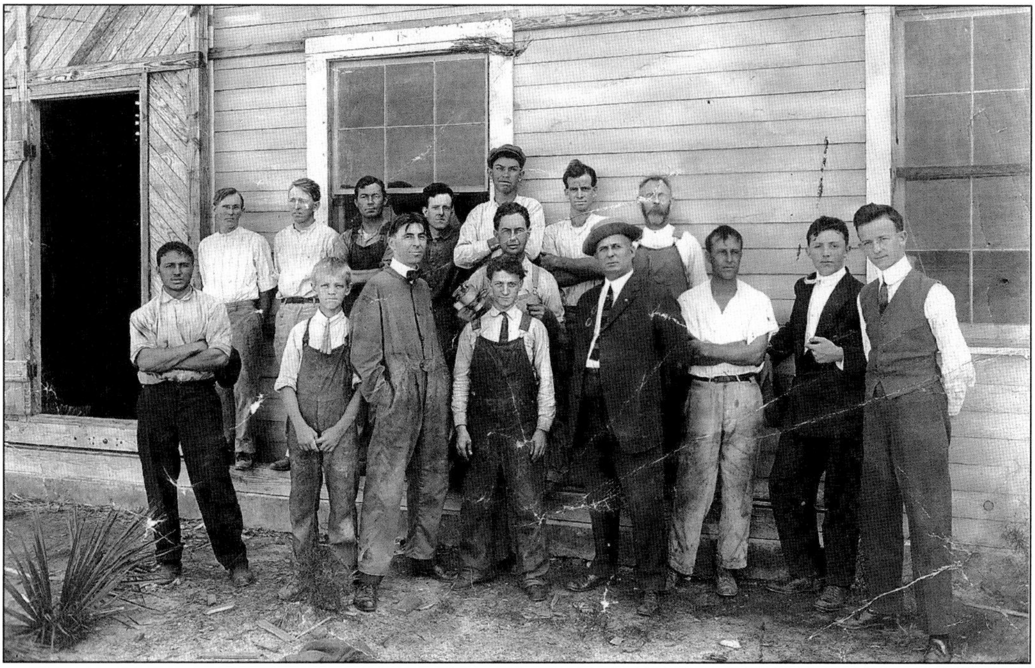

Here is the crew that built the aero-yacht. Israel Elmgren (back row, far right) was foreman of the project and a master boat builder from Sweden. His two sons, Gus and Yngve, were also part of the crew. Elmgren had such faith in the concept of the aero-yacht that he purchased shares in The Batson Air Navigation Co. Captain Batson proposed to transfer power from three engines to two propellers, a concept way ahead of its time. Most of the crew came from Thunderbolt, which was one mile away by water.

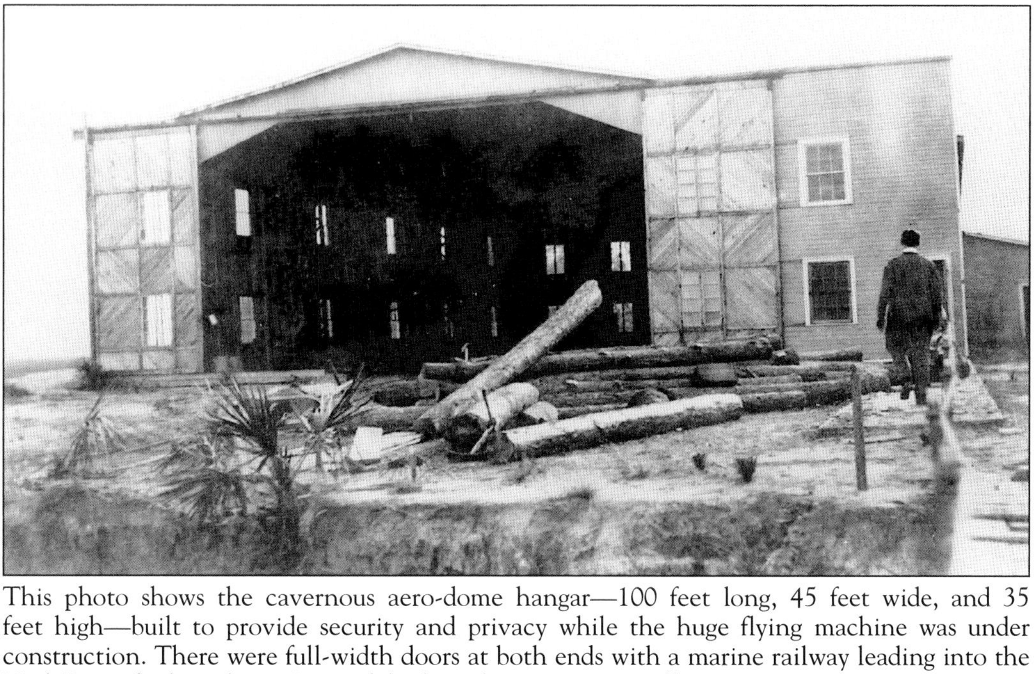

This photo shows the cavernous aero-dome hangar—100 feet long, 45 feet wide, and 35 feet high—built to provide security and privacy while the huge flying machine was under construction. There were full-width doors at both ends with a marine railway leading into the Herb River for launching. Parts of the launching ramp are still in existence.

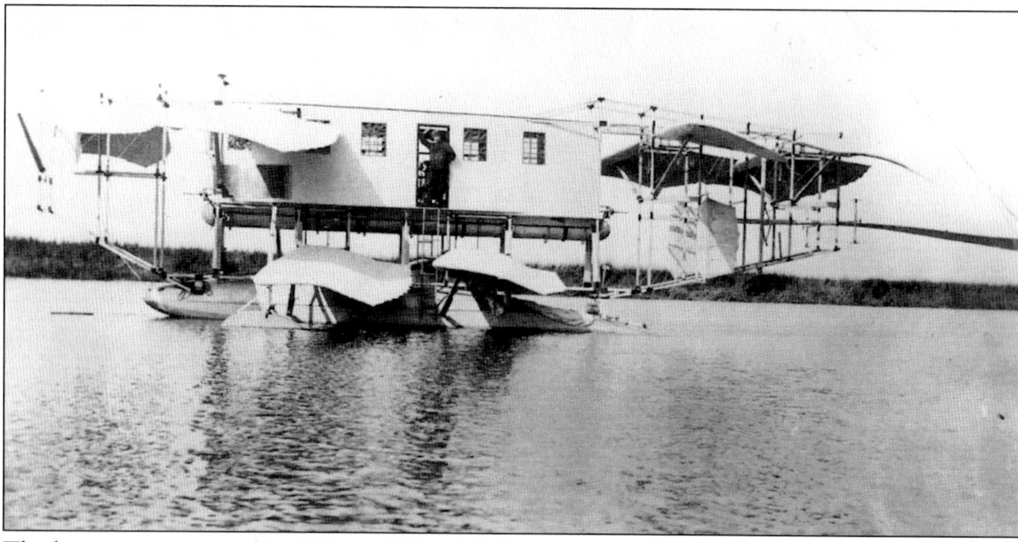

The big creature was a disappointment. Daily, engines roared in futile attempts to lift off. Flocks of seabirds flapped wildly into the air as the heavy plane ploughed up the Wilmington River, only to dock for adjustments. Attempt after attempt failed. Finally came admission of defeat. Work began at once on a smaller craft which reportedly did fly for 30 minutes at 15 feet above the water. Called *Dragonfly*, it served to provide important tests of steering apparatus. Here, the aero-yacht is pictured from the side.

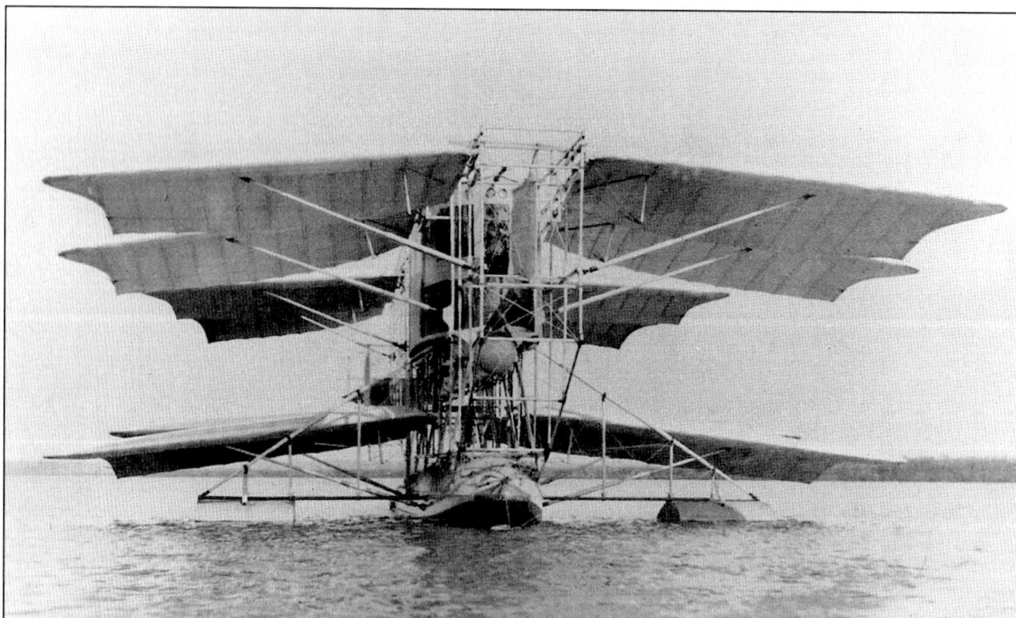

The aero-yacht had three Emerson engines, weighed 9,000 pounds, and had a lifting power of 10,000 pounds—not much room for error. The pilot's cabin was of cypress, sheathed in silk. The central pontoon had a wireless apparatus and an operator. Unfortunately, the company fell into bankruptcy before it was able to develop a final product. In 1916, Matthew Batson resumed active duty in the Army in Huntington, West Virginia. This daring man of high vision was buried in Arlington National Cemetery with full military honors.